SO GLAD
WE WAITED!

OTHER BOOKS BY THE AUTHOR

Big Lessons for Little People: Teaching Our Kids Right from Wrong While Keeping Them Healthy, Safe, and Happy

Entertain Me! Creative Ideas for Fun and Games with Your Baby in the First Year, coauthor, winner of the Parents' Choice Award

SO GLAD
WE WAITED!

A Hand-Holding Guide for Over-35 Parents

LOIS NACHAMIE

 THREE RIVERS PRESS
NEW YORK

Published by Three Rivers Press, New York, New York.
Member of the Crown Publishing Group.

Random House, Inc. New York, Toronto, London, Sydney, Auckland

www.randomhouse.com

Three Rivers Press is a registered trademark and the Three Rivers Press colophon is a trademark of Random House, Inc.

Printed in the United States of America

Designed by Susan Maksuta

Library of Congress Cataloging-in-Publication Data
Nachamie, Lois.
    So glad we waited!: a hand-holding guide for over-35 parents / by Lois
Nachamie; foreword by Debra Winger.
    Includes bibliographical references and index.
    1. Motherhood. 2. Older parents—Psychology. 3. Parenting. 4. Child
rearing. I. Winger, Debra, 1955—II. Title.
HQ759 .N27 2000
306.874'3—dc21   99-58221

ISBN 0-609-80346-8

10 9 8 7 6 5 4 3 2 1

First Edition

To my mother,

whose stunned response, "You're having a what?!*" when learning that she would finally become a grandmother when her daughter was forty-two, provided the working title of this book for the last three years.*

When everyone concerned felt that, though funny, it had a bit of a barb, it was my mother who, as so many times in my life, pointed me in the right direction, and gave voice to the best.

For inspiring this book,
for being a role model to look up to in so many ways,
and for the gift of life.

CONTENTS

ACKNOWLEDGMENTS

The author wishes to acknowledge the invaluable ideas and support of the following people and organizations:

Beth Teitelman, Director of the Parenting Center, 92nd Street Y; Barbara Katz, Director, the Nursery School at Habonim; and my colleagues Camille Ehrenberg and Cynthia Grebow, both not only outstanding teachers but also older mothers. Each of these four dear friends, in her own special way, consistently raised the bar. In the initial and subsequent drafts, with four manuscripts lined up like a Greek chorus, whenever they wrote "Lois!" in the margin, I knew I had seriously erred. Whenever they tactfully asked whether I'd considered a topic, I realized I had to fill gaping holes. Whenever they all approved with their own personal ways of showing it, I knew I had hit the mark. Although the final content expresses my views, their input, insights, knowledge, and cautions grace every page of this book.

The 92nd Street Y, one of the most stimulating and nurturing institutions in the nation of which I am very proud to be a small part; Fretta Reitzes, Director of Family Services; and all of my colleagues in the Parenting Center, with special notes to Robin Strauss and Gaby Greenberg, for providing the atmosphere where children, parents, and sitters can have fun, learn, and lean on the supportive and knowledgeable staff for whatever they may need, and where colleagues can consistently count on the same.

The many experts who shared their time and ideas so generously and who are cited in the reference section of this book.

Jane Dystel, my agent, for her unfailing good judgment and guidance; her understanding of ice boxes, Schrafft's ladies, and five-and-tens in a room full of younger new mommies was the first glimmer of the idea for this book, and her personal connection made her believe in it right from the start.

Sarah Silbert, my editor, for deftly scrambling to pick up so many different lines and still bring this book safely into port, and P. J. Dempsey, for having launched it. Janet Fletcher, copy editor, for her vigilance, refinement with language, and ability to keep the spirit of an idea while making the structure clear.

The Writers Room, with deeply felt gratitude to Donna Brodie and Bill Zuerlein, for providing the peace, coffee, clean kitchen, and community with others that all writers need; Al Lane, the librarian, for knowing how to find out anything; and my fellow writers, many of whom also happen to be older mommies, whose far-ranging fields of expertise, personal parenting dilemmas, and inspiration enrich these pages and my life.

Debra Winger, for being even more brilliant off-screen than she is on, for being such a wonderful mother, for introducing me to people whose public faces are familiar to many but whose private moments of motherhood have enhanced the text, and especially for writing such a moving foreword about the one aspect of being an older mother that I have thankfully been spared.

My sisters, brothers, and other mother, who after all these years no longer qualify as "in-laws," and Joe for the happiness he's brought.

My husband and daughter, who are the lights of my life, who both always provide me with intriguing material to write about, and who ultimately are the two people who matter to me above all else.

And finally—with a special, deeply felt thank-you to those who shared many intimate parts of their lives—all older mothers, who give this book reason to live.

FOREWORD

When I was giving birth to my first son, I endured twenty hours of early labor before the first pangs of hard labor catapulted me across the room and into the arms of an unsuspecting nurse. When the shock of this new pain wore off a little, I noticed my mother, who had been joining in for the last six hours of party atmosphere, packing up her things. In my naïveté, I figured she was taking a trip to the cafeteria to fortify herself with caffeine, and then would hunker down for the duration. Wrong. When I asked her how soon she'd return, she replied, "Oh, I'm not staying for *this*. I know what you're in for."

Many years later I reasoned that, number one, she couldn't bear to see *her* baby in pain and, number two, she was telling me once again that now I had to stand on my own. These were the kindest interpretations I could find.

Ten years later, when I was forty-two, she stayed with my husband and me from the beginning to the brutal end, as I triumphantly pushed out my second baby boy.

My mother passed away the same year that I conceived, so this put me, conveniently, in charge of her whereabouts for the blessed event.

I wanted her to see that my pain was not the same as hers was, so many years ago, when obstetricians were mostly men—and thieves at that, stealing a woman's memory of her hard work by administering the "forgetting drug," usually without her knowledge or consent.

I wanted my mother to hold that newest baby in her arms, when I was needing to rest and close, knowing that there are only a few people in the world who will hold your child sacred. This was not to be. In the first year of my son Babe's life, I experienced a postpartum struggle that I hadn't faced in my younger new-mother days. I was blue, some days beyond consolation, and I wanted my mommy. If only to feel irritated at her insistence about something I was doing wrong; something to push up against so as to feel stronger and more confident in my choices.

Our son turned two recently and, on reflection, being a motherless mother feels wholly unnatural. I know it happens all the time, and so it is as much a part of life's rich tapestry as any other condition, yet I still feel the weight of my decision to be a new mother again at forty-two.

There have been times when I've caught myself mired in a sentimental sadness about Babe's loss, his never getting to know his grandmother. We begin to see our mothers in such a different light, first when we become mothers ourselves, and next when we lose them. It is not so much the memory of what she did, but who she really, at heart, was.

When we are dealing with our moms later in life we often dread their arrivals, thinking of the many times we'll have to bite our tongues, swallow our pride, and eat humble pie. Quite a gastrointestinal assault. Yet, once we can be with who they *are*—and not what they *do*—we start to really share time.

I long to watch my mother watch my sons. Now I find myself spending time with a very quiet rendition of my mom. One who doesn't criticize, overcook, or horn in. But it is also one that I cannot hug, cry on the shoulder of, or hand my baby to.

That is why I take comfort from the wise, warm voice and occasional wagging finger of Lois Nachamie's books. Those who have mothered and still are enthusiastic on the subject have something rich to share. It is hard to hear that which we know deep down we should be listening to the hardest. But we mustn't skip over the warnings or ignore the vast experience of one who has encountered so many parenting styles.

So, lace up your boots, take your vitamins, and listen to Lois.

Debra Winger

PROLOGUE

At the Metropolitan Museum's weekend series for elementary-school children, while the kids sat on the floor in a circle, listening to the lecturer, I sat on a bench next to a woman from New Jersey.

We began to chat, as most women do in the way that amazes our husbands, and discovered quickly that we had both just turned fifty, and had both just begun the mood swings and wobbling irregularity of what were once Swiss precision periods.

She mentioned she was here with her granddaughter. I pointed out my daughter. They were both eight.

We had a good laugh.

And then, we began The Inevitable Conversation.

She said she envied me. That she'd stayed home to raise her kids and now here she was, at this age, having to decide what to do next. I felt for her. I really wouldn't want to be starting a career now. I couldn't bear to be considered a beginner. I know too much.

But on the other hand, from where I sit, there is something undeniably appealing about how free and unencumbered she is. She can take her granddaughter to the museum on a Saturday afternoon if she feels like it. Or not. She's not responsible for her granddaughter's entire enrichment. She has already raised her kids, and she and her husband are planning cruises to exotic spots. The most exotic spot we're likely to see in the near future is the Tiki-Tiki Room in Walt Disney World.

She felt that if she had it to do again, she would have waited longer. I wish I'd been a little more together so I could have started sooner. I wouldn't have minded having a couple of kids, and that is probably no longer in the cards for my biology. She wished she could have gotten a leg up on a career, but she was grateful that she didn't have to take part in the chronic balancing act between family and work that most of us are up against every day of our lives. I'm happy with my career, but I wouldn't mind being a bit freer from the constant race to keep up with my daughter's schedule as well as my own.

Judging from her polished appearance, her morning had been different from mine. Lipliner, eyeliner, perfectly blended eye shadow, and hair that holds its outline all take time in front of a mirror. I could picture her leisurely reading the paper with her coffee, then slipping into her tailored red jacket and lint-free black slacks before setting out to pick up her granddaughter.

Instead of looking "put-together," like my museum friend, many of the women I know who have young children lean more toward a "thrown-together" look when not at work. We favor looser, more casual clothes. The kind we can wear when we're down on the floor and later throw in the wash. Many of us opt for a sunscreen-tinted moisturizer combo so we can slap three things on at once. We tend to rely more on a good cut than on a hairstyle that needs too many grooming aids. Our idea of personal luxury in the morning is an uninterrupted shower.

She carried a smart, small bag for her essentials. I carried a big "mommy's bag" for all my daughter's essentials.

She wore beautiful, shiny well-heeled boots that matched her outfit. I wore the shoes I wear every day, no matter what I'm wearing. French, fabulous, a muted green Nubuck, they are so expensive that I won't reveal their price because then my husband and mother will learn how much I paid for them. But more to the point, they have soft, thick soles and are comfy. Comfort in a shoe that is not a sneaker is one of any older mom's main goals in life. Because we and our mommy shoes do a lot of walking in places you'd have to be incredibly vain, or nuts, to wear shiny tight boots to.

Although she and I were exactly the same age, her style, though not matronly, said "lady." My style, if you can call throwing on whatever is relaxed and on top of the laundry basket a style, said "built for comfort, not for speed."

We both looked like what we were. She was a grandmother, albeit a young one. I was a mommy, albeit an old one.

I met another woman on a northbound train from Florida. On her way home to Boston, she was traveling with her eleven-year-old, a delicate girl with braces, knobby knees, and the skittishness of a prepubescent. My eight-year-old was still blithely confident, too young to be a prime candidate for the heartbreaking descent of Ophelia. Seated together in the dining car, the four of us shared the immediate ease of long-distance traveling.

After lunch, we went back to our sleeping car. The girls played in one roomette. We moms settled across the aisle.

She was a beautiful woman in her early fifties with straight blond hair, high cheekbones, a simple black linen traveling dress, and understated, serious-money jewelry. When she smiled, she looked like Diane Keaton. She had just a trace of an English accent left over from having come to this country when she was ten. She was a psychotherapist.

As the train rattled along through the southern countryside, and the girls became involved in a game, it wasn't long before we began The Inevitable Conversation.

She wondered whether we'd been sold a bill of goods. Women of our generation were all so convinced that we could do it all. She confessed, as if being on a train with a stranger allowed her to say something that maybe she hadn't said or couldn't say to those close to her, that she had missed most of her daughter's infancy and childhood. She'd returned to work a month after her child was born. She *had* to, she said. Or at least she *felt* as if she had to. She was building her practice. Looking back, she wondered why she had felt compelled to go at everything so hard. Why couldn't she have taken fewer patients? Why, in fact, couldn't she have stayed home full-time with her child? Why had that option never even presented itself to her? She was, after all, a nurturing type. That was what had led her to her chosen profession, at which I suspect, after spending many hours with her, she was very good.

Empathetic, smart, comfortable financially, happily married, there she was. Questioning the path she had taken. Wondering whether she might have done it differently.

Is one path better than the other? Is it better to have your children young or when you're more mature? Is it better, once you have them, to stay home with them or keep up with your career? It is the discussion of the day. I haven't met a woman in close to a decade in her late thirties, her forties, or her early fifties who hasn't examined the timing of motherhood and its effect on her life.

Some of us conceived our children easily, others went to great pains economically, physically, and psychologically. Some adopted our children. Some of us are married, some divorced, some single. Some of us are straight, some gay. Some of us work full-time, some part-time, and some are stay-at-home moms. Some of us are well-off, some struggle to stay afloat. Yet few of the women I get the opportunity to talk with as a leader of parenting groups, and as I go about my life centered in the "mommy world," don't question the decisions we made.

There are no right or wrong answers. There are only different choices.

But when you come to parenthood later in life, there are some special joys and challenges.

I'd like to introduce you to the extended family of older moms and dads.

PRACTICAL NOTES

So Glad We Waited is divided into three parts.

- Part 1 explores how people become "older parents."
- Part 2 offers special ideas and practical tips on common parenting concerns, such as work and child care, and addresses issues relevant to the over-thirty-five parent, such as how our changing bodies affect the way we raise children. These chapters are not necessarily meant to be read sequentially, nor will all the chapters be useful for all families.
- Part 3, best read in its entirety, offers guidance on the parenting dilemmas that most older parents confront.

A recommended reading list and a list of selected Web sites are given in the back of the book.

Identifying characteristics have been changed to preserve the privacy of the women the author interviewed from all over the country. Some examples are drawn from parenting groups the author leads at the 92nd Street Y in New York, as well as from audience members and participants in lectures, panels, workshops, and less formal gatherings of parents. When several individuals had similar stories, composites were created.

Aside from an occasional father who actively sought to be interviewed, the concentration is on mothers.

Use of the he/she gender pronoun, so problematic when writing about children, was settled by the toss of a coin.

WHO WE ARE AND HOW WE GOT HERE

There is much we have in common beyond our years. . . .

PART 1

WHO WE ARE AND
HOW WE GOT HERE

There is much to learn in creation beyond our walls...

1

The Good Ship Older Parent: Who We Are

If you're reading this book, it is extremely likely that you fit the same tidy demographic niche as the rest of us. You probably had enough education of specialized training that your job, if you have chosen to continue to work, is interesting, or pays well, or both. If you don't live in the heart of a big city, you live in close proximity to it, or are an "expat." Regardless of your marital status, ethnic background, or sexual orientation, you share many common values and lifestyle choices with other new mothers our age.

The fact that we "older mothers" exist as a group large enough for many of us to identify with is just one small indicator of a society in flux.

THE TRANSFORMING AMERICAN FAMILY

Half of all marriages now end in divorce. Half of all children in elementary school or younger have mommies who work full-time. These are monumental changes in the basic structure of the family from when we grew up.

In fact, the traditional image of family that we were raised with no longer exists. None of our children will grow up expecting all mommies to stay home and all daddies to work. If not your family then certainly families your child will know intimately do not consist of a mom, a dad, and a kid under one roof. Even if you are not a gay family, by elementary school your child will certainly know a family with two mommies or two daddies. The same goes for the family whose head is a single mother by choice. Or your toddler may have step-siblings, some of whom are awkwardly close to your own age.

Gender expectations are also shifting. Work is being redistributed, although not equitably, as most women know all too well. Mommies work outside the home and daddies take on some of the work inside the home, including a greater share of hands-on parenting than they ever have before.

LENGTHENING LIFE CYCLES

During our lifetimes, major milestones have gradually shifted, some occurring a decade or more later than in our parents' generation.

Education takes longer now. Thus, being prepared for a job, a traditional benchmark of maturity, no longer occurs in the late teens, but rather in the mid to late twenties, if not later. This accounts in part for delayed marriage and parenthood, two other significant life markers.

Life expectancy has increased. There are record numbers of retirees. Boomers are turning fifty at the rate of one every thirty seconds. Because of lifestyle and medical advances, however, fifty no longer signals the "beginning of the end," but rather is now an extra decade extending the "prime" years of earning and of raising a family.

NEW PARENTS ARE OLDER

Another indicator of the shift toward "older" is that the age at which women are having babies is steadily rising. Since 1980, for example, while teenagers and women in their early twenties have had consistently declining birthrates, the numbers have risen for every other age group—and they're climbing.

Our age group—thirty-five and over—has seen the most dramatic increases. In the last two decades, the number of babies born every year has ranged from about 3.6 million to about 3.8 million. In 1980, women who were thirty-five and over gave birth to only 250,000 of those babies. By 1997, the last year for which data are currently available, babies born to women in our age group hit an all-time high just shy of one-half million. Folded into these overall statistics is the steadily swelling number of babies born to women over forty, over forty-five, and over fifty. These women have been keeping statistical pace with their younger sisters.

First-Time Births

Not only are we having babies when we're older, we are having our *first* babies when we're older. According to the National Center for Health Statistics, this has been a noticeable trend since 1975. While teens and women in their early twenties are having fewer first babies, and women in their late twenties are staying more or less the same, women starting their families past the age of thirty climbed from only 5 percent in 1975 to 23 percent by 1997.

Of the approximate 1.5 million babies born to first-time mommies of all ages in 1997, 106,973 of them were born to women who are thirty-five or over. That's a lot of older first-time moms.

Dads are right there with us. Although we never know much about the roughly 15 percent of all fathers who don't show up in birth statistics (among other places), we know enough to see a trend. Since 1980 the number of men becoming fathers under age twenty-nine has steadily declined, while that of men from thirty to fifty-four has risen. The figures for new fathers over fifty-five have remained fairly steady. We've always had our Picassos and Tony Randalls, regardless of medical advancement and societal trends.

Parenthood by Other Routes

Although no national figures exist, we know that three other segments of the population of older parents have increased dramatically within the last decade or so. First, there are more and more older couples who can and do adopt now, since the permissible ages for adoptive parents have risen throughout the world in response to our offering good homes for children. The other two groups that have skyrocketed are single and gay older parents, both male and female. Whether biological or adoptive, these new parents continue to increase in numbers as social mores and legalities alter and technology improves, welcoming them into the mainstream of American family life.

How do those numbers translate into the real world? There are a heck of a lot more women our age wearing Snuglis, pushing strollers, and scrunched down on child-size chairs meeting preschool and kindergarten teachers than there used to be!

BUT DO THEY LIKE US?

Not everybody, however, is jumping up and down about our noticeable presence.

OUR PREDECESSORS AND THE PUBLIC AT LARGE

A telling 1998 *Ladies' Home Journal* survey reported that "American women" (or at least those of a mean age of forty-four, with an average income of $43,300, who were mostly married, with school-age kids, worked, had some college, and responded to the survey) thought that twenty-five was the best starting time for motherhood and that after forty you were just too darn old.

"Young children are for young parents," sniffed an elderly neighbor recently, when I told her what book I was working on. She is hardly the first who has said that. Nor will she be the last.

Some of this sentiment may reflect both generational and class differences. As we mentioned, demographically we tend to be middle- to upper-class and urban. Many working-class women as well as suburban and rural middle-class women have their first babies when they are right out of high school or college. The vast majority of women in all socioeconomic groups who are now in their sixties and seventies started their families by their late twenties, if not earlier.

OUR PEERS

But even for those of our generation who are in the same demographic niche, there is something about us that doesn't sit quite right. For example, there is a clinical, quasidiagnostic term for us in family counseling and sociology circles: we have had our children "off-time," in contrast to the more frequent "on-time." While they evenhandedly discuss effects of "on-time/off-time" in the nonjudgmental terms required of any academic discipline, and make note of the wisdom that maturity can potentially bring to parenthood, there is a judgment implicit in the very term. Which plane would you rather have reservations for? The one that's "on-time" or the one that's not?

Educated, sensitive, knowledgeable women who are just like us in most of how we talk, think, and approach many important areas of life, when consulted for this book in their professional capacities, perhaps unaware of what was revealed by their statements, focused on elements that most of the older mommies I interviewed were definitely aware of, but weren't overly concerned with. The issue of potential disease and demise, for example, troubled them more than it troubles us. Their what-if quotient was noticeably higher than ours. In the half full/half empty department, they had a tendency to intimate that we were running on low. This is in striking contrast to how the women I interviewed are experiencing their own motherhoods and life.

Although we are no longer stereotyped as frumpy wallflowers, pathetic late bloomers, or oddballs, as older mommies were even twenty years ago, we have a new set of unflattering stereotypes that flare up here and there in the media and in idle conversation. "Pushy," "needy," and "demanding" have been heard and seen in print.

More serious, thoughtful academics point out that although most of our children are loved and cherished by mature, insightful parents, as one writer put it, if the line between ambition and maturity blurs, the child can become a mark of achievement, as typified by the golden retriever–BMW–baby phenomenon.

GENERATIONS X, Y, AND Z

The new generations of adults coming up behind us seem to have a different take. To them, "older" has a distinctly different definition.

A screenwriter in her mid-twenties had as negative a response to the subject of this book as that of my elderly neighbor. I could see it in her face. She seemed rather troubled by the idea of "older parents," though she was an impressively tactful young woman. Rather than offer her opinion, which was of course implicit in her questions, she asked what I thought about women having babies when they are in their sixties. And what about those seventy-year-old fathers starting all over with their second families?

What was telling was that, for her, the term "older parent" called to mind considerably older people than most of you reading this book. I explained that while the people she mentioned were certainly part of "older parenthood" and had very interesting issues to deal with, this book is directed toward a more mainstream group of us.

She mentioned her next apprehension. Assuming the role of spokesperson, she explained that her generation is very eco-conscious. People her age are worried about populating an already overburdened planet. Women in their forties having triplets are of grave concern.

We discussed the technology of fertility and the issues that it raises for everyone, regardless of their age, and how that, too, although a very compelling and worthwhile topic, was not really the focus of the book, notwithstanding that quite a few of the readers would indeed be mommies in their forties with twins and triplets.

We had arrived. This book isn't about the headlines of science. This book is about motherhood.

She thought about that for a while. She offered that a lot of her friends say that they'll never have children. Who would want to bring a child into a world like this?

I don't know about you, but I remember vividly being in my twenties, passionate, idealistic, armed with statistics that proved how we were wantonly destroying the planet we live on. That is the same reality this new generation is confronting. But on a more personal level, I was completely out of sorts with myself at the time. In retrospect, that was the real issue. Being in late adolescence and so totally miserable, I was right not to consider bringing someone else into the world. I was desperately trying to bring myself into the world. I sympathize with her friends who take that stance. I hope that once they get some experience under their belts, the world, although seriously flawed, won't look so bleak.

This lovely young woman leaned forward across the table, earnest now about something she feels very strongly. And I wish you could see how beautiful she is, with curling blond tendrils of hair and gorgeous, big brown eyes, so fresh, so open. If she's got an ounce of talent that can capture a fraction of her brains, her beauty, her passion, and compassion on the page, I'm sure you'll see her movies.

"I feel sorry for my friends who say they don't want to have children," she said. "I think being a mother is the most beautiful, wonderful thing in the world! I want to have children!"

She leaned back in her chair and shrugged slightly. "Just not now."

WHY WE WAITED

Although we may be painted by some as shoulder-padded Joan Collinses clawing our way through the greedy 1980s, talking on cell phones through the IPO '90s, acquiring children like fashion accessories once we can afford them, here, on the inside of "older motherhood," it is a very different feeling.

Our screenwriter is just like we were then. She is, as she puts it, "shooting for thirty." To her that is the ideal age. But as you and I know, life has a way of going faster than we notice and not always landing us where we thought we'd be when.

Take Stacey's situation. Stacey now lives in San Francisco, where she, her husband, and their six-month-old recently moved from another state. Her voice over the phone is bell-like. She sounds much younger than forty. It is a friendly, smiling voice, as if there might be dimples attached.

As she is describing how she adopted her daughter, she suddenly breaks off. "All of a sudden, I turned around and I was in my late thirties! It wasn't as if I was so busy building a career as that I was so busy living my life. That was so different from my mother. I was trying to do as much as I could.

"On my thirty-sixth birthday I said, 'I'm not at all where I thought I'd be! I've got this great job as press secretary for the governor. I'm in the paper all the time. I'm speaking for the governor. But I thought I'd have a family!

"It was a rude, rude awakening."

And so Stacey, like most of us, and like our young screenwriter and her friends of today, didn't necessarily plan on being an older mother. We just didn't plan on being mothers right away. Some of us would rather have been younger mothers, but found the wrong partners or no partners at all.

Perhaps for most women who start their families when they are younger, getting married and having babies is one of the very first things they think of when they think of what they want to do with their lives. For us, however, for the most part, there were other parts of our lives that drew us forward.

As Stacey put it so well, we weren't so busy building our careers. We were busy living our lives.

The specific events that led us to become older mothers are as rich and varied as our individual histories. But because we are older mothers, regardless of how we got here, we are at a different stage in our own lives than a younger mother is in hers.

YOUNGER PARENTS/OLDER PARENTS

DIFFERENT DEVELOPMENTAL STAGES

People in their twenties to early thirties are building their lives; people in their late thirties and up generally are already established. This fundamental difference in our personal and professional lives shapes our parenting styles.

As psychologists describe it, younger people are working on separation and individuation. To put it in everyday language, they are still learning to stand on their own two feet. Most of us, on the other hand, have probably achieved a fair amount of autonomy interpersonally and in the world at large. Whether or not we have seen external signs of success in terms of career, by our mid-thirties we tend to turn a corner internally. We move toward the next developmental stage, in which we work on issues of intimacy.

In addition, with each ensuing year, as we encounter crow's-feet, the beginning of the end of our reproductive cycles, and other whisperings of our own mortality, we tend to start holding "elemental things," as one psychologist calls them, in higher esteem. "Human love and affection, insight, pleasures of the senses, nature, and children" all begin to take on greater and greater significance.

How some of these deeply felt human passages translate into attitudes toward the home is that younger people are looking outward, as they should be, whereas many of us are much more interested in what's happening close to home, with our children being a major focus. (We will examine issues that arise from this mind-set in chapter 11, "Overindulgence: Our 'Special Hazard.'")

DIFFERENT FAMILY SCENARIOS

By elementary school almost half the children born to younger parents will have lived through a split-up and will live with joint custody or will have become part of a combined family.

Older families tend to be more stable. Although only time will tell whether all our families will stay together "till death do us part," during our children's early years we are less likely to split up. Many of us have already made our mistaken younger marriages. As one older mother of a preteen put it, "We had both been through hell before we found each other. Neither of us is going anywhere. We'll work out whatever comes along." Her comment is a personalized explanation of the 70 percent to 80 percent success rate of second marriages.

Thus our children will most likely spend their early formative years in a stable home. (See chapter 3, "Transforming from a Couple into a Family," and chapter 4, "The One-Adult Family.")

DIFFERENT STEPS ON THE CAREER LADDER

In the older family, it is likely that both partners have demanding and fulfilling careers in which we are fairly well established by the time we come to parenthood. Statistically, the single mom by choice also has a "career" rather than a "job," meaning that she earns a professional's salary. Therefore, we are more likely than younger families to have the resources to hire help. (See chapter 7, "Helping Hands: Child Care.") Because we are at a different place in our careers, our work choices are somewhat different from those of people just starting out. (See chapter 6, "Kids, Career, and Compromise.")

POSSIBLE ADVANTAGES

In addition to the financial stability and stable homes the majority of us are able to provide for our children, we tend to launch them on their own courses rather well—or at least give them options. We, as a group, eminently value education. The children of older parents are strongly represented in schools where academic aptitude is an entrance requirement. This fact quite likely has less to do with the children's innate intelligence than with their early exposure to experiences through which they develop skills that prepare them for school, and possibly for life.

Simply by virtue of having lived longer, we bring to parenthood a wealth of experience that a younger parent can't possibly have acquired. A younger parent most likely went from the family, out briefly into the world, and then into a relationship that closely replicates the formative family structure. We, on the other hand, have generally had at least one significant relationship before this; we have had vastly more experience in the workforce. In brief, we know more. Our knowledge of the world around us and our more developed sense of self give us a confidence that our children often reflect.

POSSIBLE DISADVANTAGES

Life and the body are finite. Therefore, sometimes we have less energy than younger parents. (See chapter 8, "Bifocals and Barney.") It is likely that our children will experience the death of a close loved one, such as a grandparent or even a parent, early in life. (See chapter 9, "Confronting Life's Cycles.") We may have to help our own ailing parents when our children are young enough to still be quite needy themselves. Furthermore, down the road, our children may need to deal with our old age when they are still relatively young themselves.

KNOWING JOY

Perhaps our greatest strength—and potentially our greatest weakness—is that we are parents by preference and design. Because of our age, experience, and voluntary entrance into parenthood, there is a consciousness to our parenting, an awareness, a heightened experience of being a parent. As a group, we are intense.

An older mother recently described how, that morning, her child pointed to the cows on his pj's, and said, "Dog." The mommy said, "Not dog. Cow." The child said, "Moo." And it was here that the mommy, relating the story, got tears in her eyes. "It was so beautiful. He's learning so much so fast."

This is not an unstable woman who cries at the drop of a hat. This is not an artist whose sensitivity is right on the edge at all times. This is a CPA! A woman who deals in figures and bottom lines. A straight-and-narrow, regular woman. But she epitomizes the magnificence of the older mom. Not a second of the exquisite beauty of her child's unfolding life is lost to her.

Most younger mothers love their children, adore their children, want only the best for their children. The younger woman, however, is deeply engaged in her own growth, as she should be. For better and worse—and there are most assuredly advantages—she is often so engrossed in her own thoughts and in building her own life that she simply assumes that her child will do well, will learn, will grow. She holds out a helping hand, but she is in many ways only one step ahead of her child. She cannot look at her child all the time, for she must watch where she is walking. She is, in fact, growing up side by side with her offspring.

We are already grown. That is the difference and, in fact, the essence of what it means to be an older parent. We are sure-footed enough in so many parts of our own lives that we can walk backward holding out our hands to our child.

Few of us take our parenthood for granted. Few of us yearn to be doing something else. We have already done it. Even though we may be tired to the very core of our souls, most of us are aware of our blessing every waking moment of our lives.

There can be a downside to the intensity many of us bring to parenting, and we will explore it in depth in the third part of this book.

But now I'd like to introduce you to some people whose stories may hit home for you.

2

Our Road to Becoming Parents: Mothers Speak

There isn't a woman among us who became a mother "just like that."

If we bore our children, our pregnancies were considered high-risk. We had amniocentesis or chorionic villus sampling (CVS). We had more to worry about than younger moms when we were pregnant and more of us lost potential babies than women who are younger.

If we were "assisted" in conceiving our children, our road to motherhood was even rockier.

If we adopted our children, that was one more mountain to climb.

The very fact that we are the age we are means that there may be things in our past that haunt us.

Let us meet some women whose road to parenthood may in one way or another resemble your own.

ADRIANA

At fifty-four, Adriana has quite a full life. She is a successful designer of hip children's clothes and accessories. By her own account, she has scads of friends and enjoys close ties with her parents, siblings, sisters-in-law, nieces, and nephews. This is confirmed by all the happy group snapshots tacked to her bulletin board among the fabric swatches and sketches, and by the number of personal calls interspersed among the business calls that come in before she buzzes her assistant to take messages while we talk.

She is a lot of fun to be with. A textbook example of the skinny fidgeter who constantly burns calories, she throws back her head and laughs out loud, uses her hands, eyebrows, and shoulders when she talks, swivels around on her designer's stool, crosses her legs, and dangles a high-heeled shoe from one foot. Dressed all in black, she has a lot of hair that she tosses back and forth, twists, clips on top of her head, and then unclips and shakes out.

Adriana is the mother of a twelve-year-old girl. This busy mother's face softens visibly at the mention of her daughter. She points to numerous head shots of an adorable girl with hair like her mother's and a big smile adorned with colored braces. Zoe is "doing *very* well in school, knock on wood," Adriana says, as she knocks on her own head.

She is as happily married as anyone *could* be after being with the same guy for twenty-three years, she quips in her easy, Brooklyn patter. It is the first time in our conversation that her friendly eyes avoid mine.

During our second meeting, the story comes out. Adriana, like many women, was "ready" before her husband was. "He had a million excuses. We didn't have the money," she intones. "He had to build his business. It wasn't the right time. Blah, blah, blah.

"We were one of those couples who look at each other and get pregnant." There is a silence, emphasized by her sudden stillness. "Twice," she adds.

Then her engine kicks back in and she starts to move. "Both times, he said, 'If you do it, you'll have to do it alone.' I really thought about it. But I just didn't want to take it on by myself. Besides, I knew he was the man I wanted for the father of my children.

"After the second one, I thought about leaving him." Her lively face grows sad. "Because if we're not going to have kids, why are we together? But the truth is I love him. I hate him!" She laughs out loud. "But I love him." She shrugs. "That took me through my mid-thirties. We used a diaphragm. I got serious about building my business. He had just opened his eighth dry cleaning plant when I got pregnant again. This time I just laid down the law. 'We've got the money, your business is built enough already. It's time.' I was ecstatic. He was, too," she admits begrudgingly. "I told everybody. I got on the phone to people I hadn't spoken to in centuries! Anybody who would listen. People on buses. The mailman!

"Then I had a miscarriage. You could have wiped the floor with me. But I got pregnant again easily and the rest is history. I'll tell you, though. If I hadn't gotten pregnant, I would've killed him."

She is quiet for a moment. "I know I'm not objective, but her teachers, her friends, *everybody* says how terrific my daughter is. Sometimes I just look at that child's face and I think, we could have had two more!

I always wonder what those other two would've been like." She is lost in thought for a few more minutes.

"I had another abortion in my early twenties. But I don't feel the same about that one at all. That would've been a disaster. I stayed with that guy for about ten minutes. He was so not right. Not like Gary. He really is a great father. She adores him! Every once in a while, he'll say, 'We should've had more.' I want to kill him."

When asked why they didn't have more, she shrugs. "It just gets away from you. In the first year, there was no way we could have had another unless it was immaculate conception! I was exhausted. I could barely walk. I was nursing, which kind of makes you . . ." She folds in on herself, her body language illustrating her unwillingness to be touched. "And we were both so amazed by her, I don't think we even noticed each other. Then when she was around two, we started thinking about it. By that time I was already in my mid-forties. I was pregnant a few times, but those pregnancies didn't take. Neither of us wanted to do all the fertility stuff.

"Whenever I start thinking about those other two, though, if it gets really bad, I remind myself that if I had had them, I wouldn't have had her. You know how if you had brushed your teeth two minutes later one day in 1954 then the whole universe would be different now? So if we'd had those other two, we wouldn't have made love that one night that made Zoe. And nothing, nothing, nothing in my life is as good as Zoe. And I've got a damn good life."

BLYTHE

Blythe is as different stylistically from Adriana as the Upper East Side is from the Garment Center. At forty-five, she is tall and smooth, all velvet headband, handmade loafers, navy cashmere, and pearls. She auctions rare books; her husband is in banking. Their five-year-old son is just entering kindergarten in a tony private school. With all these stylistic differences, you'd think the two families would have nothing in common. Yet Blythe tells exactly the same story.

The first time she got pregnant, her husband wasn't "ready." He didn't feel financially stable enough. Unlike Adriana, at this moment she looks me right in the eye. Her sadness is deep and palpable. "I'll never really forgive him," she admits. "I wanted that baby so much. But I just wasn't willing to do it on my own."

She, too, comforts herself with the strikingly similar thought. "The only thing that makes me able to endure what we did is Sam. He is so delightful. He is the light of my life. Had we had the first one, we never would've had Sam."

For both these women, there is a hurt from the past that colors the present and the future. Not that younger women don't sometimes resent their husbands. But their clocks aren't ticking so loudly.

Earlier abortions take on a whole different tenor when it turns out that the pregnancy was the final shot.

LIZ

Liz so enjoys being with her adopted son, recently turned two, that she is contemplating leaving her job in the personnel department of a hospital, even though that would make it very tight for her and her husband financially. Although forthcoming, even rather voluble, about some aspects of being an older mother, she is noticeably tight-lipped about her reproductive history.

Sometimes more is said in what is not said. "We wasted more money than we could afford," she says tersely when asked whether she had tried assisted reproduction. When delicately asked whether they knew what had happened, there is a silence filled with almost deafening rage and pain.

"Scarred tissue. Abortions. Jerks I shouldn't have slept with and jerks who shouldn't have licenses to practice medicine." She gets up and leaves the room. When she returns, her face shows she's been crying and she requests that we continue talking another day.

Although the road leading to adoption is often burdensome, the more people I meet who adopt children, the more their stories take on a certain deus ex machina aspect: the pairing is often eerily magical.

LAURIE

Here is a forty-two-year-old's story. Laurie and her life partner, Lisa, live in Northampton, Massachusetts, in a gentrified neighborhood of beautifully restored homes in a fairly large lesbian community. With a wide face, a sweet smile and voice, and very gentle motions, Laurie is prototypically "motherly." Both she and her partner are in mid-level corporate jobs, but at home they break down the chores along traditional marital lines. Laurie does most of the cooking and housework, while Lisa is in charge of house repairs—including major renovations, most of which she has done herself—and the car.

The first time I interviewed Laurie, home on maternity leave, it was just ten days after they had returned from an arduous trip through Siberia in the dead of winter including a three-day train ride to bring back the stunningly beautiful child in her arms.

"I always felt that I would be a mother, but I never really thought about pregnancy that much. It wasn't important, one way or the other," Laurie begins. "By the time Lisa and I reached our mid-thirties, we felt it was time.

"In college, I was fascinated by Mongolia. I studied Uzbek culture. I studied Tibet, Central Asia, and these very offbeat places.

"I had this wonderful dream at that time that I took a very long train ride to Lake Baikal, and I was on a very important mission. The mission was not defined in the dream. But Lake Baikal and Siberia in the wintertime were spectacularly beautiful. Trees covered in ice—shimmering, like jewels dripping from the trees. The visual imagery in this dream was remarkable. It was such a powerful dream. I can see it in my mind's eye right now after twenty years as clearly as I can see you.

"When we were getting close to a referral, the head of the agency called. 'I'm looking in the Russian part of Mongolia, in Oolong Uday.'

"I got off the phone and looked on a map. Oolong Uday was just a few hundred miles from Lake Baikal. It was in Siberia. I saw that the Trans-Siberian Railroad went to Oolong Uday. And I just knew.

"I called up Lisa and said, 'We're going to get a child from Russian Mongolia! I'm going to take that train journey!'"

She is by no means the only woman whose story is magical.

DEIRDRE

Deirdre, married for eight years and the mother of a four-year-old, is a copywriter for an advertising agency. She wears bangs and a straight haircut, big glasses, an oversize turtleneck, and a long, flowing skirt. Her glasses slip down her nose frequently.

It wasn't until her late thirties that Deirdre began to feel the call to motherhood. She got pregnant easily.

"The first time I was pregnant (besides an abortion when I was much younger), I was lying down resting. I wasn't really sleeping and I wasn't really awake. I had a kind of vision. I saw a vast, dark plain with a mist swirling all around. Out of the mist from far away, this very tall man came walking toward me taking big strides. He had long, shiny black braids and dark skin. He was very muscular and he was wearing a loin-cloth and thongs or straps around his arms. I had this fleeting thought that he was either an American Indian or an ancient Hebrew. There was a light far away on the horizon. The light was behind him so I couldn't see his face. I had the thought, 'This is a very ancient spirit. And he is a mighty leader.' Then I felt this overwhelming fear, that I wasn't capable of raising somebody that strong and important. I suddenly saw this place inside myself, I guess it was my uterus. I saw a bloody blotch where the baby was attached. And then the whole thing was over.

"I talked to my grandmother that night. I didn't want to tell her about the Indian/Hebrew man. I've told very few people this, because it sounds so weird. But I said I'd had a funny dream and saw some blood. She said 'Uh-oh. Blood's not a good thing to see.' Two days later I miscarried.

"I got really depressed. I told my husband that if I didn't get something little to hold and love, I was going to die. So we got a puppy. He was so cute I couldn't stay depressed too long.

"By then, I was pushing forty. We had never really 'tried' before. The idea of making a baby was a turn-on. We were making very tender love looking at each other with all the lights on. It was a very con-scious mating, which really made it special. Right at 'that' moment, our dog jumped up on our bed and started licking both of our faces and wagging his tail. We were laughing and coming at the same time—definitely a new sexual experience which I highly recommend!

"I got pregnant that very day. It sounds so dumb when I say it out loud, but I've always felt that our dog was a blessing from the uni-verse, that he somehow made up for that weird miscarriage." She laughs self-consciously.

"There's more. When I was pregnant, I read everything I could get my hands on about delivering a baby. I could have passed orals in obstetrics. Besides all the medical textbooks and popular books, I read some New Age books my friend lent me. One described imaging. When you started dilating, instead of thinking about pain, you were supposed to think of yourself as a lotus flower opening. I liked that image a lot. I was actually working on that image and feeling very calm.

"But when my water broke, I ran to the bathroom, sat on the toilet, and my whole body began to shake uncontrollably. I have never been so terrified in my life. Abject terror. I was held up once at knifepoint and that didn't come close to how scared I was right then. Suddenly, I had this thought, 'This is actually happening. There is nothing you can do to stop it. You can either go with it, or fight it, but here it comes.'

"An enormous peace came over my whole body. The shaking stopped. Our doctor said we had plenty of time and to go to bed. I lay down. When I felt the first big pain, I imagined a cloud. I climbed up on it, it went way up high, and I watched everything from then on. I must've been in pain, but I never experienced any.

"My husband, the doctor, and I told jokes and laughed during my entire labor. The only way we knew I was having a contraction was when the monitor told us I was. I never felt a moment's pain! Even at the moment of birth. I won't say it felt good. But it was like this 'Ahhhh' feeling, this total opening, and she slipped out.

"They handed her to me. I looked in her eyes. I knew we'd known each other in some other life a long time ago. She was looking back at me, but her eyes just were not baby eyes. It was as if her eyes were saying, 'Yes, we know each other.' It was so intense and so weird because I never have that kind of thing, except for that weird Indian/Hebrew stuff.

"They took her away to clean her up while they were sewing me up. She started crying. I called out across the room, 'It's okay, Sarah. Don't cry.' She stopped crying. All the nurses and doctors stopped dead in their tracks. Then my husband said, 'I guess we're calling her Sarah.' We hadn't picked a name yet. Everybody laughed and started bustling around again.

"When she was a baby, all the old ladies used to say things. An old black lady on the bus looked right in her face when she was about a month old and said, 'She's an *old* soul.' An old Chinese lady looked at her and kept nodding. 'She been here before,' she said. An old German lady with a cane was so bent over she was at face level with Sarah, who was in her stroller. The woman stopped right in front of the stroller and laughed out loud. 'You skipped being everything and went right to being old!' She nodded like she knew something I didn't and then she walked on down the street.

"Everything about my life is so regular, but everything about my having a baby was like . . . DOOdoDOOdo (she hums the *Twilight Zone* theme song and then laughs self-consciously).

"All of that stopped after she was about a year old. What do you think it means?"

I haven't the foggiest notion what it means. But every story of how families come to be reaffirms my feeling that there is magic involved in their formation.

THE TRANSFORMING POWER OF MOTHERHOOD

When I first met my neighbor, she was a rather unprepossessing woman in certain ways. Single. Middle-aged. Drab in her choice of colors. Not pretty, not ugly. Nice, smart, kind. But rather timid, the kind of person you might miss in a crowd of three. So it took me aback when she told me she had decided to adopt a child. It seemed like such a gutsy thing to do. And she seemed so un-gutsy.

The child arrived in due time. It was winter. The little face peeked out from inside a Snugli, wrapped up tight in his mommy's coat. A darling face, a wide-awake, bright-eyed face. He looked like a miniature Aztec god. But it was what happened to Mommy that was the shocker.

First a fetching maroon beret appeared, a kind of jaunty colorful accessory that didn't quite go with the rest of Mommy's look. Then a fabulous mustard-colored jacket took the place of the serviceable down jacket that had been just fine for the last few years. Then in short order, the lifeless, listless, mousy-brown hair drawn back into a tired clump of a ponytail was transformed into a glistening honey, wavy cascade that cried out for—and got—perfect makeup. Rich lipstick, glowing skin.

It was as if the love of this child transformed this woman, giving her whatever internal self-confidence it takes to toss back your long hair and laugh out loud, rather than scurry along the edges of life, unnoticed.

I have watched over the last five or six years, as mother and son have continued to grow, mature, and enrich each other's lives. I am struck, every time I see them, by how perfect their union is.

THE MAGIC OF PARENTHOOD BY BIRTH OR ADOPTION

Here's a dad, in a brusque voice over the phone from Miami:

"She had had three miscarriages. Then her doctor put her on Clomid. It turned her into a witch. Then I found out that stuff can cause a miscarriage. I was on the phone with the doctor when I heard that. I just hung up on him. I'd had it with him.

"I told my wife I was sick of this stuff. She's the one who brought up adoption. I didn't have any need to have my genes go on. I didn't even really have a big need to be a parent. My life had been pretty nice. It was my wife who really wanted to be a parent. Anyway, when she suggested adoption, I said, 'Sure, why not?'"

But even this clipped, matter-of-fact kind of guy suddenly transforms. His voice surprisingly quivers with deep-felt emotion. "I can't imagine, now, what my life would've been like without my son."

A woman from Portland exclaimed, "I am so glad all that fertility stuff didn't pan out. Because if it had, I wouldn't have this child! And I cannot imagine loving another child more."

Just as in biological parenthood, once we hold the child in our arms, the magic wand of love is waved, erasing all the pain. Am I downplaying the often deep-seated pain of couples giving up a notion that they would have a biological child? No. Am I ignoring the tension and hideous self-exposure necessary to wend your way through the process of adoption? No. Am I sidestepping whatever self-realizations, and attendant pain, accompany a single woman as she finally admits, "I am probably not going to find my soul mate this time around"? No.

But I am focusing, not on how hard, and often sad, it is before the adoption, but rather on how truly splendid it is once the trial-by-ordeal has been overcome.

Perhaps a psychologist might offer, with an empathetic smile, that those who adopt have to come to terms with the fact that for most adoption is not the first choice. They must rearrange their innards to accommodate deep disappointment before they can move on. Yet the love that I see in the groups I lead—and in the homes of friends whose children have come to them by various routes—is profound.

I am struck over and over with the feeling that there is something mysterious and exquisite about all children and parents, and about when and how they find one another.

Overwhelming love, of course, is not limited to those who adopt, nor is magic.

"The first time I held my daughter," reports one mother, "I had the funniest feeling come over me. The love was so strong and so tender. I just held that tiny thing in my arms and I thought, 'Now I am capable of killing. If anyone ever threatens my child . . .' It was such a fierce feeling to have at the same time that I felt so soft. And so unlike me."

For another mother, because of complications with her cesarean, it wasn't until the second day that she could physically get to go see her child, who had to be in intensive care. There, amid all the high-tech machinery, "I fell in love with him," she says. The simplicity of her words offsets the powerful emotion that resonates in her voice.

"There was a big medical hubbub," says another. "They kept me in the surgical recovery room all night on morphine. I was in a drugged state in this dim light, in and out of sleep. I suddenly saw my daughter's face, which I'd only seen for a couple of minutes before they whisked us apart. I knew exactly what she was going to look like when she was grown up. It was a very sensual, passionate, earthy face. She was gorgeous. And I thought, 'She looks like a Sophie.' The next morning, they moved me back to my room, I had my baby with me, and my husband came in. The first thing he said was, 'I was thinking last night. What do you think of the name Sophie?' We had never even put that name on our list before!" The magic of parenthood.

THE OLDER PREGNANT LADY

Being pregnant is intense for all women. Some are happy, some uncomfortable. Yet our age gives these feelings a stronger spin.

Here's a father talking. He is married to a woman in her late forties who was heavily involved in the women's movement way back when and whose life is still informed by it. "I should've kept her barefoot and pregnant for years! I never knew her to be so happy and relaxed." Although she never lets him get away with sexist stereotyping, she laughs along with him at this ultimate of ultimates when it comes to sexism. She agrees. "I loved being pregnant."

"I have never been so turned on in my life," exults a forty-four-year-old performance artist whose regular "being turned on" makes most of our lives look like PTA bake sales.

"I felt fabulous the entire time," a thirty-eight-year-old business consultant pronounces with relish. "But the best part started around my seventh month when I started really showing. It was the only time in my life that I loved the cat calls and whistles I got from the workmen on the street. When they call you 'Mommy,' it is just the sexiest thing ever. It makes you feel so ripe."

"You want to know why we're considered high-risk?" asks a forty-four-year-old TV producer with a stand-up comic's delivery. "You make somebody gain two and a half pounds a week, make their ankles swell, stick 'em in a heat wave, give 'em heartburn to die from, keep 'em from getting one decent night's sleep because they can't get comfortable, tell 'em they can't drink booze or coffee, take tranqs, or dye their hair! And on top of all that, refer to them as elderly gravidas. Elderly? Excuse me! High risk! I must've exploded a hundred times a day. Between the yelling and the crying, my assistant would've been luckier if I'd fired her. The way I treated her! High risk? I'm lucky my husband didn't leave me. High risk!"

A forty-eight-year-old reports that she, too, was uncomfortable physically, with indigestion, backaches, and fatigue. She couldn't sleep at all for the last month and had to rig up a pillow contraption on the couch in a vain attempt to find a position she could bear to lie in. Her physical discomfort, however, was less troubling than her worry. Speaking over the phone from the outskirts of Philadelphia, she says, "I'd had three miscarriages. I'd also had four artificial inseminations and two in vitros. There were all those hormones I had to take. Because of them, my mood wasn't great." Her laugh indicates that that is an understatement. "I was worried about the long-term effects of taking so many drugs." And most of all, she was worried to death that the baby wouldn't make it. "I couldn't wait to feel movement," she says. "And sonograms! I had so many. Every time, I couldn't wait to hear the baby's heart. Knowing I'd already lost three babies, and knowing in vitro is an even higher risk, I worried my way all through the pregnancy." She is a very happy mommy now.

LOSS

Not everybody who is pregnant at our age ends up a happy mommy, though. As you probably know from personal experience, many of us sustain the blow of miscarriage. There are no communal or religious rituals for dealing with this loss. You can ask to have a prayer or mass said if you're part of a religious group. But there is no real closure. We have no established rituals because we have not lost a child. What we have lost are our hopes and dreams about having a child. Yet the personal grief, though it heals somewhat with time, cuts deeply when it is fresh.

For some, there are even harder losses to live with.

ANGELA

One woman I met told me over the course of several hours and several cups of tea the ordeal she and her husband went through—first struggling to conceive a child and then, when they'd managed that, having to face the hardest decision they would ever have to make in their lives.

"You don't know from the test how severe the condition is," Angela says. She is talking about Down's syndrome.

"It could be quite severe. But for all you know, it could also be a child with a high ability to function. When we investigated it, what we found was that the Down's adults who were the happiest lived on their family's farms. They were productive members of their family and their community."

We sat in their loft. The walls were lined with books. There were books piled in corners like sculptures, piles of books used as end tables near chairs. There was, in fact, little but Persian rugs, plants, and books. A sparsely furnished home, bursting with ideas.

"My husband and I are both professors. Where in our world could we find a place where our child would be a productive member of our community?"

We sat in silence

She went on. "It was a girl. When they're little, there are many options. They go to school, there's a whole network of backup support. But when they're older, and they're no longer cute, the options are a lot less"—she searched for a word—"pleasant."

More silence.

"And we're older. There would be years when we wouldn't be around to protect her from all the things that can happen to a defenseless woman out in the world."

We sat in silence a third time, her bowed head and tears more eloquent than any articulation of the unspoken fears that a mother of a girl carries close to her heart.

Being a mother and taking the best care of your child comes in many forms. Guarding, shielding, keeping your child out of harm's way—that's what a mother does, even if it means that protecting your child from possible harm will break your heart.

Angela is still trying to have a child. She has tried alternative medicine and Chinese medicine in addition to assisted reproduction. Only time will tell how her family will proceed.

CORLISS

As strikingly beautiful as a high-fashion model, with shorn hair that sets off the regal shape of her head, she does not look like your old-fashioned image of a radiologist.

"I've wanted to have a child for a long time," she says early on in our interview.

But her road toward parenthood has exacted heavy tolls. It is a treacherous road that many of us have traveled. Her first husband had children from a previous marriage and didn't want any more; that was one of the reasons they got divorced.

"He's since remarried and had three more," she says, a slight raise of an eyebrow her only comment.

She remarried at thirty-nine. "My friends kept saying, 'You shouldn't wait. Try to get pregnant.' But Garrett felt like 'trying' was unromantic.

"The day we got married, I was having cramps, so I was sure I wasn't pregnant.

"We went to Sardinia a couple of days later. There's nothing there. It was wonderful. I still hadn't gotten my period but I didn't really think about it because there was so much going on. You know, a wedding, a flight, a honeymoon.

"My breasts started hurting. It dawned on us that I was probably pregnant. We were so excited. We immediately went crazy—like how long should we wait before we tell people? We started thinking of names. We were having so much fun. And being very stupid also. . . ." She drifts off in thought.

"I started to bleed after we were there for a week. There was a little hospital. It was almost like having goats in the waiting room. No one spoke English very well, and I had to try and tell them what was wrong. They kept laughing. It was horrible. They pushed on my abdomen, which is what you do if you think someone is having an ectopic pregnancy. They said, 'Don't have sex till this goes away.'"

"We have been married three years, and half the time people have been saying, 'Don't have sex.'"

She looks out the window for a while.

"We flew home. I went to my GYN first thing the next morning. She did a pregnancy test, and was all excited. She did a sonogram, but she couldn't find the embryo. She took a blood level. I was exhausted. I hadn't slept in twenty-four hours. My blood pressure was really high. I went back on Wednesday and they did another blood level. The blood levels were flat." Her voice becomes flat as she says this.

"My doctor sent me to get a sonogram at the hospital. The doctor was there for an hour. Nobody was talking. I went back into his office and he said he was ninety percent sure it was ectopic. He was very nice. I felt so sorry for him because I couldn't stop crying. To be that excited on your honeymoon and then have this happen. It was horrible.

"I went back to my doctor. She was going to try not to do surgery, because sometimes these things just go away.

"Two days later, I started bleeding. I thought, 'I'm getting my period so this nightmare is over.' My doctor did another blood test. The levels were much higher. She wanted to do surgery.

"You know it's awful. At the same time you have to think, 'Oh, I've got to call the insurance company. Can you authorize this?'

"My parents didn't know I was pregnant. The first anybody knew about anything was when Garrett called everybody from the hospital."

She collects herself until she is ready to go on.

"We had a name for the baby. It wasn't a real name. It was a silly name. It was Nearly, because it had just started. When we were in Sardinia, it was a girl. I mean I don't know if it was a girl, but in our minds, it was a girl. We'd given her this whole personality. She was very cute, and we'd see all these little bugs, and we'd tell her about the little bugs."

It is hard to watch someone cry who comes across initially as so strong.

"I'm talking like this to you," Corliss marvels, drying her eyes, "but I don't think I've ever had a conversation like this with my family."

That is why we're here, all we women, sometimes sharing more with strangers who are like us deep down inside than we can share with the ones we're connected to by blood and time.

"My gynecologist was able to save the tube," she continues. "We tried again and I got pregnant immediately.

"We thought maybe Nearly didn't make it because we called her Nearly. So we called this one Totally. Nearly was very clearly a girl. I don't know what this one was."

This, too, was an ectopic pregnancy. The doctor advised ending it by injection. "It was hard for us to willingly do that because you feel like you're killing something, but she said this is just not viable. So we did that," she says simply.

"Then we tried to get pregnant again, and that took four months. That one never had a name. That one spontaneously disappeared. So then we went to a fertility specialist."

IVF

Corliss describes the office and the procedures for in vitro fertilization.

"They still can't find a reason. The only thing they can come up with is 'You're older.' The IVFs should've worked. We did three cycles. I did everything. I was a good patient. I made lots of eggs and they would get fertilized. It was just a continuing shock that it wasn't working."

I asked the obvious: Had they tested her husband?

"They asked him to be a sperm donor!" Her humor surfaces. "Go ahead, honey! At the age of forty-three!"

She excuses herself for a minute. I sit wondering what the doctors could have been thinking to ask for his sperm. Were they that disconnected from the feelings of the people they were supposed to be helping? Couldn't they imagine that a wife having trouble producing eggs might have "issues" raised if her husband's sperm was used for another family? Couldn't they intuit that a man not able to have his own biological child might have negative feelings about having a child out in the world whom he'd never know? But whether these thoughts have occurred to her or not, Corliss has other things to share.

She comes back, slips off her sandals, and folds one long leg under herself on the couch. We have been together for what feels a lot longer than the actual time that has passed.

She starts again. "Everybody talks about IVF being this roller coaster. It's annoying and expensive, but it's rather pleasant. After they put the embryo in, you have to lie down for two days, and frankly that was wonderful. There were some really good moments!" She laughs. "For two days, people took care of me. My friend came over and brought a movie. Another brought food. You get treated like a queen!" She laughs. "In some ways it was like a six-month rest, because I couldn't stay up late, I couldn't get to work on time. It was wonderful in a lot of ways." She laughs.

THE "TAMA" CONNECTION

"I would lie on the couch and read. I read some great books, usually about women, and all these magazines. In one of the magazines was an article written by Tama Janowitz. It was a diary of her going to China to adopt a baby. It was just the most delightful writing. She's very funny, which was really helpful. She talks about going over there with all these other people. Usually you go with four other couples. You don't know them from Adam. Apparently you stay in China for a couple of weeks before you get the baby. You don't do anything. You're just *there* with the other couples. They were eating together. She was in hell! And nobody else will admit to being in hell!

"You're a complete idiot because you've never had a kid. The kid's only not screaming when it's being thrown up in the air. These kids are nine months old, they're not small. She said her husband could throw the kid in the air, but she couldn't even hold the kid up! They named the kid Willow because it was an antidote to the short, fat baby.

"By the time she gets the kid home, she thinks, 'It's just the most wonderful thing! And I want to adopt a child from India that has the little bangles!'

"Her writing was so positive. I hadn't even thought about adoption. But this article was just so funny. It made a huge impression and got filed somewhere in my mind."

BEYOND THE PROCEDURE

"I don't think the hormones are very good for your body. I definitely gained weight. I feel like my body changed in ways I'm not happy about.

"I was left feeling that I have a body that doesn't work. You just don't like your body. The residual effect for me is that I say, 'People are supposed to have sex. Okay, I'll have sex. I remember that that's something you're supposed to do.' I know this sounds awful but I almost do it because Garrett wants to and I know that's what people do."

She laughs. It is not a happy sound.

"It's weird. I love hugging, I love all that stuff. I used to love sex, so this is not my normal thing."

She takes a sip of water.

"I feel like our relationship is better and not worse because of all this in some ways [her voice goes up in a question]. Because I always felt like he was very much with me through all of this. So that's good. Rumor has it that people frequently break up over stuff like this." She coughs, and then is silent for a moment. "But I didn't, I feel like it's, I mean, I'm not *glad* that it all happened, but . . . [silence] you know. I feel like our relationship is definitely stronger. Or something."

THE NEXT STEP

"So after the three IVFs, we went to another doctor," Corliss continues. "He wasn't particularly hopeful."

She describes another IVF, other tests to see if she has an autoimmune problem.

"They couldn't figure out what was the matter, so the idea was that something must be wrong with my eggs. My eggs were no longer viable. Of course, who knows if that's the problem?

"So after that IVF didn't work—and this is the part where it got hard, so it's probably harder to talk about—I wanted a baby. It was just so clear that I wanted a baby."

EGG DONOR

"There was nothing else to do except adoption or an egg donor. We started to explore them both at the same time. Garrett really wanted to do the egg donor. But there's only a fifty percent chance that you'll get pregnant. It's more expensive than the IVF. We didn't have much money at this point. We've basically used just about everything.

"I feel selfish saying this, but I wanted a baby! I couldn't handle the uncertainty anymore. If we do the egg donor and it doesn't work, we don't have any money to adopt. I figured we had comfortably one more shot at doing something for a while, until we were able to save money again.

"I had trouble doing something that had only a fifty percent chance of working. And I think, honestly, I had trouble with the fact that it would be biologically Garrett's and not mine.

"These are things that don't make me feel good about myself, but I also have to be honest. I don't like the place that it comes from in me. 'Why should I have some other woman's child when I can't have my own?' It infuriates me. I haven't gotten past the point where it makes me nuts.

"I really tried to think about it. But he understands. Maybe I can work on it. We compromised. We said, 'All right, the first thing we'll do will be the adoption.'"

TRANSITION

"Adoption has been very hard for Garrett. He's felt such an enormous loss of control about my being able to stay pregnant, or his ability to get me pregnant. And then having all these doctors there trying to make it happen when it was something that *we* should've been doing.

"He's had a hard time, too, because he feels like he could have had his own biological child. There's nothing wrong with him—not that there's anything wrong with me either," she hastens to add.

ADOPTION GROUPS

"We spent four or five months talking to adoption counselors and getting information. And we started going to groups. He wouldn't want to go, and I would always want to.

"They held the groups in an ugly hall. It was always on Saturday night. It was always dark. It would always pour. Not a little rain, but like bad-movie rain.

"The people weren't happy. Somebody walked up to us and told us that she'd been abused as a child and therefore the adoption agency she was working with wouldn't let her adopt a child.

"And I thought, 'Why are you telling me this?' Then she said she had adopted a child, and the neighbor thought she was abusing her child. I thought, 'This is not good. I'm not having fun here.' Other people have gone to this organization and found it wonderful and supportive, but it wasn't a good experience for either of us.

"It was very hard to think of yourself as a person who's defective and can't have a child. That's what I felt in those places. Like you're in a place with defective people and you're defective and no one's happy. It just felt bad.

"So for a while, our experience with adoption was the feeling, 'There must be something wrong with you.' This is in addition to the feeling that you're ugly, fat, and not in control of your body. You're not feeling happy."

DOMESTIC ADOPTION

"Garrett wanted to do a domestic adoption. We did the home study, we got certified, we found lawyers. The state needs to okay you. You need to get documents and recommendations. We got fingerprinted! We did the whole thing.

"Garrett really felt that he wanted to choose the mother. It was very important to him. But I was really frightened that when push came to shove he'd say no to everybody, because he'd take a look at the mother and go, 'That's not what I want my child to be.'

"The other thing with domestic adoption is that you're lucky if you get one person who answers your ad. Once you get two people who answer your ad, the reality is one of them will be a druggie.

"Again, it doesn't feel good to say this, I'm not proud of any of this, but I don't know how I'd feel about another woman who got to be the mother of my child and I didn't get to.

"But I thought, 'Okay, I'm uncomfortable, but if this is going to make him happy and make him do this, then I'll do it.' But I had never forgotten the Tama Janowitz article. I can't put my finger on what was so appealing about it. It was like being handed a baby. When you get there, a doctor or nurse hands you your baby. I actively don't want to choose. Even if somebody shows us three pictures, I just don't want to choose. I feel as if it's hubris. It's tempting fate.

"We had done everything we needed to do to qualify for a domestic adoption. Then someone who's been a close friend of Garrett's for twenty years said, 'Have you ever thought about China?'"

CHINA

"I basically kept my mouth shut through this conversation and let Garrett talk to his friend. His friend had a neighbor who had just adopted from China. I let him talk.

"From that conversation, I said, 'Can we think about that again?'

"And we did.

"There's a group called Children from China. When I looked around that room I thought, 'I want to be friends with all these people.'

"That's the other thing that swayed me. You have an automatic group. You didn't get to go through pregnancy with people so you didn't get your baby group. But you have this group you can go to the playground with.

"That's what started with Tama Janowitz. That there was *someone* who was completely positive. What was so funny about what she wrote was that she was so honest. This *has* been a nightmare!

"What I experience with all these people is a wholeness. Rather than 'I can't do something,' it feels like you're whole again, not defective. It feels good.

"Who knows if you're doing it for selfish reasons, but it's nice to feel that this person might not have had a very good life, and here you are! It feels good to do that.

"With domestic adoption, if you hang in there and if you're willing to spend unlimited amounts of money, you'll have a child. But we don't have unlimited amounts of money. We could end up not having a baby because we could run out of money! The mother can change her mind. It could be three years from now.

"Now, unless something goes terribly wrong with the Chinese government, in a year's time we'll have a baby.

"I just want to be a mother!"

WHY WE ALL WANT TO BE MOTHERS

"If someone had said to me four years ago, 'You can't have children,' it would've been the most devastating thing I'd ever heard. But it's so exciting now to think, 'You're going to have a child,' and it doesn't matter where it comes from.

"All the little things. When I got dressed this morning, I wore this ring because it was my grandmother's. All the good things in life that you remember, like making pancakes, the smell of cut grass, you want to share that. I think that's what's so exciting. I made cookies the other day. We call this baby Hooligan! Garrett came in the kitchen and said, 'Are you going to make cookies with the hooligan?'

"So he's excited.

"What I want to do is be able to share family. Maybe the child's going to hate the books that I liked! I'm still in the cozy haven of the idea that the kid will like everything I like. When you go through all this you have on these rose-colored glasses. But it's mostly just about wanting to share things with my child. And with my grandchildren some day. That's what it's all about."

As I write this, Corliss and Garrett are on their way to China. By the time they read this, it will seem almost like someone else's story. Because they, like all of us, will no longer be thinking about trying to become parents. They will have done it.

Although becoming parents—for all of us, no matter how we did it—may have felt Sisyphean, the giving birth and the getting were the easy parts.

Now we have to raise them.

Part 2

Rearranging Our Lives

"*No more lying on the couch eating a pint of Häagen Dazs for dinner,*" *the forty-one-year-old mother of a one-year-old says with a laugh.*

"*I didn't realize how often I stayed late at the office until I had to start thinking about when our sitter had to leave,*" *says another mother.*

"*When you add up baby-sitting, the tickets, parking, and food, it's a hundred bucks just to go to the movies and have a cheap dinner out,*" *says another.* "*It's not worth it!*" *She is a New Yorker. For the rest of you it's only fifty to seventy-five dollars!*

From the older mother of a preteen: "*You know what I love about sleep-away camp? You can smoke! You can drink! You can run around the house naked!*"

While smoking and drinking may not be at the top of your list of pre-parenthood things you miss, with the arrival of a child, not an inch of your life is unaltered.

Rearranging
Our Lives

3

Transforming from a Couple into a Family

I wouldn't trade away one single second of the last ten years of being the mother to the child I've been lucky enough to have in my life. Not for anything under the sun.

Well . . . actually . . .

Several tantrums—and the flashing lights, blaring brass band, and big-toothed emcee screaming "Ladies and Gentlemen! She has hit the One-Millionth Phone Interruption!"—are moments you could twist my arm to part with.

And what would I trade those annoying scenes in for? Or, if I'm honest, even more gratifying times than those?

Lying in bed just one more time on Sunday morning (which was really Sunday afternoon) doing the *Times* crossword puzzle with my husband. Propped up on pillows. My head resting on his chest. Drinking in the smell that made me fall in love with him. Watching as he scribbled his idiosyncratic *E*s. In ink, oh, self-assured man I adore! My knowing arts and food, his knowing sports and politics. Feeling the rumble of his deep voice murmuring, "Okay, which section should we go to now?" My pointing to the quadrant we'd attack next.

God, what I would give to feel that sensual safety, peace, and total containment. Just one more time.

Our Sunday mornings are a bit different now.

I get up at six, which I do every day, no alarm needed. I make coffee, unload the dishwasher, take the dog out for a long run, sometimes dash to the store to pick up juice, milk, the paper, and rush home.

I hurry, no longer consciously aware of the chronic pressure of time. My husband is already up and dressed. He has to work on Sundays. We don't leave our daughter in the house alone.

Up until the last year or so, our single-digit daughter would've already been up. She and my husband would've been playing together. I would come home, bustle around, putting groceries away, feeding the dog, wishing I could be part of what was going on, feeling as if by calling in from the kitchen I was inserting my way into their play rather than joining it.

Now that she's a tween and turning into a young lady, she's still asleep. My husband and I unconsciously keep our voices low, murmuring practicalities. Don't forget this, So-and-so wants you to call, can you pick up on your way home, have a good. Luv you. Luv you, too. It is a very different kiss, this soft affectionate brushing of cheeks, from the kind we used to exchange.

And the *Times* crossword puzzle? When I asked my husband dreamily if he remembered how we used to do it together, he wisecracked, "Now it's whoever can get to it first." Our shared laughter, with so many layers to it, is a lot richer than in those early, heady days. In some ways.

I know one couple our age who assiduously staked their claim to remain "a couple," with inviolate rights. From the moment their children were born, more than a decade ago, they established hard-nosed edicts. Closed-door policy. No kids in bed unless invited on the weekends as a big special event. A bed so high that the grown-ups need a step stool. When the kids were toddlers, heavily invested in breaking rules, they couldn't get into that bed unaided when they tried.

But though their door is closed, whether they like it or not, the couple will never again be able to lie in bed the way they used to do. Even when the kids aren't home, one tiny corner of your mind and heart, like Richard Pryor's brilliant "Deer Drinking Water," is always tuned in, alert to the possible knock, call, or interruption stemming from real or imagined needs.

Naturally, time alters any relationship. Had my husband and I maintained the passion of our first few years throughout the past twenty, they probably would have had to institutionalize the two of us.

But in addition to the passage of time, the very existence of a child, as well as each child's own personality, changes the fundamental workings of a relationship. For better and worse.

Keeping the arrow pointed toward the "better" end of the scale is the essential balancing act of any marriage. Adding children simply makes the scale waver at a more rapid, sometimes violent, rate.

THE BROAD STROKES OF CHANGE: THE TRIAD

Any psychologist or marriage counselor will point out the basics.

When a couple becomes a threesome, some stress is inevitable due simply to change and the addition of another personality to the mix. We shift from a diad to a triad, in the lingo of family counseling. In the best of circumstances this requires maneuvering as the fluid relationships alter and re-form into new shapes.

It is when the balance shifts that things can go awry. Typically, the relationship between the child and one parent, usually the mother, becomes the dominant one in the home. Dad is left out in the emotional cold. Jealousies arise. Recriminations occur. Real communication and sharing between parents stop.

In addition to the emotional modifications, there are nuts-and-bolts lifestyle adjustments to be sorted out. How we divvy up the new work is a source of potential discord.

Although all marriages are altered in these general ways, the balance in each marriage tends to tilt in a slightly different direction. We might as well begin where all family sagas start. In the past.

LIFE B.C. (BEFORE CHILD)

Here's a metaphor that we throw around a lot that's very useful in comparing our new families with younger ones: baggage.

Younger couples are carrying around their parents' baggage. They may have what looks like a brand-new set that they chose, but they haven't traveled extensively on their own. They haven't learned what they need; they don't have a clue about some of the little traveler's tricks to get them in and out of places they don't like; and they haven't developed much in the way of taste. Thus, when they registered for wedding gifts, although the style and color may be their choice, they probably signed up for the make of "baggage" their parents use. And that's about all they start out with.

We, on the other hand, have a very different set of baggage. Most of us threw out our parents' stuff quite a while ago. A lot of us had to ditch a matching set from a previous marriage. Now I have my own brand. It has comfortable handles and exactly the right compartments, and it is in my favorite colors. It's also got some stickers, nicks, and scratches that remind me of some of the best, and worst, places I've ever been.

For our honeymoon, an older couple may have picked up one or two new pieces to make traveling together easier, perhaps giggling and feeling silly about how they match. But by and large, we each have our own set, and we both paid for everything we chose with money we earned.

Both of us also have a couple of battered cardboard cartons we've been dragging around for who knows how long. We're not even sure anymore just what's in them. The husband's got to haul around the wife's carton wherever they go. The wife has to vacuum around the husband's box all the time. We have seasonal fights about why we're still lugging this, or having to push around that; and woe unto whichever one of us suggests that the other throw his or hers out.

Okay, I'm sure you get the picture. Due to our age and experience, we are probably more set in our individual personal ways than the dewy-eyed couple sitting over there in the pediatrician's office whose ages put together equal one of ours.

We have more sophisticated interpersonal skills at our disposal. And we're clear about how we should run our homes.

Or so we'd like to think.

MARRIAGE B.C.

In the marriages of younger people, what usually precedes parenthood is a year or so of hot and heavy (sex and arguing). A kid just kind of comes along in the expected order of things. They arrive however many other kids they add. One of the partners may build a career and the other a home, or both may struggle in dead-end jobs to make ends meet, or one or both may go to school. But they all, regardless of careers and finances, spend the next couple of decades learning about relationships. They grow up as individuals, together or, as happens in approximately half of their marriages, eventually without one another.

The kids basically tag along for their parents' smooth or bumpy ride toward maturity.

The families that our children enter are, by definition, very different.

Many of us have our careers on track, not to mention the other aspects of our lives, including friendships, well-developed interests, and established personal routines. Not all of us, however, have ridden a smooth trajectory straight to the top. Some of us have shifted careers repeatedly, and have had a series of relationships, of which this current one may or may not be the last. Yet, by virtue of having spent several decades in what might be characterized as disorganization, we have our own system that is not as fluid as that of younger people.

Most strikingly, for couples our age, becoming parents has usually been a major driving force in our marriage for the last year if not many years.

If we had a particularly hard time, there may be residual anger, bereavement, and disappointment that must be worked out over the course of time. Adoption adds another layer of adjustment to be made. And since some adopted babies are not infants when they come to us, they present us with a different set of challenges as we adjust to our new family.

All of these elements shape the emotional landscapes of our individual homes.

But for every one of us, as for all parents, there is a moment when the excitement, drama, challenges, and struggles of trying to *become* a family are over.

We have a child. We are a family.

WELCOME TO OUR HOME: THE NEW OLDER PARENTS

Like all new parents, we are awash in powerful emotions when we bring the baby home. Ecstasy and wonder predominate in our homes; we are less likely to experience the ambivalence that many younger families feel. Yet many of us do experience negative emotions that catch us off guard.

Sometimes we are so exhausted by the emotionally draining process of becoming parents that by the time we get there, there is a letdown, all the more powerful for being so unexpected. Sometimes we are shocked by how boring the reality of parenthood is in the beginning.

Boredom is not the only emotion that may unpleasantly surprise and shame us.

Here's a woman who felt so strongly about anonymity with regard to this topic that I will omit identifying characteristics altogether:

"Those first couple of weeks, I really found myself short on patience. It really upset me. I found myself not reacting well to the hysterical screams of a small infant. And when I didn't have patience with her, I would be angry at myself.

"Crying sets me off. And for heaven's sakes! We're talking about a baby here! Babies cry! In the car, it gets to me right away.

"And then that dependence. That total, helpless dependence on me. It kind of freaked me out.

"The lack of patience feels physical to me. I feel my blood pressure rise and I feel my heart pound. It's not just a lack of something, it's a physically uncomfortable sensation. And I'm not used to feeling that way.

"You might think that I, as an older mother, would feel more patient. And have more experience. But I feel less patient. Does it have to do with being older? I don't know. I think this has been an important, valuable experience for me. But then there's always the danger that we 'older, experienced types' perhaps overanalyze." She laughs.

More of us report awe. "I have never experienced anything like those first few weeks with my daughter," marvels Ellen. Now head of a learning center for disabled children, she stayed home full-time until her child entered nursery school. "I was totally focused on my daughter. We were completely in sync. It was as if the whole rest of the world barely existed in the first few weeks. I was dimly aware of my husband. My parents and my in-laws came by at some point. But the only thing that existed for me was this tiny, amazing creature. When she slept, I slept. When she was awake, I was awake. I held her right in bed with me and never had a moment's fear that I would roll over on her. It was as if she was still one with me physically. She would burrow up against me, and we would drift in and out of this waking-sleeping time. When she was awake, she would stare at me wide-eyed, as if she couldn't draw enough in. Those tiny eyes would open up so wide. I talked to her whenever we were awake. And she listened so hard. Oh, those little fingers and toes! The newness of her. A miracle."

She thinks for a few minutes, remembering. "My daughter's six now. But those first few weeks stay with me. I don't know if other women felt this but I felt as if I turned myself over to her. Like nursing. In the beginning, I was so sore. A couple of times she latched on in the wrong place. I thought I'd go through the ceiling till I could get my finger in there and break the suction. But I bit my lip so I wouldn't scream and scare her. There's no other relationship in the world where I'd do that. Where what I feel is not as important. If I had to choose my feelings or hers, it wasn't even a choice. It was hers.

"Now that she's older, if she hurts me, by mistake or even on purpose, obviously, I let her know. She needs me to teach her. But on the big stuff, her needs still supersede mine. It started in those early days. It was like this rite, or something really spiritual. The only words I can come up with is that I gave myself over to her, body and soul.

"I marveled at that almost as much as I marveled at her. Before she was born, I spent a lot of time on myself. I'd been in therapy. I used to go to the gym all the time. I didn't take guff at work. I was clear about what I needed in a lot of areas of my life, including my relationship with my husband. I spent a long time working on allowing myself to feel entitled to have my needs met. Then all of a sudden, here comes this tiny little ball of love." She gets tears in her eyes. "Her needs needed to be met more than mine. And I needed to meet her needs more than I needed anything else in the world. That's what being a mother really means to me."

THE OLDER BEGINNER

Whether we are grappling with the distressing lack of ecstasy, or in baby heaven from day one, our adjustment to the practical ropes of parenthood has a quality that is different from that of younger parents.

Younger parents are feeling their way through many aspects of their lives. Almost everything is new and exploratory. We, however, far from Step One in most areas of our lives, are no longer used to being incompetent. Yet here we are, starting over, having to learn a whole new body of material.

Some of us joke about how awkward we feel.

"We were like a sitcom," says a thirty-eight-year-old Washingtonian with a laugh. "I run a department of the federal government. My husband orchestrates special events for some of the most important people in the world. But there we were, like two baboons, standing there scratching our heads, looking down on the changing table at all this yellowish gunk, going, 'What do we do now?'" She laughs. "It was the first time our son had made a real poopie. 'Is the washcloth still okay or are we supposed to use these wipey things?' 'Pick up his _____ and wipe under them.' 'No, *you* pick them up.' We were laughing hysterically.

"It's not exactly brain surgery. You figure it all out pretty quickly. But there are just all these things that make you feel so inept. There are the diapers, and the stroller, and figuring out how to close it up, and how to put the car seat in. It's endless! And that stroller falling over backwards business. Nothing makes you feel clumsier. Trying to hold the baby, worrying that you'll drop him, and trying to pick the stroller back up. My back is bad, so I've got to make sure I don't throw that out. Being a new parent wasn't quite like being an adolescent again, but it's as close as I want to come again in this life. At this age, you feel as if you're supposed to know how to do things. And here I was not knowing!

"At least my husband and I laughed. I met a woman in the pediatrician's office who was around my age and I really felt for her. She came in carrying her baby in the car seat. She leaned over to put her baby down. She had a huge diaper bag over her shoulder and it fell forward toward her baby. She caught it just in time before it smashed down on her child. She got tears in her eyes. I went over to help her. We were sitting in the waiting room talking. She said she couldn't wait to go back to work. She loved her baby but she couldn't take struggling with all the paraphernalia. It was driving her crazy."

Some of us bicker. Most of us read like fiends. Some do both at the same time.

"We went nuts over the umbilical chord," sighs a money manager. "When was it supposed to fall off? I liked *What to Expect*. My husband liked that AMA book. They all say the same thing, except that there are these picayune differences. Day twelve, or day thirteen. Then we'd call the doctor to settle it. We had his number on speed dial the whole first year. Then we'd fight about whether to listen to our doctor or one of the books. Every little thing would put us over the edge. We're both such perfectionists. It all seemed so overwhelming."

Some families hire a baby nurse. Hiring experts for any number of situations is more common among older parents. Many of us are more financially secure than our younger counterparts. But even when we have to stretch our budgets, older families are more inclined to value the "expertise" of others. Some of us are more comfortable in the role of manager rather than of mom. But there is an underlying element that some of us who are among the most competent in our own fields may be unwilling to acknowledge. Anxiety.

I have seen many couples defer to their nurses, whispering quietly, and nervously, together, "What does Janice say?" Our unwillingness, or perhaps inability, to address our underlying anxiety sometimes causes us to abrogate not only our authority but even our common sense, and to turn decisions about our own child over to a hired hand.

Some of us are unwilling, or afraid, to claim our babies, to say "This is mine. I am this child's mother [or father]. I will know instinctively what this child needs. And if I don't know instinctively, I will figure it out."

Some of us, once the child is past early infancy, come into our own. Others remain somewhat distant, afraid that we won't be able to know and give what our child needs.

Whether we know it or not, some of our fears about our parenting skills, as well as our strengths, may be reflections, or corrections, of our own pasts.

WHO'S MISSING FROM THIS PICTURE?

The women in a "new mommies" group were drawn together by a common theme. They identified themselves as older moms. They had come with their brand-new babies to meet other new older mothers. They ranged in age from their mid-thirties to their early forties. They ranged in type from self-possessed to somewhat scattered. They were ethnically and racially mixed. Judging from their speech patterns, they were all middle-class. From the details they revealed of their lives, their economic situations varied from struggling to quite comfortable. They were, in short, a classic representative group of us.

One woman was in her early forties. She was very poised, and even on a humid, heat-wave day in New York City looked calm and cool in a trim beige suit. She was a Wall Streeter, planning to return to work soon because, according to her reasoning, these were her peak earning years.

At one point in the discussion, she mentioned a scenario common to many older mothers. She asked her parents to wait a week or so before coming up from Florida for the birth of her child. They were supposed to come for a week. Then she added in a deadpan, "They lasted two days."

There were knowing laughs around the table.

What was striking to me was the response of the rest of the group. I have heard more older mommies than not report variations on the same theme. "I didn't want my mother there for the birth." "My husband and I felt it would be better if our parents came to the house once we were home rather than still in the hospital." "We arranged it so that they'd fly in after we'd been home from the hospital for a week." As I'm sure you know, this decision speaks volumes about having worked out a way to include our own parents, but essentially on our terms, because their terms have proven to be, shall we say, problematic.

I would wager my laptop and my entire ceramics collection that 90 percent of you completely understand all of this and all of its ramifications.

But when the same kind of statement is shared among a group of mommies who are younger, and I have seen this time and again, their responses are astonishingly different. Some of their mouths fly open. Some look sad. Some look askance. "I don't know how I would've done it without *my* mother," they say, in a tone that sounds vaguely like an accusation. Every once in a while, if a younger woman either is a trained psychologist or has been in therapy, you will see an understanding look on her face. The rest of them, honestly, are flabbergasted.

In the foreword, Debra spoke beautifully for those of us who have lost our mothers and don't have the choice. But for most of us, whether we can't or we chose not to, our mothers are not a primary source of information or guidance for getting our sea legs as new mothers.

PAST INFANCY: MOM, DAD, AND BABY

Once beyond the initial shock of having a baby, we begin to see the intensity of joy that characterizes many older families. Along with that joy comes the potential for imbalance.

In groups of mothers and their babies, I have observed an interesting phenomenon. We sit in a circle on the floor on a parachute with mommies holding their babies in their laps. Frequently a dad will take off from work and slip in for part of what is usually his child's first class.

Body language is telling. More often than not, when a younger father arrives, his wife will face him, often jumping up out of the circle. They will smile, talk back and forth, and then the younger father will take himself off on the sidelines, where he will sit down on the floor against the wall of the room and watch.

The older family usually presents a very different tableau. The dad will come right in, sit right down in the circle, and take the baby in his lap. He and his wife will communicate through touched shoulders as they sit side by side, beaming at their baby. It seems safe to infer that in other situations, including their homes, older couples are noticeably less fixed on one another and more riveted, in concert, on the child.

This small but telling moment in the newly forming family structure illustrates graphically the imbalance each group is prone to.

YOUNGER DAD / OLDER DAD

A psychologist offered developmental reasons that may explain why we see the older dad more comfortable taking his baby and sitting down in a circle with a group of women and babies, whereas the younger dad may be more at ease on the sidelines. (By the way, the "older" older dad, who we'll mention in chapter 11, usually opts to *stand* on the sidelines, or in some instances finds a chair to sit on, which I believe tells a different, interesting story about his relationship to his fatherhood. But here, I am focusing on the majority of older daddies, who range in age from their late thirties to early fifties.) Men, your son included if you have one, psychologically have to separate from their mommies in order to achieve their manhood. This normal growth pattern plays out most noticeably when they're adolescents. They usually exhibit a deep desire to distance themselves from all things womanly, sissy, girly, and soft.

If you watch a group of teenage boys, most will bang into each other, smack into each other, and "be cool." A classic example is a moment in the movie *Grease* where the character played by John Travolta is delighted to see Sandy—and then, remembering that his friends are present, retreats into "cooldom." Softness is considered unmanly.

By the time a man reaches his late thirties, however, he is sure of his own manhood. This internal knowledge allows him to behave in a more nurturing manner, in all aspects of his life, but most notably with regard to his child.

Thus we see middle-aged men on summer mornings in pale blue shirts and ties, jackets folded neatly over their arms, carrying their briefcases, holding hands with their preschoolers, sometimes kneeling in front of them to wipe away a real or imagined hurt. We see other middle-aged daddies, slightly paunchy, in jeans and T-shirts, what's left of their hair a bit unruly, their mustaches thick, their babies strapped to their bodies.

It's not that younger daddies, too, don't hold hands with their kids on their way to school. Younger daddies certainly carry their babies, prop their children on their shoulders, provide the strong arms needed at the end of a long day at the beach.

But there is an internal assurance of his own adulthood, and manhood, that allows the older dad to let his tenderness be visible. His maturity enables him to be comfortable entering a circle of women and sitting down on the floor because that is where his child is. He has no need to be off on the sidelines of his child's class. Or, by extension, of his child's life.

All this is played out in exaggerated form in the different kinds of imbalance that can occur in both homes. The younger dad is more likely to stand back, because he still has a vestigal need to avoid show-ing what he feels.

The older dad is more likely to show how deeply engaged he is with his child. He is as attentive to the child as the mother is. He may not, however, be paying so much attention to her. On the other hand, she may not even notice. Because they're both paying so much attention to their child.

ONE CHILD/TWO ADULTS: SLIGHTLY OUT OF KILTER

I tossed off a line earlier about how the kids of younger parents basi-cally tag along for the ride as their parents grow up. Not only don't our kids tag along for the ride, in many cases, the kids *become* the ride.

All first babies begin as only children. Since so many of ours, even those with older step-siblings, will live most of the time that way, let's look at how their singleness colors the family structure, and thus potentially the relationship between the couple.

I'd like to compare a family with a car trip. In families with more than one child, the kids interact on a kid level in the backseat while the adults interact on an adult level in the front seat, with occasional calls for a referee or instructions issued between front seat and back. In an only-child family, there is no metaphorical front seat–backseat separation. Mommy turns her head a lot; Daddy talks while keeping an eye on the rearview mirror. Both parents include the child in the conversation as well as in much of the decision making. Not only is the child included as an equal, but frequently, interactions get tilted *toward* the child. We often see the parents actually defer to the child as the dominant member of the group. This goes on without anyone ever noticing how it came to pass—or even the very fact that it exists at all.

Thus, unlike the textbook skewing of the family, where the mom-kid duo takes over, leaving the dad as a figurehead, we often set the child up as the focus of the home, and the driving force, rather than as a member of the family in good, albeit subordinate, standing.

In the words of one older mother who was herself the daughter of an older mother at a time when it was much more of an oddity than now: "I wasn't the Princess. I was the Queen."

Of course, with the addition of a child—a third person, a new family member—things will change. They have to change. In fact, they should change. But sometimes, if we become too child-focused, the change that occurs may not be the change we would have intended.

SEX? I'M SORRY, COULD YOU REPEAT THAT?

When did you become "Daddy" and I become "Mommy"? When, exactly, did we start playing only Raffi in the car? When did we stop eating sushi and start making mashed potato mountains with broccoli trees? When did we both start getting home from work and, instead of racing to strip off our clothes and lunge at each other, start elbowing each other out of the way to lift up our child and dance around the living room laughing and smiling in soft-focus twilight?

Where did our passion and lust go?

So many of the women I interviewed, when I asked them about sex, got sudden stinging tears in their eyes. They seemed caught off guard by a topic they'd pushed down deep, somewhere far away from their immediate concerns.

"I'm still nursing," said one thirty-eight-year-old. "The last thing I want when I fall into bed is to have my breasts touched. I am crazed for privacy, crazed wanting my body back to myself."

"Are you kidding?" one older mother guffawed. "I don't know what planet you're on, but . . ." She trailed off, unable even to imagine having sex with her husband. She stared off for a moment, seeing whatever images were hers. Then she said, "It's not like he's into it either, you know. We're both bone weary."

Almost all new parents are "bone weary." Almost all nursing moms yearn for physical space. Almost all women need time to recover from vaginal delivery or cesarean surgery. Yet it seems that younger women are more likely than we to regain their sex lives once past these early new-mother stages. Whether we bore our children or not, our hormone levels are changing. (See chapter 8, "Bifocals and Barney.") Many of us have been with the same partner for quite some time. Raising young children and keeping up with our jobs at the same time that we're experiencing hormonal shifts may combine to push lovemaking decisively to the back burner.

Wouldn't it be fun if in the "Helpful Hints" section I could give you a snappy *Cosmo*-style bulleted list of ways to get that zing back in your bed? But what would they be? Pretend you're strangers and pick each other up in a bar? One of you dress up in a costume (aproned maid-ette, muscle-bound bellhop, your choice of whichever dominant/submissive sex-money-power combination appeals to you!) and jump out from behind the door? Meet in either of your offices and do it on the desk? With the window washer watching? Get real.

"He's my best friend. We're more like brother and sister than any-thing else," says one woman who's been with her mate for close to twenty years. "I don't know what our sex lives would be at this stage without kids. But I do know that after the girls were born, we basically said good-bye to sex." Her twins have just turned nine.

"By ten or ten-thirty I'm wiped. My husband lies on the couch with the remote control till Letterman and Leno are over. Sometimes I wake up to go to the bathroom, and I can hear him switching back and forth. We don't go to bed at the same time. We used to love the morn-ings. But when you're trying to get two kids and two adults out of the house by seven-fifty, the morning is not exactly prime time for a snuggle, let alone anything else. It just doesn't happen."

"Since the kids came," says another woman, "I feel like my husband's my roommate. Somebody I live with and share space with. But some-body who has disgusting habits!" She laughs.

One woman, forty-five and the mother of a four-year-old, who's been with her husband for a decade, feels the lack deeply. "I wish it were no longer a need. It would be so much easier," she says. At least she and her husband are close enough that they can joke about the fact that for several years they've both been finding relief in masturba-tion. Yet that is an inelegant solution. "It takes the edge off. For maybe five minutes." She tries to laugh. She has a fragile, haunting beauty. Black hair, crystal-blue eyes against black lashes. Lines in her face, suggesting hurts other than this. "Lately, it's been making me feel so lonely."

Ever thought about an affair?

"Who has the time?" jokes the mother of twins.

"Eww," says another, sounding repulsed. "I already can't handle my life. Who would want a complication like that?"

Another looks thoughtful for a moment and then confides, "You want to hear something really sad? I don't even *fantasize* about doing it with somebody else, let alone have an affair. On the rare occasions when I do fantasize, it's about my own husband. How sad, or romantic, is that? Even so, somehow, by the end of the day, neither of us is really into it."

For many women, it's not really about sex. It's about love. And we love our husbands. We just can't seem to find the time—or the desire if we do find a moment—to make love with them.

Predictably, most women seemed surprised that others were going through the same thing. Each felt that everybody else was having a wonderful time, and that there was something wrong with her.

Whether there is "something wrong" or not, the lack of sex seems to prevail in many of our homes.

"I just never feel comfortable," says another. Her son "sleeps like a log." But, she says, "I always have one ear out that I'm going to turn around and he'll be standing there."

"I think one of the reasons we don't anymore is because I'm so physical with my child," says Gail, a mother in her late thirties with engaging dimples and a great, husky laugh. "I hug my son, I grab him, I hold on to him. My husband actually said to me recently that he couldn't remember the last time I just came up and kissed him on the back of his neck. I put most of my physical stuff into my child."

As we age, the sex drive diminishes for some. The harder we work, the more tired we are. The more needs we meet for others, the more the need to draw into ourselves for peace and privacy grows. For some women, there is also an appropriateness to shifting priorities, needs, and desires as we mature.

"Sex," says Cheryl. "You want to talk about sex."

A tenured professor in the humanities department of an Ivy League school, she is fifty-three. Her children are nine and eleven. She and her husband have been together for fifteen years.

Her thick chestnut hair is cut in a wedge that shows off her long, aristocratic neck. She wears an elegant cream-colored silk shirt, black trousers, a belt with a bold sculptural silver buckle, and the surprising touch of strappy, high-heeled, turquoise lizard sandals that she props up on her desk when she leans back in her chair to talk.

Her skin is staggeringly beautiful. I'm dying to know if she's wearing any makeup, and if so, what brand. I'd also like to know what moisturizer and hand and body lotions she uses. I want skin like hers. But drat! I have this series of questions prepared. This one leads us to the grown-up version of getting together to do our hair and talk about boys.

"I'm am artifact," she begins. "I was a hippy. I was at Woodstock. I was at Radcliffe when Tim was there [she means Timothy Leary, who was experimenting with LSD at Harvard]. I was in consciousness-raising groups. I was in SDS [a radical campus group in the 1960s]. I went to Washington to pull it down brick by brick if I had to, to end the war in Vietnam. I lived in a commune. During that entire period, we were all balling anything that moved, if you'll pardon my French.

"In the current climate, that sounds so crass and stupid. I feel for my students now. They'd be crazy to do what we did, even though I know a lot of them are experimenting sexually. I find myself with my own children connecting love and marriage every time sex comes up! Not that I'm a hypocrite, but unless they find a cure for AIDS, I really don't want my children to be too active sexually when they reach that age.

"But for us, it was a time of true liberation and experimentation. It was a heightened, sensual way of living in more respects than just sex. But sex was a big part of things. With men, with some women, in some groups. There was a freedom then of coming out of the restrictive fifties into this paradise of openness. Not wearing a bra was definitely a political statement. But it was also incredibly sexy. It was basically being turned on twenty-four hours a day!

"Somewhere toward the end of grad school, and certainly by the time I had my first teaching job, in my mid-twenties, I graduated to serial monogamy, with an occasional one-night stand. I lived with one guy for a few years, I dated the rest. Sex was great. There was one—we used to act out operas naked. There was an impassioned sculptor who lived in a little shack by the beach. I had my requisite tortured writer. He was riddled with a million idiosyncracies. That's really a kind word. He was as neurotic as they come. But really fabulous in bed. He used to do this little humming thing . . . but I'm not sure that's what you're asking about! I even had a fairly serious affair with another woman. That was a whole other kind of passion that was intense—although it wasn't ultimately for me. This is an aside, but you want to know the truth about women? I've never been with anybody as possessive as she was. It was so disappointing, because you think, well, a woman's going to be . . . a woman! You know, somebody you can be rational with." She shakes her head knowingly. "Guess again."

"Anyway, somewhere in my mid-thirties, I just kept going home alone.

"Then one night at a party, I saw this man literally across a crowded room. Everything you've ever heard in every hackneyed, trite romance book happened. Our eyes met. Within thirty seconds, he'd made his way through the crowd. We left the party, went to my place, tore each other's clothes off, and afterward he said, 'I know you've never had anything like that. Neither have I.' I hadn't. Then he said, 'I guess we're getting married.' I'd chalked marriage off long ago as an anachronistic institution. But I said, 'I guess we are.' I didn't even know the man's last name! He never left. We've been together ever since.

"As it turns out, we come from incredibly similar backgrounds. If I didn't know better, I'd say it was tribal, really primitive and primordial. We really are mated. We didn't have any trouble conceiving, even though I'd had four abortions during the course of my life and by that time I was already in my early forties. Sometimes I think it's because our gene pool was just strong. I don't know. But never, in all those years, did I ever have sex like I had with my husband."

And now?

She shrugs. "Can't really remember the last time." She brings her feet off the desk and leans forward. "But this is where I think people need to step back and think. There's a cycle to life. A time for things. This is a time in my life that I feel very much in my mind. I'm thinking about a lot of spiritual things, reading things I haven't read before. My husband is pursuing his own interests. We're awfully good companions. I'm really glad we had the kind of sex we had, and if we hadn't, I think things would feel empty now. But my life and my marriage feel full.

"We were in our forties when our kids were small. Sex became less of a pressing need. Maybe I'm suggesting that people are being sold a bill of goods—the idea that their lives aren't full enough and they should read a self-help article if they're not having sex all the time. Maybe it's okay—at least if you had it when you were young, like I did—to grow into the next role. To say, 'I was a girl, then I was a libidinous woman, and now I'm entering the next stage, where I know a lot and can think about things. Sex has diminished in importance.' And to not only be all right with that, but to exult in it. To revel in the next stage on the ladder of development.

"It's just a thought," she adds, smiling.

"I think, for me," says Miriam, a mother of two in her early forties, "it's that the intimacy with my children is more intense. It's impossible to replicate. When I first fell in love with my husband . . ." She smiles, shrugs. "I think that at this point, the flaws of your partner are readily seen. But the flaws of your children are just not important."

She has touched on something that gets into so many homes where we're juggling too many balls at once. "The last time we did it," she goes on, "all I could think of was how angry I am at him. I'm angry because he doesn't earn enough money. You read that everybody's so rich. We're certainly not. I'm mad that I've got to work so hard. I'm mad that he doesn't do a lot around here. Once you get angry, all the things you never noticed start to be real clear. Like his 'love handles.' They do not look like 'love' to me. Of course, I'm sure my thighs don't look so great to him anymore." She bursts out with her fabulous laugh. "It used to be that sex would drive everything else from my mind. But now, it just brings everything right out there." She pauses for a minute. "I wonder what *he* was thinking? Here I was engaged in this big fight in my head, and he was probably thinking about some model!"

She repeats my question: "How often do we do it?" Her face gets sort of sheepish. She hazards a guess. "Every two weeks." From the people I've spoken with, they've got a hot-and-heavy thing going.

I ask her to try and remember the last time they did it. When she tries to remember when it was, she can't quite. Maybe it was three weeks ago. . . .

When I tell her that at least according to the women I've talked to even once every three weeks sounds respectable, she laughs with delight. "And I bet he thinks that all the other guys are getting it a lot more!"

This is not true for all of us.

One forty-two-year-old mother of a two-year-old, whose birth came a year after his parents had met, laughingly said that she and her husband had just gone out and bought condoms to stash all over the house. "We're so spontaneous, and I just don't think I want to do *this* again at *this* age," she said, laughing as she jumped up and reached her son just as he was about to heave his second salvo of pebbles from the driveway into the border of flowers.

A forty-nine-year-old mother of a ten-month-old (and a veteran of five years of fertility treatments) laughed lustily. "I am finally enjoying sex! For the first time in my whole life, I'm not worried about getting pregnant or not getting pregnant!"

Here are two more. In their late thirties, they are friends of another woman I've interviewed, and have kindly agreed to meet with me. They are so striking, these two, with their halos of curly hair, one dark, one light, that they make me wish I were a painter. Or, better, a photographer. Because a painter might miss what a camera couldn't. How bright and dancing their eyes are. One with a wide, wide smile. The other with a delicate, sensitive face. Judged on the basis of bones and features alone, both of them are pretty. But the expressions on their faces, the intelligence in their eyes, and the sensitivity in what they have to say make them beautiful.

At the question about how often they have sex with their husbands, one's face lights up. "A lot! Every day sometimes for a week." She stops for a moment, thinking. "But then, I guess sometimes we don't do it at all for two weeks." She considers that for a moment, but then adds smilingly, "We always do it every day when we're on vacation."

"Where do you go?" asks the other. "And can I go there?" We laugh. But, like all jokes, it is telling.

What if your daughter's with you on vacation? I ask.

"No. Not as much then."

"It's hard to find the time," the other takes up. She has two young children. "In between when they go to sleep and when you go to sleep there are so many things to do. And then, you're sleep-deprived. . . ." Her voice trails off. But she offers hopefully, "We did finally get the sleep thing together! [As you probably know, 'the sleep thing' is a major accomplishment in most homes.] But finding the time is always so hard. Even when you do find the time . . . The other day, my oldest was at a birthday party and my baby was asleep. I had to drag my husband out of the basement. He was fixing something. We both always feel as if there are so many other things we have to do."

I think of Miriam, and how juggling so many things makes her angry. "Do you not do it because you're angry?"

"Who knows what's the chicken and what's the egg? Whether you don't do it because you're angry, or you're angry because you're not doing it. But when you finally do find the time, it's so special." I cannot replicate on the page the almost reverential way she says "special."

"Oh God, yes," agrees the other. "It's mating. It's the father of your child. There's nothing like that in the world."

And what they have expressed that we all know is that there is more to it than frequency. More to it than urgency. And while we all may wish we had the same abandonment that we may have had when we first met, or the "spontaneity" that only one of the women I spoke with felt was still a part of her life, there is something deeper, more meaningful. Something, as the two so beautifully put it, that is special. It is mating. With the father of your child.

Some families consciously work at building a time for intimacy into their lives.

"We go out every Saturday night," says one couple, "and every other weekend, our son stays with his baby-sitter. She's got two kids near his age, and he loves it. So do we."

"Every three months we go away for the weekend together," says another.

"Every Wednesday night, come hell or high water, my husband and I have a date," reports another.

But how does it happen that if we don't lose each other, we have to be so fierce and unyielding about holding on to what should, by all rights, be ours? Why should we have to regularly schedule what ought to be a spontaneous welling up of emotion? For other families, like the couple with the closed-door policy, when did they become so ferocious about treasuring their time together? How did it happen that in order to maintain our personal, private space, we have to make rules and guard them vigilantly?

How do all these subtle shifts occur, causing us to either stand firm or cave in?

The answer is that we have become a family.

TODAY'S NEW FAMILY

The kicker is that "family" no longer is necessarily the family we grew up in, perhaps railing against, but nevertheless fundamentally understanding. Family is a brave new world wherein we are trying, against a backdrop of deeply ingrained responses, to forge new relationships.

A large number of us have different cultural backgrounds from our spouses, and others also from our children. As the darling All-I-want-for-Christmas-is-my-two-front-teeth classic seven-year-old announced proudly, "My daddy's from Hawaii, my mommy's from Singapore, and I'm from China." A generation ago her statement would have been shocking. A generation hence it will probably be a nonissue. Even for younger couples born twenty years ago, her statement is only mildly significant. But for those of us who either bucked tradition strenuously or caused ripples of readjustment as both sides got used to the idea, and even for those of us in our generation who come from exactly the same culture as our spouses, the narrow focus we were raised with is not what we want to inculcate in our children.

Those cultural expectations were in many ways limiting. The clichés about the Italians having strong family ties, the Irish being tearfully poetic and attached to their mums, and on and on, are no longer useful. Most of us either can't, or choose not to say to our children, "*We* don't do that," and by "we" mean whatever ethnic group we feel part of. Yet those strong groups used to offer parents stable expectations about acceptable behavior. Furthermore, they used to offer spouses common expectations of behavior in the home.

THE CHALLENGE OF "MIXED MARRIAGES"

From the most mundane areas, such as who sits at the head of the table, to much more serious issues, such as how we work out conflicts between the adults, during every interaction we are improvising.

If our spouse responds to our child in a way different from what we grew up admiring, we may be stumped. Perhaps most distressing, we may even feel ourselves aware of age-old hateful prejudices that surface within the family. I have heard jokes that were just this side of racist traded back and forth between spouses. Although everyone laughs, what do those jokes reveal as to how partners feel about one another? And how do they translate to the children?

Tensions are typically caused by traditions and holidays. My family does it this way, your family celebrates that, our child's culture involves thus and so.

Not only are we denied the easy way out of establishing family customs. Gender expectations are a free-for-all.

A Lot of What We Worked Out No Longer Works . . .

If you go way back, *pre*-pre-baby, we were a fairly evolved couple. We had worked out nifty ways of talking. Tidy ways of divvying up the chores. We were fulfilled by our jobs, liberated from traditional stereotypes. Not a single element of our lives was present simply because it was expected of us. Our lives were predicated on choice.

But whatever life you had elegantly sculpted for yourself, the moment they put a child in your arms (excuse me for being the voice of reality), there's The Mommy, The Daddy, and The Baby.

Suddenly you are in an emotional arena that you left behind several decades ago. You are thrown back into the entire, tired issue of gender, role expectations, and who takes out the trash.

Which Takes Us to Housework

A major stress in any family is the stupid housework. The addition of a child increases the number of household chores unimaginably. But in the established home of the older parent, housework takes on a new hue.

While we had worked out many satisfactory ways of dealing with housework pre-baby, once the baby comes along, not only is there a lot more to do, but either the woman will do the "woman's work," and all that that implies, or the partners have to *work* at doing things differently. (By the way, here I'm really only talking about domestic duties. There's an emotional aspect of being the "mommy" that I have taken up in chapter 6, "Kids, Career, and Compromise.")

Study after study, wasting good money that should've been spent hiring cleaning people, thereby giving jobs to people who need them and freeing already working women from the drudgery of their heavy load, has corroborated what we all know. Women are still responsible for between 70 percent and 90 percent of all work that goes on in the home, including that related to food, clothing, cleaning, and, of course, child care. Men, when polled, naturally think that they do 50 percent. Because if they do any it's a lot more than what they grew up thinking they'd have to do.

After several decades of obviously idle chatter, it is still the woman who is either down on her hands and knees scrubbing the bathroom floor or making sure there's Comet in the pantry and cash on the dining room table for the person she hires to do it.

I hear a good deal about how couples are sharing more of the responsibilities, domestic, financial, and now those of parenting. I know for a fact that financial responsibility has become quite equally shared. We women work. And while only about half of all younger women work outside the home while their children are young, for the most part, we older mothers continue with our careers.

When asked, many families report that they have stitched together careful plans for who's in charge of what, seeming to divide the responsibilities. When I hear couples announce that they share responsibilities, the announcement rarely jibes with what I observe. It is the woman who knows what's in the mesh stroller bag.

Furthermore, when was the last time you heard a woman brag about how she does the cooking? Boast that she picks up the kids? Trumpet that she did the wash? Yet in families that "share" domestic duties, both wife and husband almost gloat about whatever work the man takes on around the house.

The sheer volume of mundane, boring, repetitive laundry–cooking–cleaning–play-date-making–lunch-packing-arranging–dentist-appointment-making drudgery generated by the advent of a child is overwhelming. And even when you have the resources, and the inclination, to have many hired hands, again the woman is still ultimately in charge of it all. Or so much of it that why bother to talk?

Who does what in the home is generally a source of major conflict in households where both parents work. But it is we older women who are the most galled by the whole thing. I mean, haven't we already had this discussion ad nauseam?

What is unnerving is that with the advent of motherhood many of us find ourselves on a seesaw: from self-righteous refusal to do it all, which is accompanied by hideous waves of guilt, to great soaring arcs of having to do it all, and do it well.

Here's a family that is representative of one of our subgroups: The woman is the major breadwinner, the man stays home and takes care of the kids. Many of the families that have reversed traditional roles in this way also have the interesting footnote that the men are younger than the women. Of course, this set of circumstances can result in many interesting ins and outs of family life. But here I just want to look at chores.

In this family, among all the other at-home chores he does, the husband packs the child's lunch. But listen to the wife: "It took me three years to stop looking in my kid's lunch box to see what he packed." You don't hear a man saying he needed three years to work through the emotional need to peek in a lunch box. You don't hear the dad reporting that he sneaks into his wife's briefcase to make sure she has everything in there that's supposed to be there.

Many men have trouble taking on duties traditionally done by women. But many women have trouble letting go. We don't have readily available models for men as we'd like them to be, for women as we'd like them to be, or for families as we'd like them to be.

I don't know about you, but not all that causes stress in our home can be swatted away like flies by carving out personal space to go to the movies.

Becoming a parent dredges up antediluvian ways of behaving. No matter how enlightened you are, you find yourself suddenly slipping into a traditional mode of interaction that you thought you'd left behind several decades ago.

WHAT'S IN A NAME? OUR IDENTITIES

You held on to your name. *Your* name. Maybe you hyphenated your name. But it was yours, what people in your profession called you.

I received a phone call recently from someone whose name I didn't recognize. When I returned the call and found out who it was, I was shocked. I have known this woman, who is in her mid-forties, for the last four years. By *her* name. But now that her son is in nursery school, she said, it's just too hard to hang on to all those names. She has started using the same last name as her husband. And more significantly, the same name as her son.

For better and worse, they have become a family.

Does it mean you're not a family if you have hyphenated your name, or still use yours exclusively?

Of course not. A family, as we're all discovering, is any constellation of people who cleave to one another and identify themselves as one.

Yet there are age-old relationships—husband, wife, and child among them—that reverberate with a powerful force. Those of us who are older, who fought so hard to establish individual identities of our own, are often overwhelmed and saddened by having to tread the same territory once again.

It's heavy stuff, this forging a family. Particularly for those of us who thought we knew a lot.

HELPFUL HINTS

In this section, I want to address some practical issues and see if I can offer you ways to reconnect with your spouse while keeping your family growing. There's the practical end of things and the emotional one.

DEAL WITH DOMESTIC DUTIES

If you feel that you are doing more than your share around the house, there are some techniques that you can try.

The obvious one is to hire as many people as you can to do all the work that must be done that neither of you has the time or inclination to do. Most people, though, can't afford to have a live-in maid, a live-in housekeeper, a live-in laundress, a live-in cook, a full-time social secretary for each member of the family and another for the family as a whole, a person responsible for all routine and emergency medical events, a liaison between school activities and after-school activities, a live-in chauffeur, a live-in bookkeeper, a live-in receptionist, a live-in military strategist to supervise the entire staff, and, what the heck, as long as we're making a wish list of what it really takes to run a home with three people in it, a live-in masseuse/personal trainer/manicurist.

In the event that the kind of support staff necessary to free you to parent your child, make pleasant chitchat with your husband, see a friend or two, hold a job, and think one uninterrupted thought a day is beyond your means, there are other methods available to you.

- Let your housekeeping standards slide. It is more important to read a story to your child than it is to clean out the silverware drawer.
- Teach your child to help out with chores. This will have enormous benefits for your child as well.
- Make a chart of everything that has to be done. Go through it with your husband, each of you saying what you absolutely refuse to do, what you like to do, and what you wouldn't mind doing. Pray that somehow the lists mesh. Compromise where it doesn't.

Now let's look at the emotional side of things.

GAME: WHEN DID THIS HAPPEN?

Here's a silly game to play if your child is past the first year. Since every family is different, your baby might be only three months old and you might be feeling a lack in your life. But at least by your child's first birthday, there are certain kinds of things you might want to start thinking about.

Think, for example, about the last five conversations you had with your spouse. What were the topics? Did you talk about movies, politics, art, work, friends, or hobbies? Or were your children's accomplishments, calamities, and practicalities the mainstay of your dialogue?

When was the last time you . . .

Had sex?
Saw a movie (that wasn't animated)?
Went out with only your friends?
Went out at all?
Held hands?
Sat on the couch next to each other?
Hugged when it wasn't a greeting or a good-bye?
Had coffee together during the day?
Strolled along going nowhere?

If all of these activities are dim memories of an ancient life, maybe you want to rethink and rearrange.

Here are some techniques that may feel artificial but sometimes help out.

A SPECIFIED TIME TO TALK

Talking is an important part of any relationship. As you may have noticed, however, gals like to talk and guys like to grunt. Don't you detest stereotypes like that? But don't you also notice how it's often the case in your home that the wife wants to *discuss* something while the husband says there's nothing to discuss?

Both partners have their points . . . of view. This method can satisfy opposite needs.

Or perhaps yours is one of the homes where both partners are "talkers." You, too, would benefit from this technique until you get some balance.

- *Agree on a time to talk.* Specify a time of day when you will talk about whatever the issue of the moment is. In this way, the "talker" gets to "talk." This can include talking about what needs to be done, or about what everybody agreed to do . . . and didn't (a frequent argument in homes where people are feeling put-upon, with too many things to do and not enough time).

- *Agree on an amount of time to talk.* In this way, the one who doesn't like to "talk" is reassured that the conversation will not go on interminably. After the agreed-upon time, there is no more talk about who did or didn't do what. This gets rid of obsessing, spinning your wheels, and wallowing. Furthermore, it ensures that you talk about something else!

- *Keep a journal.* This will help if the "talker" is not satisfied by what feels like too short an amount of time.
- *Give yourself a specified amount of time to write in your journal* about the current problem. After that, make yourself write about other issues in your life.

There really are other issues that matter. It is very important to hold on to that.

WAYS TO RECONNECT

In order to find your spouse again, try to spend more time together without your child. Go to the movies. Go out to dinner. Spend time that's not special, doing something as simple as sitting in front of the tube for an hour together. Making sure your child gets to bed at a specified time each night helps. Carve out time where you talk about topics unrelated to your child.

GET AWAY

The best, most tried-and-true way to really reconnect with your spouse is to go to a hotel without your child. At the first moment that you can possibly afford it, and can bear to be away from your child (the timing depends entirely on what you feel comfortable with), go somewhere where all the worries of home are not piled in front of your face on your bureau. It doesn't have to be fancy and it doesn't have to be far. Although fabulous resorts are fabulous, businessmen's hotels downtown in the city where you live are just as good. There you will use the phone only in an emergency. There you will not have to think about who does the sheets. There, you will have a chance to make love in peace and quiet. There on your "getaway" you will be free to drop your nightly battle cry, "Get away!"

BEYOND TECHNIQUE: HOLD HANDS

We may know enough to make charts to divvy up the work. Sometimes we succeed. Sometimes not.

We may know enough to schedule time together.

But while dividing the work equally and going out are terrific, necessary, and certainly more than mere pop-psychology gimmickry, they don't add up to a cure-all.

It is the subtle attentiveness to one another that we mourn. The shift in focus. The fact that we sometimes forget how to protect our marriage, and each other's feeling and needs, in our all-consuming passion to respond to the needs of our child.

I offer you some odd ideas to try out.

Think of something you know your spouse likes. (Mine, for example, likes chocolate.) Call your spouse at work. If possible, it's even better to leave a message. If there's another person answering the phone, say, "Tell my husband I bought him some chocolate. He'll know what I mean." The idea, in case you didn't get it, is to reconnect as romantic partners.

When you go somewhere, shoo your child ahead and walk hand in hand together.

When you go to a kid's movie, take along a playmate for your child. Sit in the row behind them. Hold hands.

Not all restaurants you go to necessarily have to be Chuck E. Cheese. Not all music you listen to has to be Raffi. Not all movies have to be Disney.

If you find that you have slipped into the unfortunate place where your child's preferences basically dictate how you live, start with the obvious. "Tonight it's not your turn to choose what we eat," for example. While you're at the table, make sure you have some conversation that is with the man you once noticed out of all the other men in the whole wide world as the one who was the neatest, funniest, best-looking. Treat him like that.

If you are to be a family with a healthy balance, sometimes you need to turn your headlights away from your child and focus them on the other adult in the room.

4

The One-Adult Family

"I like to call myself an independent parent. I know everybody doesn't agree with me, but sometimes to me 'single mother' sounds so pathetic. We're not a pathetic family. You should see my daughter. She's spectacular! Of course, that's me talking," laughs Ruth. She was forty-eight when she adopted her daughter, who is now four.

She is speaking on the phone from Los Angeles, where she is in the development department of a major film studio.

"I don't have that feeling of 'Poor me, poor me, I didn't meet Prince Charming. I don't have a man so I'm going to have to do this alone.' I've never felt like that. I'm not a single mother by default. I'm a single mother by joy!"

Ruth decided to start her family after the death of her own mother. "I was looking at a picture of Mom when she was about seven. She was with her sister, brother, and cousin. Something went through me, that everything she gave me, all the love, wisdom, and devotion . . . it seemed to me a tragedy to let all that die with me. I needed to pass that along."

Oh, courageous independent mommies! I admire you so.

Such as Rosie, an acquaintance from way back, whom I ran into recently. As a child, Rosie had polio; it left her with a body that needs help to take care of a lot of daily functions, but a spirit filled with resourcefulness and a marvelous sense of humor. She was standing, wobbling a bit as she does, breathing noticeably as she does, and simply beaming. Next to her stood a tiny boy. He appeared to my fairly trained eye a good deal smaller than the twenty months she said were his. He had the straight black hair of South America, and he wore a little man's hat. In this country only a few short weeks, he looked serious as he stood taking in the activity of a raucous costume party for kids. Nearby stood Rosie's helper—Rosie has always had the most wonderful luck with helpers because she is so delightful herself. This one was a lovely girl who was bilingual and helping now not only Rosie but her brand-new son.

Or such as the forty-four-year-old with the grin from ear to ear who said her last boyfriend didn't want kids. He wanted horses. She left him to his horses. She is now the mother of a baby girl.

Or another mommy, forty-two when her son was born, unbeknownst to the biological father, a man with whom she had a fleeting affair. Talk about an affair to remember.

THE BROAD STROKES OF BEING A SINGLE MOTHER: THE TWOSOME

Just as family counselors use "triad"—a word that resonates with meaning—for the home with two parents and a child, so do they use a nifty word for the one-adult home. The "twosome," as psychologists refer to your relationship, has its own tendency toward imbalance. Where things can go awry emotionally in your home is that sometimes it's hard to keep a clear perspective about your respective roles. As in the three-person family where the tendency to allow the child to dominate exists, so, too, in a two-person family is it possible to have the scales tip out of whack and create the illusion that mother and child are peers.

This imbalance can occur easily, particularly as the child matures. This is the person you come home to and talk to. This is the person you spend the most time with outside of work. Like most children of older parents, as we shall see in part 3 of the book, your child will probably have a sophisticated vocabulary and way of interacting, making it even more of a challenge to keep in mind that you are dealing not with a peer but rather with a child.

The challenge for you in parenting, as is the case for all parents, is to make sure that your child knows that you are in charge so that your child feels safe and secure emotionally. Much of this has to do with setting limits, which we will look at extensively in part 3.

The challenges you face as a mother, as a woman, and as a parent without a partner are in many ways the same as those faced by all older parents. They are just intensified.

PRACTICAL CHALLENGES

If all older mommies are a bit more tired than our younger sisters, so are you. But there's no other adult to trade off with.

If most of us are juggling careers and motherhood, so are you. Only the stakes, as you know, are a good deal higher. You either earn enough or you and your child starve. Furthermore, although some of you have very high-paying jobs, proportionately more of you feel a tighter crunch about money since you are, by definition, a single-income family.

Roz is a social worker whose regular monthly expenses, including a baby-sitter for after school, and saving for summer camp, college, and her own retirement, allow for very few luxuries. "There are times after work when all I want to do is go out to eat. I just want someone else to put the food in front of me and clean up. But all I can really afford most of the time is pizza. My daughter loves it. But sometimes, I just wish I could go to the restaurants I used to go to."

"I used to treat myself to a cleaning lady." She smiles. "No more. Thank God for my sitter. She does a lot of the cleaning, but I do most of it."

Like all of us with child care, you've got to juggle the baby-sitter relationship. But because you are single, and therefore a hundred and ninety degrees more dependent on help, the quality of this relationship can potentially become more intense than is useful. So you either have to deal with that relationship getting out of whack, or you have to expend just that much more energy and work to ensure that it stays on track.

That, in the end, is the key concept. You have to work a little harder. At everything.

Besides being responsible for the housework, it's also just you taking care of the typical "men's" stuff. The garbage. The car. Hanging shelves. Dragging the bookcase from one room to the next.

And when an emergency—or even something fun, such as a school play—comes up, there is no other adult in the house to share taking time off from work.

EMOTIONAL CHALLENGES

The fact that there's not another adult in the house presents single mothers with a variety of hurdles. There isn't anybody else to buffer anything, no one to help get you out of sticky emotional globs that happen in any relationship.

There's no one to bounce ideas off of, or to help make decisions. "No one who's going to sit and obsess with me for hours and hours and hours," as Ruth puts it. There's no built-in other to whom you can voice your private, sometimes paranoid worries, nor is there anyone to share that bragging, swaggering pride we all feel for our children but are justified in wanting to keep rather private.

DEBBIE

A jewelry designer in Westport, Connecticut, Debbie has a home that is like a fantasy from the Arabian Nights—cerise and chartreuse silk drapes, painted carved furniture, filigreed brass lamps, all gathered during her extensive travels in Bali, Nepal, and Thailand. Judging from the framed photos lining a small hallway leading to the bathroom, art and furnishings weren't all that Debbie collected. In each shot she smiles with a different hunk, his arms around her. Some of the guys have backpacks, one wears a flowing white shirt. They all have romance written across their rugged faces.

When I asked her how she had decided to become a mother at the tender age of forty-five, she shrugged. "When I was younger, I had a lust for life. I hit my forties, and bam! I suddenly had a lust for *another* life. I felt a biological imperative to be a mother, like an instinctive desire. I had a blind faith that everything would be okay. I didn't worry at all about the repercussions. I jumped in." She rolls her eyes.

She then goes on to describe how, when her son was born, it became clear that he had special needs. He had immediate visual and auditory problems, and now that he's a toddler it appears that he has some cognitive problems as well.

"I sat with that for all of about twelve minutes." She laughs. "I started talking to the doctors in the hospital. Then I called every friend I had. My sister was with me when Jared was born, and my parents came in. But I suddenly thought, 'You know what? I don't have to be a hero. I don't have to be a stoic. I just need to take care of my son.'

"I hauled my tush into therapy. Not because I thought there was anything wrong with me, but because I really felt like I needed one other person who was going to be with me, who I could run decisions by, and who could help me deal with everything I was feeling. I don't know what I would've done without her. She's been a godsend."

Debbie has found a solution to one of the largest challenges of the single parent, whether the child has special needs or not: having someone you trust and can count on to talk to about your child.

There is another pressing issue that all one-adult families have to deal with in one way or another.

THE "DADDY" DILEMMA

Whether her child is adopted or biological, every mother raising a child without a partner is confronted with the challenge of how to deal with the absence of a father. As with so many of the new ways to form families, the only known element is that secrecy is ultimately harmful. Yet there are no tried-and-true methods. We don't as yet know when the best time is to tell our children or even what to tell them about the variety of ways that families come together. Every family is essentially winging it, drawing on the experience of women whose children are only a few years ahead of our own.

Ruth, with her marvelous outlook on so much of life, has her own take on the "Daddy" issue.

When her daughter was three, another child—as frequently happens—asked, "Where's your daddy?" Sara answered brightly, "Don't you know? I have a mommy! I don't have a daddy!"

"Right around that time," continues Ruth, "she said to me, 'I want a daddy.' And, oh, I got all uptight! I tried to tell her all the things that our culture associates with a father." She drops her voice, mimicking a reassuring male. " 'I will always protect you, I will always blah, blah, blah.' Then she just looked at me and said, 'I want some ice cream.' " Ruth laughs uproariously. "She wants a daddy, she wants some ice cream, and I know she wants a dog! It's not as big as what we make it. We project a lot on our kids. Of course, I don't know what's going to happen in her teens when she wants to be like everybody else. But every kid has their own issues. I had my issues in what appeared to be a *Leave It to Beaver* upbringing."

Not everybody is so sanguine about the whole "Daddy" issue.

ELEANOR

"There are no easy answers." Eleanor is a family therapist. She is also a single mother.

"I was put off by one meeting of single mothers I went to," she continues. "I didn't like the dogma. This particular group seemed to have a knee-jerk response. 'Tell your child this.' I even heard some people say, 'My child says, "I don't have a daddy."' That concerned me. Everybody has a daddy! How will that translate when the child is older?

"My child is less than a year old. But I think what makes the most sense is to wait until he asks. When he asks, I'll tell him we don't live with Daddy because I never lived with him. When he asks how he got born, I'll tell him I borrowed something from a man so I could have him.

"What concerns me the most about starting young with a pre-arranged answer is that you're not really listening to your own child. You learn to listen to your baby's cry. Is he hungry? Is he sleepy? You learn to listen and respond to what he needs. It's the same thing with regard to 'Daddy.' Listen to your child. Answer when he asks. Give out the information that you think he's ready to handle.

"Some books tell you to say a certain thing. Some groups have party lines. But I think every parent needs to decide for their particular child what that child is ready to hear and when."

She leans forward earnestly. "First of all, every child does have a daddy. It's not good to have children saying they don't. Whether they live with them or not is a different matter. But there's a broader issue. If you use dogma, or have an already formulated answer that you make up without responding to your child, what you're really indicating is that this is an issue that's off-limits for discussion. But we know that this is really fertile ground for there being unpleasant emotions later on. The child may feel jealous, for example, that other kids have daddies. If you're too dogmatic, and you don't let him lead the way in this discussion, then you may communicate that he's not allowed to talk about negative feelings. You risk communicating that you're afraid to talk about all 'unpleasant' emotions, not just this. Then he might be afraid to talk to you about what's on his mind.

"Every child is different. I think it's best to listen to your child rather than to have a ready-made script about where 'Daddy' is or isn't."

NEW MOMMIES PROBABLY DON'T DATE

Robin is fifty-four and her daughter is thirteen. Robin is about to be married. "I started dating when Jesse was eight," she says. "Before that, I was too engaged in her life, and she was too needy for me to even entertain the idea of having another significant relationship in my life, not to mention the logistics of it.

"Once she hit school age, I started noticing men again. It was as if they really hadn't existed before. Like I had blinders on. All I saw was my little one. But when she got more independent, I could, too. I met Bob. He'd been divorced for quite a while and has two sons. So we're going to be another statistic!" She laughs. "We used to be a single-mother statistic, now we're going to be a joined-family statistic!

"Bob dated a lot of other women before he met me. It's obviously easier for the parent who has the children on the weekends and once during the week than for the parent who has them the most. I don't know why he decided I was the right one. He keeps quoting the maxim that second marriages are the triumph of hope over experience!" She laughs again. "I don't know why I decided he was the right one either! It just feels right."

A new single mother added, with a hopeful smile, "Now that I have my daughter, I feel open to relationships in ways I never was before."

The majority of new older mommies just don't seem to be getting much sex at the moment. Whether we are single or married, the relationships with our children are front and center during their early years.

HELPFUL HINTS

There are a number of practical and emotional ways that you can alleviate some of the pressures of being a one-adult family

PRACTICAL HINTS

What you may lack by not having a partner, you can make up for in part by building a support system and by enlisting your child's aid in running the house.

Build a Support System

In addition to keeping in touch with any extended family you may have, particularly sisters and brothers with children, it is helpful to connect with others in your situation, not solely for emotional support, although that is wonderful, but also to help each other out, to go places together, to celebrate holidays together, and to expand your family experience. Here are some options.

- *Single Mothers by Choice.* If you didn't know about this group, now is the time to find your local chapter. Members laughingly characterize themselves as Murphy Brown mothers—women who are mostly between the ages of thirty-five and forty-five; single, and educated, and whose biological clocks ticked too loudly to ignore. Many children will not have fathers who they know, whether they are adopted or biological. As with any national organization, some of the local chapters will be more to your liking than others. Often, however, the best part is that you will find one or two families you feel very close to, with whom you can build a real support system.

- *Parents without Partners.* Many churches, synagogues, Ys, and community centers have these groups. Their activities range from parenting workshops tailored to address the needs of single-parent families to family get-togethers held on a regular basis and for holidays. Most of the members will be divorced, a few widowed. Some of them may resent your having chosen what came to them through pain. Although in any group there are always one or two people you don't feel drawn to, if the general feel of the group is negative, you don't need me to tell you that this is not a good place for your family. However, if you do experience a negative mood in the group, chances are that other women in your situation have felt this as well.

- *A group you organize.* If established groups seem unwelcoming, it would be worth your while to try to organize another group locally. Group dynamics being what they are, it's quite likely that other single parents would embrace a different group. Sometimes, one or two negative people are able to bring a whole bunch down, but nobody knows how to get out of it. Your sign in the grocery store, in the playground, or on the Internet just might be what everybody was hoping for.

- *Groups for adoptive parents.* In the adoptive community, there are groups for many cultures with whom you probably connected before your adoption but who become like extended family over the years. If you are not already part of such a group, whether your child was adopted domestically or abroad, any large adoption agency will have the resources to put you in touch with groups in your area.

Get a Handle on Running the House

To keep your house from running you, consider these suggestions. In addition to giving you some breathing space right now, they will help your child grow up with excellent skills.

- Include your child in household duties. Start this as soon as the child is walking. A toddler can help put cans on the shelf when you come back from the market. Toddlers love to put clothes in the washing machine. As your child's skills increase, let him or her sort by color.
- Make your household democratic. Don't just assign chores, encourage your preschooler and older child to feel part of things by choosing which chores they take on.
- Teach your kindergartner how to set and clear the table and empty wastepaper baskets, for example, so you eventually work together to run the home as your child matures.
- Don't beat up on yourself if every meal is not gourmet.

EMOTIONAL HINTS

Since you have to make a living and care for your child, there often don't seem to be enough hours in the day to do both, let alone refresh yourself. But as for all parents, it becomes important to regenerate yourself. Here are some tips in addition to those in chapter 8, "Bifocals and Barney," and in the resources section in the back of the book.

Take Time for Yourself

The more you have adult relationships that meet your adult needs, the less inclined you are to tip the crucial balance in your home by unknowingly engaging with your child as if the child were your peer.

- Make sure you get some quiet time every day, even if it's just for fifteen minutes. Write in a journal, meditate, or enjoy some other peaceful activity.
- Find a way to decompress in between work and home. Some parents take a few minutes just to read the paper; others take a ten-minute walk. Find a way to shift gears so that when you get home you're ready to be "on."
- Try to get in some exercise. Most kids will love exercising with you, if you set it up right. They like to stretch and do floor exercises, for example.
- Talk regularly to other adults. Even if it's just a quick coffee date, it's important that you have an adult to talk to and have a social life away from your child.

Set Limits

Many older parents, as we will discuss at length in part 3, find limit setting to be a challenge. For single parents it's potentially tougher. Single parents wear multiple hats: you're the mother and the father, the disciplinarian and the consoler.

Sometimes it's the intensity of the relationship that makes setting limits harder. If you're not careful, you'll start relating to your children as friends because you spend so much time with them. If that happens, it's often difficult to act like the parent, so in that context it becomes difficult to discipline. A child who is overly close is difficult to discipline because you may not have the distance you need in order to mete out consequences.

It is in everybody's best interests that once you set a limit, you stick to it. Here are some typical areas where all parents, but especially single parents, sometimes waffle and then feel they're in over their heads. Allowing boundaries to disintegrate gets everyone into trouble.

- Allowing your child to continue to watch TV "for five more minutes." Then for five more minutes. Then for five more.
- Staying in the store, at the playground, or in any other fun place beyond the time you set to leave.
- Not sticking to a regular bedtime and not maintaining separate places to sleep. Either can become a major battleground. Many parents are conflicted about sleep. They don't know whether to let their children cry, or whether to allow them into their beds. They are unsure about how to handle the normal, long-term developmental area that is sleep. In fact, contrary to what some experts espouse, there is no prescription for sleep that is perfect for all children. For the single parent, however, allowing the child to sleep with the mother on a *regular* basis is not a good idea. It is important for each of you to have space apart from the other. You, the parent, need your own time and place to refresh yourself.

BEYOND TECHNIQUE: TREASURE YOUR PEACE

Although being a two-person family obviously presents a sometimes tricky set of difficulties to deal with, there is the other side. Some find that a home with an independent parent is more peaceful than a traditional family setting.

Leslie is an older mom who's seen both sides. A secretary who is now forty-nine and the married mother of a ten-month-old, she was thirty-seven and single when her first child was born. "Now, I've got a husband, the cooking, the cleaning, the groceries, the laundry, two kids. I even have a house. And a dog! I'm my eighty-year-old mother's main support. My husband watched the baby last month so I could go help my mother move. That was my free time!" She laughs long and hard. "Before? There were no other responsibilities. It was just him and me! Life was a breeze!"

There are without doubt moments of true loneliness and longing in being a single mother. But you can find excellent places to share some of those feelings, as well as to learn practical strategies that other single mothers have successfully employed.

5

Our Mothers / Ourselves

As all writers do, I sometimes sit struggling to find a way to introduce difficult topics. While I was writing and deleting paragraphs (the modern version of crumpling up a paper and taking out a new sheet), looking for a way to tackle two complicated aspects of being an older parent, happenstance had it that I finally connected with a woman with whom I'd been playing phone tag for some time. I'd like to introduce you to somebody who feels like an angel to me.

CAROL

Carol lives in Chicago. Now the divorced mother of a teen and a tween, she had her first son at thirty-eight, her younger one at forty-two. She is now fifty-two.

As Carol spoke, she happened to hit on a topic that I'd been dancing around.

"My mother was a really selfish person. She had, in quotes, 'help,' for which I'm grateful. I was raised by a couple that worked for us. I think that's why I turned out [she laughs] as *relatively* healthy as I am, because of this couple who lived with us. I consider them parents of mine. I just lost Ethel this past spring. Jack is very dear to me (my father died when I was six) and will be ninety-one in March.

"My mother was a wealthy, nonworking woman who was a club lady. Garden club, bridge—she was very active socially. She's pretty devoid of values and pretty superficial. But she can be charming! She's funny, she's got spunk. She's very gregarious.

"Her response to any feeling I had other than happiness was, 'Don't be ridiculous! Stop feeling that way.' I never felt in any way heard, or attended to, or that she was tuned into what was important for me.

"I really hated her and acted it out. I didn't talk to her for years. I had nothing to do with her for quite some time when I was in my middle years, from about twenty to thirty-five. When I got married, at thirty-five, I started seeing my mother more.

"We've had this evolving relationship. I'm very close with her now. Close in that I talk to her every day. I'm kind of a caretaking person for her."

I asked Carol how she had made the emotional leap.

"I accepted my mother." We sit for a moment in silence, on the phone, the power of that simple statement reverberating.

"Somehow or other, I don't know, I feel badly for her. If my mother's on Lake Shore Drive and there's a completely blue sky and somewhere in Skokie there's dot of a white cloud, she'll say, 'Oh my God. It looks like rain. I don't know if we can go out.' And that kind of sums up who my mother is. She's terrified of life. And I empathize with her. I can identify with her fear of being alone. I'd like to make her life as full as I can.

"I don't let her get in my way. And I don't respond to her neediness. She would like me to be over there all the time and I just don't do that."

Did becoming a mother herself make Carol more sympathetic toward her mother?

"I don't think that having kids made me feel better about my mother. Not at all. Now my mother can hang out with my children, but I could never leave my children with my mother overnight because she wouldn't change their diapers.

"My mother's just not a nurturer. When they go to her house they eat what I call 'gold food.' Fried fish sticks, macaroni and cheese. I'm not an organic-milk-and-tofu nut but I do try to encourage them to have vegetables! My mother just absolutely has no idea how to raise a child, so I didn't have good feelings about her when my children were young. No, it wasn't having children that made me feel, oh, loving toward my mother. I think it was a perspective on life and aging.

"She's going to be eighty-five. It'll be sad for me to let my mother go. Which of course sometime in the near future I'll have to do.

"I could dump my mother, yeah, but a lot of who I am has to do with her. I look like my mother. I'm sociable like my mother—which I passed on to my children because their father is not that way at all. I can be selfish like my mother. Turning fifty made a huge difference for me. I've been confronting my own mortality. I feel lucky to have my mother around. We can always let go of things. But to me, the value of life is in the connections that are made."

COMING TO TERMS WITH OUR MOTHERS

Some of us aren't as enlightened as Carol. Some of us haven't yet reached the point where we're ready to allow ourselves the chance to let go, to accept, to take in, to turn the tables and let the love flow from us toward our mothers. The way we couldn't when we were little, defenseless, and scared.

Now, they no longer threaten. What could they possibly do? We have too much experience, too many other people and moments validating our lives in ways that they may or may not have been able to do. Their sticks and stones no longer seem sharp or heavy. We can deflect them almost with our eyes closed. What we are left with, then, is the connection. A lifetime together. A chance to love.

Many of us have good relationships with our mothers. Some have fits-and-starts between us. Some of us have already lost our mothers' physical presence; others are witnessing the end of their days. Quite a number of us have had histories that are similar to Carol's, perhaps not in their drama, but in their essence.

Yet if we are to grow, to mature, to stand up tall and whole in the world, and if we are to be the kind of mothers we want to be, we all have to make it our business to treasure—as Carol so beautifully put it—the "connections."

As she so insightfully acknowledged, we are products of our mothers. Some of our qualities were inherited, some taught. But whatever the process of how we become who we are, no matter how hard we "work" on ourselves, and no matter how much understanding of the past we are able to glean, it is not until we reopen the gates, if we have shut them, and allow compassion for our mothers to flow freely from us toward them, that we will fully mature.

In terms of our journey, and where we are in our lives, the very fact that we are the age we are means many things. The reality of time has special significance with regard to the charged relationship that was the model for our own motherhood. Although in part 3 we will mention some parenting challenges we may face based on our histories, here I am addressing how we feel as daughters.

Those of us who have already lost our mothers need to treasure their worth as women in their own right and hold fast to the strengths, no matter how large or small, that they passed on to us. To the women who walked the face of the earth and bore us, we owe our very lives. To the mothers who raised us and allowed whatever is the finest in us to grow, we owe our hearts and souls.

Those of us who still have our mothers have the chance to allow our own children to grow up registering subliminally that we have accepted our mothers, instead of their learning to live with the tension that often exists in younger homes.

Being at our stage in life means that if we still have our mothers, we would be wise to seize the time to make amends, to make peace, to accept them, and therefore ourselves, while we still have the chance.

SELFISH MOTHERS

Carol has also introduced a topic that I've been hard pressed to address. Her mother was selfish. Her mother did not attend to her needs. Her mother was busy having a good time in her own life. Other people raised Carol.

This is a scenario that can also be found among our homes. I'm sure you know families, as I do, who seem to treat their children more as acquisitions than as family members. Unlike the overattentive family that changes their entire life to dance to the tune of the child, these families barely register a ripple in the surface of their pond that would indicate that a little pebble of a child has been tossed in.

In chapter 7, "Helping Hands," I mention ways we can all increase the connections in our homes.

But here, because of what Carol has shared, I want to try and address a deep hurt that I see. A kind of middle- and upper-class neglect.

Whether they are deeply involved with their work, or taken up with amusing themselves, as Carol's mother was, there are families who have not only an all-day sitter but a nighttime sitter, and even a weekend sitter. I'm sure that you must have seen families like this, where the parents are marginal to their children's lives.

The danger that I see for those children is that very few of them have the same people with them all of their lives. While Carol may have been emotionally estranged from her mother, at least she was connected for a lifetime to Ethel and Jack.

Most of the children in the families in question do not have the benefit of such a connection. They have a series of baby-sitters. So, in short, they have no deep emotional connection. With any living soul.

It is something to think about, in case you know people who may have set up their lives in such a way that their children are not active parts of the lives of their parents. If there is no one to whom the children are emotionally attached for their entire lives, no good can come of that.

Sometimes we see the separation in the way the home is set up.

One family I visited lived in a fabulous apartment on Central Park West. For those of you who are unfamiliar with the nuances of New York locations, this is a very fashionable address. The apartment, which had a view of the park, had been gutted and redone. All that had been left untouched of the original grand layout were the maid's quarters. It was here, in two tiny rooms with a shared bathroom located off the kitchen, that the baby-sitter and the child lived.

I visited another home, much less affluent but solidly comfortable. In this home, the master bedroom and bath had been given to the child. It was a spacious room, and when I was there during the day it was sunny and cheerful. It was decorated from its parquet floor to its crown moldings in darling little-girl touches. Amid shelf after shelf of neatly arranged toys there was an entire corner for Felicity, one of a series of American Girl dolls. The doll had her own complete set of beautifully made furniture. In the center of the room there was a hand-painted, child-size table, set with a single place mat. There was a cunning plastic drop cloth with dancing, fun-loving alphabet letters under the table to catch crumbs. There was a television. It sat on a swivel base so that the child could watch when she ate, and watch when she went to sleep. There was not a trace of the child in any other part of the house.

We make choices, and each of us has to decide how to spend every day. But for those of you who have set up your lives so that your child is a distant family member, what you lose is love.

If you really listen to Carol, what she says is so revealing on so many levels. She has become a grown-up with a powerful ability to connect and love. Think what her mother might've gotten, had her mother let that little empathetic creature into her lap.

There is something that seems so lonely in the homes where the child and the parents are not connected. There is something that seems sad about a home where each member spends his or her time not in the company of family members but apart, seeking only limited, controlled contact with others.

If I am in one room on the phone, and my husband is in another room on the treadmill watching TV and checking his stocks, and my child is in her own room watching videos—or when she's older, cruising the Internet—why are we all living together? Why not simply have studio apartments spread around town? That way, we wouldn't even have to have the momentary unpleasantness of brushing against one another, of getting in each other's way. We can make dinner dates! Pencil them in! Change them if need be.

Life would be so much richer for those families were they to include the amazing little people now living on the outskirts of their homes.

6

Kids, Career, and Compromise

If I ran the zoo, all families upon the arrival of a child would be offered a two-year hiatus from ordinary life. If they chose to exercise this option, they would be provided with enough money so they wouldn't have to give it a second thought.

They could then putter around together, hunching down to watch ants at work, slowly and leisurely hanging laundry on a line with all the time in the world for a toddler to stoop, pick up a clothespin, drop it, be told in a loving voice to try again, hand it to Mommy, be approvingly patted on the head, and watch with fascination as the wind snapped the sheets on the line.

If the family included a dad or another mommy, he or she would be humming over in the garden. Soon, everyone—including a tail-wagging dog and a purring cat—would convene to pick string beans and tomatoes right off the vine for lunch. They would plop down on a soft blanket under the big elm, drop off for a little snooze, all resting heads on one another's bellies, wake up and take their bikes down to the beach to watch sandpipers chase the receding waves, the shadows of their long legs growing even longer in the late afternoon sun, the cry of sea gulls poignant, the smell of ocean and sunscreen sweet.

They would stretch, pedal back home, sit on the front porch till it was twilight, wander into the kitchen and sing while they rustled up some grub, eat out on the back porch, pick peaches from the tree, and laugh as the juice dripped down their chins. Then they would all toddle back into the house and take a nice bath together. The parents would plop the baby in bed, say nighty-night, turn out the light, go into the living room, play an intensely competitive game of Scrabble, lie down on opposite couches, read novels for a while as classical music played, then wander off to bed, make long languorous love, turn out the lights, and wake up when everyone was rested.

Several nights a week, they would be joined by other new families. The grown-ups would lounge on chaises out in the backyard, the sound of ice clinking in their glasses mixing with the sound of the children playing beautifully together until the lightning bugs came out. Then everybody would carry their own children home, the little arms and legs dangling in the blissful rag-doll flop of deep sleep.

This arrangement would be optimal for teaching children what they need to learn during those important first formative years. It would lay the groundwork for all future intellectual development, including the acquisition of facts, the encouragement of innate curiosity, and the foundation of language and communication skills. But most important, it would give the children the chance to feel secure, as a result of learning how human beings who love one another interact and how lovely life truly is.

At the end of the two years, the child would be emotionally and intellectually equipped to enter a cozy, stimulating group environment. The parents, having enjoyed to the hilt living at a child's pace, would return to the same position and salary that they had left, refreshed, revitalized, and filled with new energy and ideas.

We are obliged to tailor the first few years of our children's lives to a slightly less optimal lifestyle.

What is tantalizing about this fantasy scenario is the lack of stress and the way it would meet everyone's needs. It would allow the parents the pure joy of being around for every moment of those first few special years. It would allow the child the benefit of separating from Mommy at a slower, more biologically appropriate pace. And it would allow both parents to continue in the growth and development of their own lives. It would be a win-win situation.

As modern life is constructed, however, for families with limited resources and crummy jobs, it's a lose-lose. For families that appear on the surface to have everything in the world, it's more often than not a draw, with no one's needs being met completely and compromise the order of the day.

THE BROAD STROKES OF THE WORK DILEMMA

There is no right or wrong answer to the work/don't-work discussion. Many men have the option of some kind of paternal leave; most of those who have the option don't exercise it. Some women don't have a choice economically; others don't have one temperamentally. Some fields are easier to leave on a temporary basis; some not only keep you down with a glass ceiling but prevent you from shifting corridors once you're hemmed in by the maternal wall.

Men are not forced to choose between having a career and having a family, even though some do.

All women, whatever their age and whatever their profession, must make a decision—which they then, crossing their fingers, must hope was for the best. Those who continue in their careers, slotting the child into their free time, run the risk that they will miss being a real part of the child's life. Those who opt to be stay-at-home moms run the risk that they will miss being a real part of their own lives. They will miss the stimulation of work. Furthermore, as history has shown us only too well, they risk finding themselves later in life in the unpleasant position of having to support themselves at a competitive disadvantage, having been out of the labor force.

In short, if you work, you have to leave your kid; if you stay home, you have to leave your career. Furthermore, as even high-ranking women in large industries are only too aware, the very act of becoming a mother impinges on your career, either overtly or subtly in ways your husband doesn't have to face. So that even if you make yourself 100 percent available, at the expense of not being with your child, you are perceived as no longer genuinely in the running. If you acknowledge that being a mommy is as important as your work, you run the risk of being relegated to less interesting and less remunerative positions. If you work part-time, which would appear to be the best of both worlds, in many jobs you are no longer treated as a team player. Working in a "helping, humanitarian" field or having a female boss who's a mother herself doesn't necessarily mean that if your kid has the flu, you will find it any easier to leave work than if you had a male boss and worked in a profit-making concern. If you drop out of work for your child's early years, while this is certainly a lovely option in terms of how your child's days are filled, you have chosen yet another rocky road. Many fields make it hard for any mommy to get back in. But our age puts us at a further disadvantage. Why would a company hire someone with a lot of experience, therefore able to command a high salary, when it can get some bright-eyed, bushy-tailed gal who's happy to take the job at entry-level wages?

As is manifestly clear to any woman who values her work as well as her family, we are over a barrel. From a societal point of view, the only way that lives will improve is if there is systemic change. There needs to be public policy that offers viable child-care solutions; there needs to be corporate policy that values families and organizes work in such a way that people don't "owe their souls to the company store." And there needs to be massive change within each family so that both partners view their careers as equally affected by the advent of children, and both are conscious of and equally responsible for devising and carrying out all that needs to be done to keep the home running.

But until such utopian changes take effect, each of us has to search her soul, and possibly her checkbook, and try and come up with what meets the needs of as many people in her family as possible.

As with every other family issue, we older moms have the same concerns as everyone, but our age intensifies the experience. We have more options—yet more at stake.

Here's a story that touches on all the work/motherhood dilemmas—and then some—of the older mom.

REARRANGING YOUR CAREER

ELLIE

Like most women who marry later in life, Ellie had a rich work history and personal history. When she was forty-one she gave birth to Lauren. But a year and a half earlier, Ellie had stepped into a more complicated motherhood when she married Stephen. In a series of heart-wrenching twists and turns, Stephen and his first wife had adopted a baby, Janie, from Russia. Less than two years later, Stephen was a widower and Janie was motherless once again. When Janie was just over two, Ellie entered her life, legally becoming her mother when Janie was four. According to Ellie, since Lauren's birth she's been a better mother to Janie. It is hard to imagine how much better a mother this caring woman could be.

For Janie's sake, Ellie left the kind of job many women dream of. She was a high-ranking executive for one of the network evening news shows, "a really exciting, social, fun, intense, rewarding world," as she describes it.

Ellie felt compelled to leave her job after one particularly telling episode. One day, shortly after Ellie became her mother, Janie came into the bedroom and said, "Mommy, I have to show you something." Ellie, perpetually "at work" whether at home or in the office, was monitoring TV for breaking news. She answered, "I can't talk to you now. I have to watch television."

At this point in her narrative, she gives a long, loud laugh still full of the shock of sudden insight. "I thought: 'Hold it! Something's not right with this picture!' This kid got gypped out of a mother the first time around. I wasn't going to take it away from her again."

Ellie echoes what so many women feel. "I was exhausted. It was a demanding job. It was easy enough as a single person. I could come home and collapse. But for a mother, there is no collapse time."

Another mother of a two-year-old, an industrial analyst, says for her the hardest challenge is "the minute I walk in the front door. I have to be on."

All working women must make the daily transition from worker to mother. For some it is easier than for others. If we are teachers, whether in nursery school or in college, the material and our students stay in our heads and frequently require work to be done when we're not "at work." If we are artists, writers, therapists, or doctors, regardless of how many hours we put in away from home, all we've been dealing with rattles around in the back of our heads. Those of us in business, law, or any fast-paced field drag our work home. Just like Daddy, who "had a hard day" and needs to be "left alone," so do we. Only we're the moms. If the child leaves both of us alone, who does the child live with? And so for the most part it is Mommy who must walk through the door and be "on."

Ellie's story in some ways reflects both the advantages and the disadvantages of coming to motherhood later in your career. Because of her skills and her time in the workforce, she was able to transfer to a career more supportive of being a mother. She took herself out of the mainstream of her profession and became a university professor, with less demanding daily hours, and summers and holidays off. But although she finds being a professor rewarding, Ellie experiences academia as more "isolating and quiet" than the world of television.

So it is not quite win-win. It is certainly not lose-lose. After all, she has a job that pays well, although not as handsomely as the other. It keeps her mind active, gives her a sense of satisfaction and mastery, and at the same time allows her to have the kind of hours that are much less stressful than her former job. But it is not the career she set out for when *she* was the bright-eyed bushy-tailed gal, eager for any salary that would let her do what she loved—as we all once were. Although satisfactory, it is a compromise.

Furthermore, glaringly, there is a missing piece. Stephen. While it would be unrealistic to expect him to leave his banking career, for better or worse, right or wrong, he did not feel the emotional pull to make major changes in his professional life to compensate for, ameliorate the needs of, or just plain take care of a needy child who'd been given a raw deal. Stephen is an attractive man, and as I'm sure all of you are well aware, a solvent, attractive man in his forties has a darn good array of choices when it comes to picking partners. The fact that he already had a daughter was a bonus for him—though it would not be one for a woman in the same position. To his credit, he took care of his daughter beautifully. He chose, out of all whom he might've chosen, a woman who had the capacity to be an extraordinary mother. And so from a traditional point of view, he more than adequately fulfilled his paternal duties by finding a really good mom for his kid. In the end, however, it was Ellie who rearranged her entire life.

STAYING AT HOME
GRACE

Grace is a renowned actress. She's a serious artist, not a mere entertainer. "It would've been easier if I'd had a regular job to quit. I would've known what to quit," she says, laughing. While her fame and the caliber of her work offer her options that many of us don't have, in that when she is ready to return to work she will certainly be able to, nevertheless she manages, as she does with her roles, to touch us deeply by reaching the very heart of the dilemma.

"A lot of people are terrified. They're scared of pain of any kind. They start off being terrified of the pain of childbirth. I know some people who ask for cesareans, they're that scared of experiencing anything. Then they're scared of being home alone with their child. Their intuition is right. It's terrifying!" Here there is a deep laugh of self-recognition. "I find myself hoping that I can keep up with my daughter intellectually!

"My child is basically going to be acting out every single relationship she'll have for the rest of her life. Every love affair, every fight. She's going to learn how to deal with every indulgent person, every person who finds her annoying. Insignificant. Rude. Every single type of relationship there is, like playing dollies. She's going to act out everything with whoever spends the most time with her!

"My friend was saying she'd slit her throat if she stayed home. If you're afraid that you can't trust your own responses, that you'll slit your wrists or smack your kid, why assume that whoever she's with is going to be more enlightened than you? Somebody's going to have her limits tested. And that's whoever is spending a lot of time with that little kid. . . .

"Having your baby and going back to work in three weeks? What does that say about the miracle of life? Yet I feel so empty some days, like my life is going to be over like that [she snaps her fingers] with nothing to show for it. Sometimes I think, 'How am I going to sleep tonight? I haven't done anything!'

"But having my child makes it worth pushing that stroller around."

Even completely free from the worry of money and the fear of cutting yourself off at the knees in your career, staying home is hard. Knowing how important those days may be to your child, and to you, doesn't always ameliorate the tedium of the day-to-day moments spent with a young child and the lack of tangible movement in our own lives.

And so we see, once again, with Grace's situation, that the choices we make in motherhood are not necessarily win-win. Once again, we see a choice made from compromise.

MORE AT-HOME MOMS

Most of the mothers with full-time jobs, once you really start to talk and peel away the outer layers, reveal that they are conflicted. They are not conflicted about working; most enjoy their work and get satisfaction from it. They are conflicted about not getting to spend as much time as they'd like with their children.

Many at-home moms, although clear that what they are doing is the only right choice for their family, nevertheless express a rueful lack.

Here's one who left a powerful behind-the-scenes position in fashion. "It was right out of a made-for-TV movie," she says with a laugh. "My daughter was two. We were coming out of Central Park. I had stupidly given her one of those red-white-and-blue popsicles. It was the end of a long day and she was in a meltdown. She was heaving backwards in her stroller. There were red-white-and-blue drippy gobs everywhere. I was kneeling in front of her stroller. I don't even want to think about what I looked like. And then, out of the corner of my eye I see, standing next to the stroller, these shoes. Manolo Blahniks. Oh, please! I looked up, way up. There was a group of people I used to work with. They'd just finished lunch. They didn't even try to cover up how much they were laughing. We all laughed, but after they left, I thought, 'What has happened to my life?'"

Here's another woman who had been a headhunter for financial executives: "Walking down the street, pushing a stroller. I was still nursing at the time. I was wearing sweatpants and sneakers. Coming toward me was someone I used to work with. She was wearing a silk shirt and pearls. I started to sob."

It's not the clothes qua clothes, of course, that gets these women. It's what the clothes symbolize. That you are a "somebody" in the world.

Because in truth, notwithstanding that perhaps there might not be any work more important in terms of civilization at large than taking care of young children, it is a job that carries very little prestige.

SELF-ESTEEM AND THE AT-HOME MOM

Sociology, psychology, and various clinical family disciplines have documented fully how a woman's self-esteem plummets when she becomes an at-home mom. In addition to carrying very little status out in the world, because her day is spent in the company of small-fry, her conversation and concerns can sound limited, particularly to the ears of people who spend their time in what they consider to be larger arenas. This happens even to the twenty-two-year-old who has not yet had a chance to do much out in the world. For many of us, who *have* had a chance to do something out in the world, it is often experienced as quite a big step down.

Maybe we would like to think that we're above all that. But why should we be "above all that" when nobody else is? The self-esteem of the full-time mom does not come from her place in our society. It must be created by her. She simply does not get rewarded by the world at large for the important job she's doing.

Many at-home mothers use their skills by volunteering. Is being a kindergarten class mother or the head of a school auction as important as running a lab that's searching for the cure for cancer? It depends on how you define important. If you mean by important that the activity will directly save millions of lives, then no, it is not as important. But suppose you define important as being one simple factor that will enrich your child's life and that of your child's friends, and will make their school experience a happy, satisfying one. And suppose that experience will then provide them with the kind of internal self-confidence and external caring, commitment, and attachment to their community at large that will make it possible for them to grow up to be productive members of a thriving society. Then perhaps you have done as much in the long run for the world as the person who spends her days looking in a petri dish for the hidden mysteries of disease.

A MOM WHO DECIDED TO TRY BOTH: TERRY

Terry is a forty-six-year-old social worker who has recently adopted her second child. She worked full-time after the birth of her first child, and decided with this second one to stay home. Here's what she has to say.

"I'm not having the fabulous time being a stay-at-home mom that I thought I would. I've been working nonstop for almost twenty-five years. I thought, 'This is going to be fabulous. I'm going to stay home. I'm going to make soup. I'm going to do things around the house. I'm going to do my résumé. I'm going to write an article about the trip and about the adoption. Finally, I'm going to have some time to myself!' But the reality so far has been very different. That we've been able to sit here and talk like this while the baby's sleeping is a first! David and I haven't been able to sit and talk like this. This is a gift. This is adult conversation about me and my family. I thought there was going to be a lot more of this. I'm starting to get the rhythm of being an at-home mom now. And it has nothing to do with making soup!" She smiles.

She talks about how stressful she is finding her child's neediness and how slowly her days pass. "I miss the stimulation of work," she says ruefully.

"I think back to when Cara [her first child] was a baby. It was such a different experience. When I came home, I wanted to spend all my time with her. It was such a magical, wonderful time. When she cried and was fussy, I could handle it because it was a finite amount of time. Weekends, and holidays. I have regarded that model of mothering—the part-time mom—as severely flawed. But I'm now willing to consider that it's something that works very well. Albeit that it's sometimes very difficult. I don't regard it as a compromise way of mothering as much as I did before. Because I think that model allowed me to be the best kind of mom I can be. Maybe I'm saying that twenty-five years of working was a way of having a side of me that my mother so desperately wanted and didn't have. And I could be a mother at the same time. I wonder how successful I'm going to be as a stay-at-home mom. This is impressionistic because I've only been a stay-at-home mom for six weeks." She laughs.

Terry, as you might suspect, returned to full-time work.

THE PART-TIME SOLUTION

"I feel lucky, like I have the best of all worlds," says a lawyer who took a major cut in pay and started working three days a week. Of the women

I've spoken to, part-time presents itself as close to win-win, allowing the stimulation of work and quantity of time with our children.

But even part-time is not perfect for some women. "I don't really feel like I'm doing either," says one, laughing. "I kind of can't get a routine up in either place."

In what may be the most telling statement of all about life for the at-home mom, one woman admits, "I am a million times more tired at the end of one of my mommy days than at the end of a day when I work."

A WORK-AT-HOME MOM: BETH

"Sometimes I just can't play with her," says Beth, a single mom who lives on the outskirts of Washington and works from her home. "I say, 'It's your time to play and Mommy's time to work.' She usually understands, because it's always been like this. I work out of my home, so she's seen me at my computer since day one."

When asked what her daughter does when she works, I can hear Beth smile over the phone. "She imitates. When she was younger, she imitated what I do. Write letters, talk on the phone, sit with a calculator." She laughs. "Now that she's four, she likes to sit on my lap and write her name on the computer. But usually, because her day is structured and full at her day care center, she loves coming home and playing with her dolls. She's a very imaginative child. She will get very deep into her own little world. She and her dolls go to Africa, or on an airplane trip, or to the doctor. She's been able to play on her own from day one."

By temperament, Beth appears to be a very easygoing person. The word "usually" has crept into her conversation twice in a very short time, with the implication that her child does not understand "always." We have seen a darling four-year-old, leggier and larger now than a toddler, writing her name on Mommy's computer. Beth is obviously not hard-pressed to withstand the normal interactions that occur when an adult and a child are in the same space.

Evidently the temperament stars were aligned when they made this particular match since her child seems to have the facility to play on her own.

Not all parents and kids are as comfortable sharing time and space engaged in parallel activities. Perhaps more to the point, not all children spend a good part of their day in day care.

A WORK-AT-HOME DAD: PETER

"I can't bear it," moaned the dad in one of my classes.

When his wife was pregnant, it seemed the perfect idea that she continue her job, complete with nine-to-five hours and benefits, and that he, with the looser hours of a writer, should be the at-home dad.

"When he was a baby, it was a snap," reports Peter. "Now that he's a toddler, I can't plunk him down anymore with some toys like I used to and lose myself in my work for an hour at a time. I'm going crazy. I'm having a hard time meeting my deadlines. I'm not going to be able to earn a living if I don't figure something out."

THE WORK-AT-HOME OPTION

Although working at home would appear to be the best of all worlds in many ways, for most of us, it is as fraught with compromise as any of the other configurations of parenting and working at the same time.

In a gathering of new older moms, we were discussing the work-at-home concept. One of the women was sharing what so many women report. Once their children are past babyhood, if they are in the house they want their mommies. If they have a baby-sitter, even one they adore, it doesn't matter. They want their mommies. If mommy closes the door to the room where she works, they pound on the door, sometimes screaming, sometimes crying, sometimes calling out quite playfully. They want their mommies.

In our discussion, I offered that I found "the closed door" an inelegant solution. Like the advice you sometimes read in parenting books to close, or even lock, the door, so you can have "marital intimacy," it never sits right with me. It sets up a funny feeling in the home. It seems unnatural and unkind for a child to be confronted, particularly during daytime, waking hours, with a glaring closed door.

A mother in her late thirties sitting next to me at the table gasped. "I'd forgotten that!" she exclaimed. "I used to hate it when my mother was finishing her dissertation. That closed door! I hated it." Tears came to her eyes. (Incidentally, she then marveled at how motherhood can make you so much more aware of your own past as well as your child's present. One of the footnotes of parenthood: If we're observant, we have the chance to see so much more. One of the footnotes of older parenthood: So many of us seem to be so observant about so much more.)

There may well be things in our homes as we grow up that we hate, and in fact we can argue that this is at least as valuable as always having everything rosy. We learn how to live with what we do not like, a meaningful lesson indeed. We can argue further that it is important, and perhaps even more important for girls, to see that mothers have lives, interests, work, and an integral connection to the world around them.

But where it gets tricky is if our children perceive that we are choosing our work over them. That given the choice—and to a small child who doesn't truly understand what work means, if we are in the same house, we do have the choice—we could very well play with them. We just don't choose to.

In addition to Beth's temperament, the reason she and her daughter can so happily and smoothly spend several hours in the late afternoon in happy tandem occupation is that they have both had long, uninterrupted hours to do other things. Beth has been able to get the lion's share of her work done. Her daughter has been stimulated enough that she's happy to spend some time in her own fantasy world. It is, in fact, darn close to win-win. The mother can put in enough time to get her work done, but she is free enough that, if necessary, she can attend to her daughter's needs.

For the rest of us looking at working at home, here are some things to consider. If you have a baby-sitter, have the sitter take your child out. Arrange your day like any other working family. You all eat, get dressed, and get ready to start your respective days. Your child goes out. That way your child does not feel as if you might be rejecting him and you are not faced with banging on the door.

THE "WORK" OF MOTHERHOOD IS NEVER DONE

For all of us, whether we spend all our time with our child or most of our time at work, there is something that we cannot find a "cure" for. In motherhood, unlike work, there are no hours. Furthermore, we cannot set a goal and reach it. In the short term, we are lucky some days simply to get out of the house. In the long term, we have no way of gauging whether our parenting is a success at all until we have spent so many years doing it that if we have failed, our children will be obliged to pick up the pieces on their own.

There is no desk to clear, no file to put away. There are no discrete tasks in parenting such as there are at work which we can say we have finally finished. There is no praise, there are no raises. There are no sick days, no vacation days—even when we take a vacation. We cannot ask for a raise. We cannot be fired. We cannot quit.

Whether we work out of the home or in the home, we are all full-time moms.

There are no perfect solutions.

THE OLDER FAMILY'S RELATIONSHIP TO WORK

Recently I got an e-mail about a reunion from my high school boyfriend. He is a grandfather. He and his wife have already sold their acreage in the Carolinas in preparation for retiring to Florida.

Although my husband and I daydream about winning the lottery so we can play all day, the concept, the word, the idea of retirement is completely out of our sphere. Among most older families with children younger than late teens, retirement is not something that occurs to them. Not so much because they can't afford it, although certainly having to keep earning in order to support their child's needs comes into play. But more important, retiring is "an old people's idea." And I don't know a soul who has young children who identifies with being "old." Or at least the kind of old that "retires."

A mother of a twelve-year-old brought up an issue that's been on my mind—one that most of you will probably come to. As a natural progression of life, many people in their fifties start to look inward. Somehow you get philosophical. You get less introspective about what makes you tick, having explored it so much that frankly there's nothing very interesting left to think about, and you become more curious about "the meaning of life." It is a more mature search than the important adolescent search for meaning that most people experience in their late teens and early twenties. What is telling is that this desire to turn inward is never linked with "retirement."

This mother expressed it best: "If my husband and I could, we would probably go to the country to paint and meditate and write. Of course, we won't. We still need to keep earning as much as we have been for college, and more important, we need to keep our son in his school with his life going ahead. Going to the country is not a crashing need. It's just what I think we might do now if we didn't have our son's needs to think about." Although she and her husband were in fact fantasizing about radically changing their lifestyle, "retirement" as a word or concept never came into her conversation.

Another friend, who is the same age as my husband and I and who like us has a ten-year-old, was just offered a fabulous new job on the other coast. He grabbed it, since it is an extraordinary opportunity for him to grow. One of his best friends is furious that he's taking a new job. He was yelling, "You should be thinking about retirement at this stage of your life, not new jobs!"

My friend asked me with a kind of bafflement in his voice, "Do you ever think about retirement?" He was relieved to hear that it is not a need or even a fantasy for us. Yet so many people I know who are the same age as I am, but whose children are older, are marching along, planning and moving quite rapidly toward retirement.

It's possible that the fact that we chose to have our children at a later age means that we approach life very differently. That developmentally we are slow. I think, however, that it has more to do with the fact that we are the kind of people who did not follow the expected projection, and that therefore "retirement" is a kind of closing-up-shop, a move toward the end, a diminishing rather than expansion that seems foreign and distasteful. I feel very much in the prime of my life and nowhere near the end.

Everyone I know with young children is going full steam ahead, growing, learning, following new lines of inquiry, completely in the thick of life and moving upward rather than tapering off, perhaps going inward, but certainly not slowing down. We are in the work-force for the next several decades. For better or worse.

HELPFUL HINTS

There are some tips that might help you if you work full-time, others that will help the at-home mom, and still others for the work-at-home mom. Refer to chapter 8, "Bifocals and Barney," for ways to refresh yourself however you spend your days.

THE WORKING MOM

There is an entire, and much needed, industry of books, magazines, and Web sites (see the lists in the back of the book) devoted to helping you juggle multiple full-time jobs: mother, whatever paid work you do, and wife, if you are one. In addition, here are some practical and emotional hints to help you manage what is essentially an unhandle-able situation.

Practical

SET DOMESTIC PRIORITIES

You really cannot do it all. Nobody can. Since you already have a full-time job, the hours necessary to keep house the way a house "ought to be kept" are no longer available unless it's at the expense of spending time with your family. Many people find that the best solution, or more precisely the least of all evils, is to let domestic standards slide.

Ellen Bravo, head of Nine-to-Five, an organization dedicated to making the lives of working women better, has a slogan. "It's more important to have your life in order than your closets in order, as long as you can make your way to the closet!"

GET HELP

Whether you're married or single, if you have the money, obviously you don't need me to tell you to farm out as much of the domestic work as you can, to free yourself for all the other parts of your life.

As soon as your child is a toddler, begin teaching and expecting your child to participate in running the home by doing age-appropriate tasks. Not only will this become helpful in actually getting chores done, but it is very important in terms of teaching your child responsibility, cooperation, and self-reliance.

If you're married, it would seem obvious simply to share taking care of running your home with your husband. This solution is elegant and satisfying—in the homes where both partners are in intellectual and emotional agreement with this plan. As we discussed in chapter 3, "Transforming from a Couple into a Family," however, this is not always the easy task that we would like to think it would be. Notwithstanding the logical notion that your entire family only stands to benefit from your husband being an equal partner in running the home, it is a "should" that in some homes becomes more of a burden than a help. Not all husbands will take over a fair share and not all wives will let go of the control of their homes. Therefore, each of you has to evaluate honestly what participation is reasonable to expect and what expectations are in fact unrealistic and therefore setups for frustration, anger, and despair—none of which make a home run more smoothly, not to mention feel better.

Once you and your husband have come to common grounds on what he is responsible for, back off. If he folds the towels in slap-dash squares instead of in fluffy, rectangular thirds, learn to love squares.

Emotional

FIND WAYS TO REFRESH YOURSELF

Going from work to home is such a major shifting of gears that it exhausts most people. Try to give yourself time in between, a buffer zone where you can decompress from one activity to be ready to go to the next, a way to let all your loose ends from work be tied up in a ball and put into a bag so that when you open the door, you are ready to face the little face.

Think about something other than work or your child during your travel time between both worlds. Notice the changing scenery. Notice other people around you and make up stories of their lives. Sing at the top of your lungs if you're driving. Read a novel if you're on a bus or train. Find a way to give yourself a time when you are off-duty from both work and being a mommy.

LEAVE WORK WHEN YOU LEAVE WORK

Many working mothers feel like they're never fully in either place. As one put it, "When I'm at work, I'm thinking about my son. When I'm at home, I'm thinking about work."

In the early years, for most women it is almost a biological imperative that their child's well-being and very existence form the bedrock of their marginal thoughts. Advice to put your child "out of your mind" while at work would be remiss and unrealistic.

But advice to put work out of your mind once you leave it is an idea that will prove useful. There are some practical steps to take to ensure that business doesn't creep into your home.

Before you leave work, make a list of the things you need to do tomorrow. Put the list in the same place every day. Leave the list at work.

Although occasionally you may have to make a business call in the evening, make the vast majority of your nights business free. There are no e-mails important enough to be read or returned while you're nursing your child. There is no strategic move, snappy comeback, or savvy maneuver that needs to be swirling through your mind when you're reading to your child.

Leave work when you leave work. Your work will be there next year and ten years from now. If it's not, there will be some other work. Your child will only nurse, or take a bottle, and snuggle next to your body and look up at you with those eyes filled with complete trust and fascination for a very short amount of time.

Here's the experience of an older mother who runs a large legal department: "As soon as I decided that I would only work when I was at work, I became much more efficient. I made up my mind that I would leave at six. That meant that I had to get everything done. I worked harder, because I took away my safety valve. I used to figure I can always finish up when the office is quiet. Now, if I have to do some work that requires concentration, I shut my door and turn on my voice mail. I finish what I need to do, and I move on. I've gotten ruthless about reaching people during working hours. It has completely boosted my productivity."

BE AT WORK WHEN YOU'RE AT WORK

Some women find that not having their child's picture displayed in their work space helps make the separation easier and allows them to concentrate more fully on the job in front of them.

Limit your calls home. A daily, or more frequent, "check-in call" often makes you, your sitter, and your toddler feel worse than no call.

Refer to chapter 7, "Helping Hands," for many ways to enrich the time you do have to spend with your child, which may make spending time away from your child less of a conflict.

LEARN TO SAY NO

You do not have to host every holiday dinner at your house. You do not have to bake from scratch, *and* make the soup, *and* make the homemade cranberry sauce, *and* make the sweet-potato casserole to assuage your guilt that your sister-in-law is having Thanksgiving at her house this year. You do not have to be the only person your colleague trusts to help choose upholstery fabric for her couch in her den. You do not have to continue all of the volunteer work you did pre-baby. You can return once your child is older. You do not have to have dinner with the couple that both you and your husband find boring but somehow have gotten into the habit of seeing on a regular basis. You do not have to feel obliged to have your cousin's Italian friends who are traveling around America stay at your house for a weekend—even though you still have a spare room and may have adored having guests pre-baby. You no longer have to be the person at work who always buys the birthday presents, organizes the parties, and collects contributions for wedding showers.

Although these kinds of suggestions may seem practical and more along the lines of setting priorities, the truth is that for those of us who are "givers" and "doers," giving up this role is often an emotional challenge. But every minute you spend doing anything that is not actual work is a minute that you cannot spend with your child, your husband, or in much needed self-refreshment. The early years of your child's life are few. Cutting back on activities that are unnecessary—even though they may be nice—is a useful way to manage your time to include your child.

THE AT-HOME MOM

Your "job" is very difficult. If you're not careful, you may be hard-pressed to know what you "did" all day. Here are some hints.

Practical

- Aim for a week at a time rather than having a must-do list of chores for any given day. This will allow you to alter your plans, as is necessary when you're with a young child.
- Keep in mind the reason you're no longer working at your job. If you spent most of your day doing housework, and squeezing your child in among chores, you didn't do such a hot job.
- Let your housekeeping standards slide while your child is young. It will take the pressure off everybody.
- Plan one activity a day with your child, leaving you the rest of the day to "go with the flow." Planning more than two activities a day starts to put pressure on everybody.

Emotional

- Make sure that you get a break sometime during the day when you are not "on," and when you are not doing something else that is necessary. In other words, make sure you have about an hour a day, even if it means getting up at five in the morning, where you can read the paper, or lie down staring into space. But where you are not on duty with your child.
- Build a life. Make friends. (See chapter 10, "One Is Silver and the Other Gold.") Most of your friends, as you know, have either older kids or no kids. You really need companionship during the day. Take toddler classes. Besides being a hoot for your child, they will give you a specific place to be at a certain hour, and a potential place to meet people. They will hook you into the "mommy world."
- Consider part-time child care, such as a local college or high-school girl for a few hours a week. If you're an at-home mom with full-time help, chapter 7, "Helping Hands," may speak to you.
- Try to keep up with your husband's life in a meaningful way, not just in half-hearted questions attended to with half an ear. I know

that sounds like "Betty Crocker" advice, but don't forget, "Betty Crocker" advice stemmed from the fact that in those days most women were home all day with their children.

- Hold on to the fact that these few years are short, fleeting, and all-important. I saw a mommy on the bus a day or two ago. Her little boy was about two. She was making a raspberry sound in his ear and he was laughing with delight. The hug that she was getting in the middle of the afternoon was priceless. There will come a time very shortly when her child will not need her, or any other adult, the way he needs her now.
- Hold and hug your child.

One last thought—or perhaps caution. We approach at-home motherhood with a variety of styles. Some read like fiends about child development, for example, and this often leads them back to graduate school in a related field once their children are old enough to start school. Others, once free from the hours of a job, pick up a variety of highly marketable skills, including everything from furniture refinishing, antique collecting, or fine arts to financial or real estate expertise or the basics of other small, home-based businesses that can flourish with time.

Others throw themselves into their child's life. By nursery school, they are on every committee, volunteer for every classroom job, and take every group to the park every day. If you find that you are spending every hour that your child is in school on activities related to your child's life, perhaps you have tipped the balance a bit. I am not at all suggesting that work in the schools is not important, both for enriching the schools and for making a powerful statement to your child that his mother is actively part of his life. I am suggesting, however, that if you put more than one hour a day, on a consistent basis, into volunteer work related not to your child but to your child's life, that does not provide you with a marketable skill, you might do yourself and your child a service by finding another outlet for your talents.

THE WORK-AT-HOME MOM

I know one writer who is extremely successful (an Academy Award winner) and who works from home. He has a large room in his home that is empty save for his desk. And he has a wife.

If *you* have a wife who will take your child out, defrost something for dinner, clean out closets and drawers, put away laundry, make sure that no bills or scribbled notes regarding play dates and birthday parties end up on your desk, and when she and your child come home in the afternoon from the playground will whisper, "Shhh. Mommy's working. Let's be as quiet as little mice," chances are you can smoothly and successfully have a small child and work from home.

But should you happen not to have a wife like that, you may find that working at home is difficult. It's hard to plan time, as it is for the at-home mom. But also, the lines between work and home have a tendency to blur. It is tempting, when you have a moment, to jump up and throw a load in the washer rather than make a difficult call or finish a boring part of a job. For many people who work at home, life seems somehow to seep into an unending pit where they're never really at work, and never really at home. Add to that never really being with your child, and you have the potential for feeling terrible, not getting your work done, and ending every day completely dissatisfied.

There are some practical things that can help.

- Keep your work space, whether it's a room or a desk, off-limits from the rest of your home. Keep all home messages, bills, records, and so on somewhere other than your work space.

I love those TV commercials where they show beautiful women and handsome men in clean, uncluttered surroundings, leaning back, their feet up on the rail of their deck, their T-shirts and the bottoms of their socks clean, working on their little lap-tops. Who are they kidding? Many people at home drag around in their robes! That's one of the real reasons lots of us like to work at home. You don't have to wear panty hose! However . . .

- Get up, get showered, put on clean clothes and set a time that you must be at your desk, as if you had a boss watching the clock.
- Take a midmorning break, when you leave your desk. Do not do domestic chores. Use your break, like any working mom, to exercise, write in your journal, or take a moment for yourself.
- Take a lunch break.
- Set a time for work to be over. Shut the door. If you don't have a door, close down your computer or do whatever tidying up your particular work calls for, to signify that it is now the end of the workday.

Obviously this nice schedule does not include a child in the house. Have your sitter take your child out to play. There are libraries and bookstores and other indoor options, including play dates with other children, should the weather be bad.

If you do not have a baby-sitter, or the option Beth had, day care, it is unlikely (although not impossible) that you can successfully run a full-time business from home for the first few years of your child's life without being extravagantly tired or without ignoring your child. I am sorry to sound so bleak about that but I presume you share my opinion that a young child needs to be attended to during the day.

There is another very valuable option to consider. If you are in a large enough town, there are probably other work-at-home parents struggling the same way you are. If you can pull off the logistics and can afford it, I recommend pooling your resources, renting a space together, and teaming up to get a baby-sitter for a few children. Although difficult in the beginning to organize, this arrangement will give you a chance to be free from corporate constraints and be your own boss, but also to leave work when you leave work, which ought to be a human right.

There can be no right or wrong answer to such a complicated problem as whether you "should" or "should not" work, how much you should work, and where. Every life is different. Yet here is a philosophical approach that I feel often gets lost in the debate.

child has enough of the skills necessary to function in the
—skills given mostly by you—you will find that while you are
ng, you are actually able to have a complete series of intelligent
hts uninterrupted by the dread that your child is dead—or the
ory of a particularly darling smile!

u also find with time the interests you must keep in your life and
that no longer beckon so strongly. Just as the last incarnation of
"self" was more mature and developed than your adolescent
" so will your new role of "mommy" start to take on a richer
a with time.

BEYOND TECHNIQUE: "OWN" BEING THE MOMMY

Many older new mothers, both those who work and those who are at
home with their children, report the unsettling feeling of having "lost
themselves."

"I don't know who I am anymore," says Rachel, a forty-two-year-
old whose son is eighteen months old. Although the specifics of her
life may be different from others, the massive change is typical. She
has cut her business as a financial consultant down to the bone, going
from fourteen- or sixteen-hour days, including being available by
phone on the weekends and evenings, to two or three six-hour days.
She is trying to keep alive the business that she worked so hard to build
while she spends as much time as she can with her son. She is supervis-
ing her family's move into a larger home. She and her husband are trying to have a second child and therefore going through the stress once
again of fertility treatments, including the added strain of beginning to
discuss adoption. She is trying, although she feels not successfully, to
pay attention to her husband and allow their marriage of a few years
to grow. Somewhere in all this "domestic bliss," so radically different
from the life she led just a few years ago, she has "lost herself," as she
describes it.

Like Rachel, we all had a decade or two under our belts to define
"ourselves." We developed interests, friendships, and fields of expertise. We were able to take care of ourselves by taking classes, going to
the gym, going out with friends, and traveling. If we were building
careers, we could devote ourselves to them, being available for whatever was called for. The drastic change in priorities and lifestyle that
parenthood cries out for is often felt more keenly by us than by
younger people who had less highly developed lifestyles pre-baby.

Not only do we miss the "selves" that we feel we've lost, we're not
always so happy with our new "selves." Motherhood, whether we
work full-time or are home, can have the effect of turning us into the
manager, if not the "cop." We herd the flock where we have to go,
remember to pick up the milk, remind everybody to get their lunches
off the kitchen counter. We are often cast in the role of the bad guy,
the one who says, "Bedtime," and on and on into the infinity of vexing
chores that we have to stay on top of if we want things to run.

While it's important to strive to have the husband take on a good 50 percent of those chores, which is possible in some homes, there is an emotional element that sometimes gets obscured by the struggle to juggle domestic duties, as well as all the other parts of our lives.

Rather than offer you palliative Band-Aids for refinding your "self," I'm going to suggest looking in a new direction.

The truth is that the "self" you used to be really is lost. You were not a mother before. Being a mother changes you on a very fundamental level. It requires that you knowingly put the needs of another before your own on a regular basis. It requires scaling back on meeting some, and perhaps many, of your needs during the first few years of your child's life and later on not having the luxury of time to take up all that you suspended. It requires sometimes choosing the needs of your entire family over your own. This transition is not always an easy, smooth one. It is not always fun. For most of us, it is more pleasant to get a massage than to give one. In order to allow your new "self" to emerge, however, it is not necessary to assume a martyr-like stance. "Don't worry about me, I'll just sit here in the dark." Instead, you have the chance to take on a new, possibly larger, possibly emotionally enriched "self" than the one you miss.

Somebody has to be the center of a family. Somebody's got to be the ballast. Somebody's got to be the fulcrum. Somebody's got to be the heart. And that somebody is the mother.

What you have lost—and make no mistake, you have lost quite a bit—is autonomy and a certain kind of freedom. What you have the potential to have gained is the chance to be deeply connected. Both are magnificent states. You worked hard to grow into your last "self"; this new self, too, will require work, and readjustment, until you wear it as comfortably as you wore the last.

Here is Grace describing how she defines her new role: "The mother is the center—the spiritual, psychological, and emotional center—of the family. And the family is the center of society. Spiritually, psychologically, emotionally."

Ellie, oddly playing with the same imagery, expresses the same meaning from her own perspective:

"I turned my life over to my children, as much as I could. I still have

a job. I kept that for myself. But when I'm with them them.

"A lot of young mothers still seem to me to have a tence. The younger mother puts herself in the cent Her child becomes a spoke, her husband become work—if she works—her friends, and whatever it is still the center of her life. But I think when you're ol and children become the center. That's your prima everything else gets the scraps. I feel lucky to know tha

There are so many complicated relationships even in three. There are alliances and loves, there are favorites get taken. In a family that has a strong, passionate conn another, it is not simply about dividing household cho can maintain our autonomy. That is not a family. That is i

Roommates can be marvelous. I had some way back are still my best-beloved girlfriends, notwithstanding ho to stay out of each other's hair sometimes and to do our the kitchen. We took turns doing the shopping, and we other's likes enough to get each other treats when it w Each was responsible for taking care of her own room, and we were responsible for keeping the common areas livable it was marvelous, it was civilized and rational, and it wor was roommates. When each of us found the partner she we went to start our families.

Families need an emotional center. Once you "own" that bility and right, juggling the various practical pieces of an life becomes a bit easier. You manage to keep your eye on ball—your family—and your work, while exhilarating, cha and inspiring, becomes just one of the other balls.

Whether you have chosen to be an at-home mother or to b work, I can offer you a lovely experience to look forward to.

As your child matures, so do you. As your child takes ste from you physically, so are you able to be apart. With each d mental stage of independence from you comes your own indepe from your child. Usually by kindergarten, the work/mom di loses the emotional pull and becomes more a matter of logistics

7

Helping Hands: Child Care

We see them as we open our doors wide, indicating that class has begun. Some toddlers stride into the room, their smiling grown-up trailing in their wake, greeting the other grown-ups by name as they hang up their coats, patting a little shoulder with a friendly hand, urging the toddler to go play, sometimes offering a pleasant call across the room warning of a potential danger or social mishap, sometimes close enough to avert a wrong turn. Other little ones are tugged or prodded into the room, their grown-up greeting some and snubbing others. Some "lap sitters" are held in strong arms until they are confident enough to wiggle down to go play. Others are pushed off laps as if they were offensive pieces of lint. Some of the grown-ups we see here are sitters. Some are moms.

Sitters, like moms, come in all sizes and shapes in terms of temperament and emotional availability to their charges.

Some of us are single working parents who by necessity rely heavily on full-time child care. Some of us work full-time in two-income families—a situation that perhaps gives us more leeway in how we organize our help. Some of us do not work outside the home but choose full-time care in order to have the flexibility to keep up with other parts of our lives. What you need from the caregiver you hire will of course depend on your situation. But there are some common issues for all of us who add another person to our household.

THE BROAD STROKES OF CHILD CARE

If the mother or father does not take care of a child during the day, obviously other arrangements must be made. A relative, group care, or individual care are the options.

I am assuming that you are a resourceful person who, if you have not already sought out the information necessary to make the right arrangements, will take a look at the resources in the back of this book for leads about the best ways to hire, pay, and manage whomever you chose as your caregiver. I don't think it's useful for any of us to rehash the advice that you can find already clearly spelled out in other places.

In this chapter on child care, I want to address the issue specifically in terms of how our age, experience, and lifestyle affect some of the day-to-day decisions we make.

The first obvious place where we differ from younger parents is that we do not automatically turn to our own mothers as the logical choice.

IT'S NOT GRANDMA

A large percentage of younger working parents opt to leave their children with their mothers. In addition to the "comfort level" of having a family member take care of the child, money is frequently a deciding factor. In any number of homes where Grandma is conscripted, she is the only viable solution.

Even though some of us are lucky enough to have our mothers baby-sit from time to time, typically, most of us do not have them take over full-time child care. There is a practical reason. Our mothers are older, just as we are. In happy circumstances, some are still working in their own jobs; others are playing tennis in Boca or bingo in Arkansas, or are finally able to spend as much time as they want in the garden of the house where we grew up. Sadly, many of us have already lost our own mothers; for others our mothers have become full-time caregivers for our fathers or are in need of care themselves. Most, given the stage of life they are in, are simply not available to play with a baby forty hours a week.

But even if our mothers were willing and able to take on the task, unlike younger women who tend to be more emotionally dependent on their mothers, we are inclined to want to avoid the sticky interpersonal web that can potentially be spun around such a daily joining of lives.

One forty-eight-year-old woman expressed the quandary that mothers our age face when our own mothers become part of our daily domestic lives. She became seriously ill after the birth of her daughter, and needed the help of her mother, an energetic woman in her late sixties. Now, months later, our older mom is having to "deal with" extricating her whole family from under the stylistic domination of Grandma.

"I feel like I'm twenty again!" Her discomfort with having to retrace her history of growth to independence contrasts with the genuine delight of younger mothers I've heard exclaiming about what a blessing it is to have Mom around.

GROUP CARE

I would love to persuade you to try out group care. When it is good, it is very, very good, whether it is provided in a corporate setting or in someone's home. But I know that very few of you will exercise this marvelous option. Should you decide that the regularity, reliability, predictability, and intellectual and social stimulation of a good group care situation are appealing, in the "Recommended Reading" section you will find books that have sound information to help you select.

INDIVIDUAL CARE

That leads us to the child care arrangement in approximately 75 to 80 percent of the homes of older parents.

We hire a sitter. I'm more comfortable with "baby-sitter" than with "nanny," a professional title conferred on people who have fulfilled specific course work, including three thousand hours of training.

For this discussion, readers, I want us to close the door, kick off our shoes, curl up on the couch, turn on the answering machine, and talk. Just between you and me. I want to be cozy and private—not because I have anything terrible to say, but because I want to give us all the chance to drop our defenses. Once we abandon our public stances, which we all need and maintain for various reasons, I think we might give ourselves the chance to come to a more comfortable place.

Here, I want to try together to get to something deep. Something that is very hard to discuss because it's so threatening. The reason it's so threatening is that it's so complicated and there really is no right or wrong. There are degrees. It is a compromise that we must make in modern life. The repercussions of the compromise will be far-reaching for everybody concerned.

In the other chapters, I have relied on others to share their views. But in this chapter, the only way that I am comfortable having this discussion is for me to share the decision that I made when I was a new mom. I think that will give you a perspective to evaluate what I have to say on your own terms. You may find that you disagree with me, but at least you will know clearly where I stand.

So, as in the other chapters, here we find the fifty-two-year-old mother of a ten-year-old sharing part of her life.

ONE MOTHER'S CHOICE

I had the luxury of having a choice. We had enough money—although not nearly as much as we would have if I'd worked full-time—that I was not obliged for economic reasons to work when my child was young. Teaching is a field that is not as hard to get back into as many others. Writing is something that you just continue to do and do and do and either you have lots of success, a little success, or no success until you're dead—if then. But neither is an occupation confined by glass ceilings and mommy tracks. In short, I was free from many of the external pressures that may be impinging on you.

When my child was eighteen months old, my husband came home one night to find me, still wearing the purple sweat suit that had taken me through pregnancy and was now safety-pinned in a big glob at the waist, mopping the floor and sobbing. Surely, there had to be more to life than sitting on the floor doing sixteen-piece puzzles of kittens with my child. Again, I was lucky. I was hired to lead a group that met for one and a half hours, one day a week. Hardly a backbreaking workload. But it gave me a place to have to be at a certain time, it gave me a situation that required my getting dressed, it gave me a sense of belonging, the chance to feel as if I had something to offer in life, and, although quite small, a paycheck. When my child was two, I was lucky enough to sell a proposal and coauthor a book; again, the amount of time required was manageable. It was not until my child was three and a half and in nursery school full-time, and therefore in a situation that I felt was completely nurturing, that I took on more work, both in teaching and in writing. By the time she was in kindergarten, I was back to putting in full-time—and then some—hours.

I know how lucky I have been. Because I am a teacher and a writer, I was able to tailor my professions to become a paid part of the mommy world. This is a route that many women take once they become mothers if their temperaments, interests, and chosen occupations can be retooled to earn a living and gain intellectual satisfaction while raising their children. I was not constrained by a nine-to-five or longer workday. I was completely free to meet the needs of my child and myself, to not work when I felt she needed me not to, and to work when I felt that I would either shrivel up or go mad without it. I know that you are probably not in such a dreamboat situation. Your choices are probably much harder. Many of you are up against a much more difficult either/or situation.

For me, hiring a full-time caregiver was never something that I had to do.

But I want to go on record as saying that it was also something that I would never have chosen to do.

The reason that I am sharing this is certainly not to win popularity contests. It is far from a popular position in our world. But I am uncomfortable about how most writers, psychologists, and other parenting experts are either adamant about their position, admitting no possible good to come from the other side, or walk on eggshells, careful to be neutral and evenhanded about one of the most difficult, complicated, and troublesome issues in modern life. They offer strategies and take great pains not to make anyone anxious, yet never reveal where they stand personally.

I feel it only right to say that I do not feel neutral about the subject. I have opinions borne out by experience.

After working closely with over a thousand families and observing countless others, I have found that while many baby-sitters are caring, and a tiny fraction even have some form of training for their jobs, there are very few people hired to take care of children who do the same kinds of things and who teach the same kinds of things that you would. This does not have to do with intelligence or personality but with their own backgrounds, early childhood experiences, and the model of mothering that they were raised with. I have spent considerable time with many baby-sitters whom I genuinely like a lot, and whose company their charges clearly enjoy. They are lovely people with a lot to offer. Yet, for the most part, they do not share fundamental values with the family for whom they work.

Are the children all right? Certainly. They're fed, and they pass their days pleasantly. Are they learning as much as they should be at a tender age? They are learning an enormous amount. Children are sponges. *What* they are learning, however, is different from what they would be learning if they were with you. And I think that this is at the core of the issue.

THE EARLY YEARS

During the first three years, an enormous amount of cognitive development takes place. Language is learned. Example: Scientists showed pictures to a group of eight-month-olds. "Show me the dog," said the experimenter. All the eight-month-olds pointed to the dog. "Show me gub dog," said the experimenter. All the eight-month-olds looked as confused as you were when confronted with the gibberish word "gub." By eight months a group of babies had already learned enough syntax and vocabulary to recognize when a simple sentence has been disrupted. In response to stimulation, the physical pathways and synapses in the brain are ignited to fire properly during the first year. The connective thought processes necessary to build the intellectual foundations for understanding physics, science, mathematics, and the nuances of meaning and emotion conveyed by both verbal and body language are all established during the first three years. The underlying bases for how we interact with others, how we share, how we know what is right and wrong, how we modulate our voices, how we touch, how we hold our bodies, what we laugh at, what we value, and who we love are all laid within the first three years.

I think you know all that. That is why we have our defenses built. That is why we do not like to talk about this too much. It is easier to talk about the how-tos—how to hire, how to check references, how to set up weekly meetings—than it is to address the fundamental reality that if we are not careful, someone else, who probably does not share our values or our approach to life, will be raising our children.

Basically, we have to pretend that those things do not matter or hope that they can be attended to later on in order to run our homes the way some of us currently do.

Before you start hyperventilating, or throw the book across the room, I am not suggesting that you quit your job and fire your sitter. That is not a viable option for many of you, and for others it is simply not what you would choose to do.

I am suggesting, however, that you may have to rethink various aspects of the way you've arranged everybody's lives to make sure that everybody's needs are being met.

WHO DOES WHAT?

Start by taking a few minutes to think about what your sitter does with your child and what you do. Start from the moment you awake until the moment you go to bed. If your sitter lives with you, think about a twenty-four-hour period.

Do you divide child care so that your sitter takes care of the chores, freeing you to be the one to spend fun time with your child?

For example, do you play with your child in the morning and then let your sitter feed your child breakfast while you get ready for work? At the end of the day, does your sitter give your child dinner, bathe your child, and get your child ready for bed so that when you come home you can play with and read to your child before lights-out? Does your sitter go to your child when your child awakes either in the morning or the middle of the night?

If you have set up routine events in this way, you may have unwittingly denied yourself, not to mention your child, some of the most intimate connections of motherhood. All the repetitive, seemingly mundane tasks—feeding, dressing, bathing, and sleeping—are not drudgery and chores to a young child. They are life.

LIFE THROUGH YOUR BABY'S EYES

The person who picks the child up from the crib, whether first thing in the sunshine of morning or in the dark in the middle of the night, is the person the baby smells, smiles at, nestles into. The person whose strong hands lift the child out of the tub is the person the child snuggles up against in the cozy embrace of a big, cuddly towel. The person who chatters, making up stories about taking the bowl from the cabinet, is the person whose imagery, word choice, and worldview are laid down like strips of information on a magnetic tape. The person who sits on the other side of the high chair smilingly offering a yummy piece of banana has the face the child will lovingly study, the expressions the child will devotedly mimic, the intonations the child will carefully try to repeat, the presence that spells out safety, comfort, hominess, and joy.

Although the reading of a story is vitally important, if it does not follow as a logical, integral activity, as immediate and pressing as the rest of the real "work" of the baby, the dinner, bath, and pj's part, if you come breezing in like some splendid big-name star, you might as well be the librarian, a videotape, or a favorite aunt brought in to a drum roll as a special event to brighten up the day of the child and the child's primary caregiver.

"Quality time," although there really is no such thing, has to do with emotional and intellectual connections. And connections get made doing what may seem to us the everyday, oh-this-again activities, but to the child are rich with their repeated phrases, rhythms, smells, and feels.

Young children are tactile little beings whose range is close to home. If you take them to the zoo to see the polar bears, they will focus on the fly on their juice pack. If you take them to the Met to see Renoir, they will marvel at the pattern in your skirt. If you take them to the opera, the sound of your voice will be music; all the rest will be vaguely alarming or vaguely appealing background noise. Whatever is not within arm's reach might as well be on Mars; whatever they can touch or hold is the universe. Whatever is new may or may not be of interest; whatever is known is held dear. The closer you stay to your child during the safe, secure, routine parts of life, the stronger the connection between you.

INTIMATE MOMENTS IN YOUR TODDLER'S LIFE

With that kind of perspective in mind, here are some questions that bear introspection.

When your child wakes up, who goes to him or her in the middle of the night?

Who comforts your child for physical or emotional hurts?

Who stays with your child when he or she is sick?

Who will toilet train your child?

Are you out more than four nights a week? If so, who puts your child to bed?

Who puts your child to bed when you're home?

If you have the kind of work that frequently requires you to be out past your child's bedtime, I have two recommendations. The first is to make it your business to see that you get up with your child, feed your child breakfast, and then get yourself ready for the day so that you are allowed that important, intimate time to connect. You would be wise to consider cutting down on evening events for a few years so that, in general, dinner, bath, and bedtime are spent with you. Evening events have always gone on and will continue to do so. Your child's early years are finite and brief. You really don't have that much time to establish that you are the one who will always be there for your child.

YOUR CHILD'S SOCIAL LIFE

In addition to the intimate, visceral moments that make up a young child's life, there is another element that I'm afraid we lose sometimes while keeping up our busy pace. The issue, from the child's point of view, is this: When I am out in the world, who do I belong to? Who is my protector? Who do I follow like a little duck? Who do I turn to if I'm not sure what's what? Whose social world am I part of? I think by now it's clear that Mommy is the one who ought to come to the child's mind as the answer to those kinds of questions.

Here, I'd like to present another set of questions for you.

Who arranges play dates?

Who goes to birthday parties?

Do you know the other children your child plays with?
Do you know the parents of the children your child plays with?
Do you know the caregivers of the children your child plays with?

I've had mommies not exactly brag, but let's say share with pride, that their toddler's social lives are so full and that the mommies don't know their friends. While it is dreadfully important for your sitter to be able to navigate through her day with autonomy, and to arrange fun things to do for your child, it is equally important for you to actually lay eyes on the people in your child's life. Otherwise, you may intimate by your total absence that you and your child inhabit different social worlds. The unpleasant extension of that later in your child's life could be that you are not interested in who your child's friends are.

If your sitter has a network of people that she and your child hang out with during the day—and this should be encouraged—make it your business to meet the children's parents some weekend. You also might consider stealing a lunch hour here or there and meeting the other caregivers with whom your child is spending time.

Even though you may view getting your child to a birthday party as simply a logistical problem, from your child's point of view, if the sitter always takes the child, you may appear to be not particularly interested in where your child goes or with whom your child socializes.

Your Child Out in the World

Here are some other questions a child might ask: Who speaks for me? Who safely ushers me through exciting, yet sometimes unnerving, experiences of life?

I'd like to counter that with questions for you.

Who takes your child to the doctor?
If your baby-sitter takes your child to a toddler class, do you attend at least one class each semester?

Although perhaps routine, and possibly viewed again as a logistical problem of getting the child to the appropriate place on time, doctor's appointments are essential to your child's health. Pediatrician's and dentist's reports and recommendations are too important to be filtered through your sitter. Furthermore, in the context of creating and sustaining connections, if your child has to have an injection, and you are not the one whose lap your child sits in and who comforts your child afterward, you have once again missed an intimate moment, one that, although it may be unpleasant, is part of motherhood.

If you cannot find the time to attend at least one session of your child's toddler class, you have managed inadvertently to convey that what your child does in an institutional setting, how your child interacts in a group, and what individual is in charge of teaching your child are not vitally important to you. I would imagine that's not how you feel at all.

If most of the activities mentioned are taken care of by your sitter, your family balance is off and you need to make some scheduling adjustments. Your child needs you to be more actively involved in his or her life. Whether you admit it to yourself or not, you need to be more involved in your child's life—for you as well as the child.

YOUR OLDER CHILD

Here are some questions in a similar vein if your children are past their toddler years.

Who takes your child to school?
Who picks up your child?
Who talks to the teacher about what's gone on that day?
Who takes your child to lessons? Who oversees practicing?

Let's just look at lessons, seemingly a sideline of life. Perhaps, on closer examination, even lessons are not as marginal and unimportant as they may seem.

If your baby-sitter oversees practicing due to everybody's rigorous schedules, you have lost a valuable chance to teach your child many important lessons in life. In addition to the actual content, which is a richer experience for your child if you are familiar with the piece of music, there are many things that music lessons are teaching over and above Schubert. For example, when practicing becomes a struggle, you can help your child learn the habit of doing something that's hard to do, of learning how to stick with something. Most of our children are learning how to play an instrument because it enriches their lives, not because they will be professional musicians. Yet if the parent is not hands-on involved, we lose the chance for the real enrichment. "We don't walk away from challenges," is a lesson that gets taught week after week when a child practices an instrument. We are given the opportunity to reward them when they have success. If you are not the one who is instilling these values, who is?

If you relegate the entire duty of overseeing practicing to your sitter, everyone is going through the motions. We may feel as if we are providing lessons. We are certainly paying for them. We have arranged to have our child taken to the lessons and brought home and we have arranged for our child's schedule to include practicing. However, we may be kidding ourselves into thinking that we have offered the opportunity for enrichment. We have provided the trappings. The stage set. But we have missed the substance. The parenting part of the experience. The shared struggle and triumph of doing something that's sometimes distasteful until we have mastered it.

On something as simple as lessons, if you have backbreaking schedules during the week, you might consider ensuring that at least one practice session takes place on the weekend and that one parent is within earshot to offer kudos when appropriate and suggestions to try again if needed.

Homework

What about homework? Who is overseeing that? Although some children are able to simply sit down and do their work, most need some adult help from time to time. From a purely academic point of view, a parent is more likely than most baby-sitters to say, "What do you think this means?" rather than just supply an answer.

Some of us hire tutors, not because our children are failing, but for the express purpose of making sure that someone who is academically equipped will be guiding their learning. But in the same way as with music, children are learning habits as well as content when they do homework. Having the parent involved with actually getting the homework done imparts a very valuable lesson. There are compelling data which show that those students whose parents are available to help with homework not only do better in school but do better socially. But you don't need scientific studies to tell you that the child who feels important to his family feels important in the world, and to himself. He feels connected.

Shopping

Let's look at something boring and chorelike, such as shopping. A family where both parents work full-time may not want to push their way into the Saturday masses to buy shoes, for example. They may feel that that's the kind of task that can be taken care of by their sitter. They may prefer to spend their weekend day going to the zoo.

But so many issues are raised by the simple act of buying shoes. What if your child is finicky? What if the shoes you specified don't feel good on your child's foot? If you don't specify which shoes to buy, then you are leaving it to your baby-sitter to teach taste and style. If you were there, maybe you would see a pair of shoes on sale and encourage your child to try them. What about fads? What about fashion? You are asking your baby-sitter to inculcate many values by the simple act of buying shoes, including how we behave in stores.

Although low down on the list of glamourous things to do, planning regularly scheduled weekend times to take care of homework, practice an instrument, and provide for our children's basic needs may prove in the long run to be much more satisfying and enriching than any single, special event.

If your schedules are such that you are essentially unavailable for the majority of the kind of parenting activities we've been discussing, you might want to rethink, reprioritize, and reschedule. Developmentally, there are two periods when a parent's presence is especially meaningful: during the first three years of your child's life, and during the preteen to teen years. We basically have a very limited amount of time to make a lifelong, strong connection.

VACATIONS WITH A CHILD OF ANY AGE

Here's a question that's interesting to me because I know so many people who do this. Do you take your baby-sitter with you on vacation?

I am reminded of various friends whose sitters were at their beach houses or country houses when we all gathered for parties. It was indisputably more pleasant to have somebody else taking care of the kids. You can finish a sentence, balance a plate on your lap, and lie back and look at the sunset much more freely when undisturbed. I can't pretend I didn't like it. I loved it!

But on one vacation when several families joined together for several weeks, one brought their sitter along. I began to be aware of how the adults and the children inhabited different universes. They overlapped from time to time, but the emotional spheres that we occupied were distinctly different. Separate. We did not share the same jokes. We did not share the same food. We did not share the same table. We did not share the same schedule of when we arose and when we ate. We did not share much of anything except that we were plunked, somewhat like strangers in a public park or at the beach, in friendly proximity to one another's group. Each group had its own ebb and flow and agenda.

Because of the capable presence of the sitter, there was very little need for the two groups to interact. There were occasions when one adult would peek into the little people's world, or when one little person would venture into the grown-ups' world. But that would only occur once the sitter had expended all her skilled resources in keeping the children occupied, as if the grown-ups were to be approached only for something extreme. And when a child did draw near with the need for a lap and a hug, it seemed somehow inappropriate if it went on too long, as if they should be having so much fun in the kids' quarters, because we were having so much fun among ourselves. And so in short order the little one would be led back to the kiddie corner to be duly entertained where he or she belonged. Which was certainly not among us.

TRAINING OUR CHILDREN NOT TO NEED US

If our children are trained to be separate from us, emotionally and physically, when they are toddlers and preschoolers, to not need us to attend to them, but rather to rely on whoever is assigned and hired to take care of their needs at the moment, how very distant they may well be by the time they reach their teen years, when developmentally they need to distance themselves. I should think by then the gap would be unbridgeable. There will be only fragile ties from times gone by, half-remembered feelings of a yearning to be near. But there will be no strong connection, no common assumptions, no pull to stay near, no feeling in the teen years that they are missing that closeness and wish to keep it intact—if they never had it.

And so if you answer, Yes, we have organized our life with the assumption that we take our sitter on vacation, I ask you to think about restructuring. Perhaps she can stay nearby and show up for the evenings if you want to go out. Or perhaps you should restructure who does what. If you have enough money to afford someone else to go along, more power to you. There's nothing noble about wiping counters, nothing uplifting about scrubbing a tub. Farm out every piece of repetitive housework that you can. But don't, as the cliché says, throw out the baby with the bath water. Don't relinquish your chance to hang out with your child for an entire twenty-four-hour period, attending to the unsavory moods along with the fun.

We all need breaks sometimes, and sometimes it is so good to get away. In that case, take a vacation without the children. A family vacation, however, should be just that.

Although it is not good to oversimplify, as we see more and more disturbing events, such as the shootings at Columbine High School, we begin to feel a need to discover how the fabric of human connection has become so frayed. Clearly "things like that" can happen in "nice" neighborhoods, where children have "everything." Neighborhoods like ours. I might be wrong but I don't think such events are as likely to stem from families where the children feel their parents' presence as a benign, intimate, crucial part of their everyday lives. Where they feel a strong connection.

We all might consider spending less time planning the logistics of our children's and our own lives and more time actually connecting with our children from the time they're very small. And we need to make that connection not only doing things that are splendid and fun, but engaged in the mundane chores and events. Eating, bathing, sleeping, going to school, coming home, being together, arguing, making up, and doing it all over again the next day. These are the real rhythms of life.

YOUR SITTER'S JOB

With all that in mind, what do I see the sitter's job as being?

The fun gal! The person who arrives to pick them up, like a date, when they're all dressed, looking good, and ready to party. To take them out to have fun, to do a lot of nifty things, to come home, grab some lunch, give them a nap and straighten up the toys and kitchen (because this isn't a real date, you know!) have a little downtime, go back out, run an errand, do something else fun, and then to bring them home, as at the end of any date. To say a loving good-bye and deposit the child into the warm embrace of the family in time for dinner, bath, and the end of the day.

If in order to have that occur, one parent has to leave work every single day earlier than 7:00 P.M., or not leave for work until 8:30 or 9:00 A.M., so be it. If it means that you have to cut back drastically on any work that does not occur during business hours, so be it. If it means that your nightlife has to be seriously curtailed for a few short years, so be it. If it means that you have to get up at the crack of dawn and be dog-tired for a few short years to be able to spend those early hours with your child, so be it. If you are single and it means that you have no social life to speak of for a few short years, so be it. In a two-parent family, if it means that one of you has to take a job that is less pressing and pays less, and that some of the luxuries of life that can be bought may have to be put on hold in exchange for intangibles, so be it.

That is what I believe it takes to readjust the balance and connect with our own.

A RED FLAG

Although many families find that it takes one or two weeks of false starts with several sitters before finding "the one," if you have a constant stream of sitters, or if sitters don't last longer than a year, something's wrong. The "something" is wrong with your home, not the sitters. If they are quitting on you, do yourself, and especially your child, a favor. Ask the last quitter for a favor. It is likely that you may have already used up your favors, which is why she is quitting. Nevertheless, ask her to be completely honest about why she's quitting.

Although what she says may make you mad enough to spit, listen to her. You are doing something that is making it impossible for people to take care of your child.

When other people's sitters come to me quietly, their eyes nervous, asking if I know of anyone looking for someone, their reasons are always the same. The hours are unpredictable. The parents are never home. The children have no rules.

If your home has few rules for your child—which can easily occur in homes where parents work full-time and therefore are loath to have disagreements when they're home—you may find part 3 of this book especially helpful.

The sitter who is often unable to go home to her own life when she's expecting to will eventually quit, causing your child to have to get used to someone else. The live-in whose hours stretch longer and longer, no matter how much she is paid, will eventually be asking people if they know of anyone who needs someone. You may remember Carol's story in chapter 5 about how thankful she was to have been raised by Ethel and Jack. If you are not going to be an active player in your child's life, it is important that you at least have the decency to fulfill your parental obligations by figuring out a way to keep your help so your child can connect with someone.

THE CONNECTIONS WE CAN MAKE

I will spare you the bragging moms who justifiably rave about their sitters. If you're lucky enough to be one of them, congratulations. And I will spare you what most of the mothers and sitters privately share. Long, involved, Byzantine sagas of nitpicking, and interpersonal quicksand. On both sides.

Sitters and mommies both come to me, some with sad eyes, some with eyes that are flashing. She did this. She did that. She said this. She said that. I don't know what to do about her always doing this. And that. They are the normal problems that can so easily occur, be worked on, patched up, and forgotten between any two women interacting on a daily basis, compounded by differences in culture and class, and centered on the love and welfare of a child.

A mother of a twelve-year-old, whose son is away at camp for the first time, said that she had shared an aha! realization with her husband. "Being parents," as she laughingly put it, "is only a phase!"

She was not laughing, however, when she said, "It is such a short period, those eighteen years, in the context of eighty to a hundred years. You can do so much in your life on either side of those few short years. But you can't replace that time."

In terms of your child's development, your presence is priceless. In terms of your own emotional enrichment, you only stand to gain.

Whether you need a sitter in order to live, or you have a sitter in order to free you to feel as if life is worth living, consider who does what. I urge you, no matter how marvelous your sitter may be, not to relinquish your rights or rites of motherhood to even the most capable hands. Allow yourself the luxury and gift of sludging through the drudgery and weathering the nastiest storms as well as sailing through the sublime. Hold fast to the only thing that ultimately matters: the connections we make with our own.

8

Bifocals and Barney: Our Changing Bodies

The one-liners you've all been waiting for. After each one, please supply a comedy-club ba-da-*bump*.

How do you know you're an older parent?

When you need your bifocals to see if your nursing infant is properly plugged in to your nummy.

When your two-and-a-half-year-old wants to ride on Daddy's shoulders so he can see his face in the mirror on top of Daddy's head.

When you're watching the pre-ballet all-pink tutu extravaganza, the pee-wee league soccer meet, or any other little-squirt show-off event and while camera bulbs flash all around you, you're trying to hide your hot flashes.

How do you know you're not only older, but out of shape?

When your eighteen-month-old, following Mommy's model, bends from the waist and grunts to pick up a piece of paper from the floor.

When your four-year-old is surprised to see a grown-up get up off the floor without having to roll over on her knees or be hoisted up by her husband.

And, of course, the biggest sidesplitter of them all:

How do you know you're an older parent?

When somebody calls you Grandma.

If you're thirty-five, nobody's going to call you Grandma. At forty, you're probably still safe. As the *Newsweek* cover declared, making what we all know official, forty is the new thirty! You really have not yet reached Grandma status.

By forty-five it starts to get iffy, and by fifty it may just be a question of time. At water parks, at Disneyland, Sesame Place, or any "kid place" where a cross section of the population gathers, we are definitely contemporaries of many of the grandmas standing next to us, waving, and taking pictures of the kids going round and round on the tootle-train.

But whether anyone out in the world calls us Grandma or not, there are certain physical aspects of being an older parent that affect our family. Let's take a look at what is on our plates and the various ways we can cut it into palatable, bite-size pieces.

THE BROAD STROKES OF BEING
OVER THIRTY-FIVE

While all humans, from infancy till death, are constantly learning how to readjust to a changing body, we have taken on the task of raising a young child at the same time that we are likely to be engaging in some major physical changes ourselves. Notably, our reproductive systems will alter and our energy sources may diminish.

PHYSICAL ASPECTS OF BEING OUR AGE

Let's start with some of the physical ramifications of no longer being in our twenties, and I hope you will indulge my sarcastic tone.

As was so clearly pointed out to those of us who were pregnant (and frankly I felt rather meanly harped upon!), with each ensuing decade there is an increasing mathematical likelihood that we will suffer from bad tickers, clogged veins and arteries, glucose out of whack, and the general decline if not total conking out of various vital organs.

In addition to the increasing possibility of serious physical problems, there is the normal, gradual change in our bodies that can potentially flavor our parenting.

For men and women alike, our bodies, when left untended, have a proclivity to widen, wrinkle, drop, and gray.

All of these self-esteem boosters can be dealt with—and in fact should be, for your future health—by sensible eating habits and exercise, which we will talk about in the "Helpful Hints" section.

While it's on my mind, let me mention that a good hair colorist can turn out to be one of your best friends. (Yes, Paul, I am talking about you.) And speaking of friends, my closest circle of girlfriends are in their fifties. We have always been virulently opposed to plastic surgery as another aspect of the degradation and infantilization of American women. Always, that is, until recently. So if you would like to join us in our search for a plastic surgeon who will give us a good group rate at a really nice spa where we can recover together from having gotten rid of our wattles, please come along! Ba-da-*bump*.

CHANGING REPRODUCTIVE SYSTEM

For women, as in every other aspect of our entire lives, there is an additional complicated matter to deal with. Hormones. Gradually declining. Beginning for everyone right around age thirty-five.

Some of us will feel it more than others, some not at all. For some, the hormonal decline begins gradually and the effects don't kick in until after fifty. For others, menopause drops like a bomb in their forties. But whether you have not noticed any change, are just beginning, are in perimenopause or in menopause itself, the decades we are in right now can be as hormonally bumpy as adolescence. Thankfully, our coping mechanisms are more highly developed.

The effects of hormonal decline have the potential to challenge our day-to-day interactions with our children. A young child can run faster than the wind, might wake up nineteen times a night, and needs, more than anything else in the whole, wide world to test behavioral boundaries and your tolerance for tests. At the same time, due to hormonal changes, you may be experiencing sleep disruptions of your own, compounded by possible weepiness, forgetfulness, and mood swings.

Another possible change due to hormones is a decline in sexual appetite. Combined with the challenges of having a young child, this may account somewhat for the lack of a love life that so many of us reported.

In addition, metabolism slows. Therefore, if you did put on too much weight when you were pregnant, it may be harder for you to drop it than it is for your Lamaze friend who was twenty-eight. If you didn't bear your child, all that Ben & Jerry's you ate while waiting to hear from the Chinese consulate may now be sitting firmly on your hips and not easily dislodged. Not only might you, if you're not careful, be downright pudgy, but it's possible that you'll be angry about it, perhaps crying about it, and sometimes forgetting what you're crying about!

I really hope you don't mind my joking about all of this. I suppose we all have our ways of dealing with change. I am extremely happy with my insides based on having done a fair chunk of living; I'm not having as much fun with my outsides.

SELF-IMAGE

While research indicates that at-home mothers of all ages tend to experience a drop in self-esteem, for us motherhood may have just the opposite effect.

One parenting expert noted when talking about all older mothers, but particularly single older moms, we often see a transformation "from chronic disappointment to chronic satisfaction." Our self-image often rises with the advent of motherhood. This was vividly displayed, if you remember, by a neighbor of mine whom I described in the second chapter. The one with the maroon beret? Yes, that one.

But there is another factor with regard to our self-image. Because we have become mothers later in life, we may experience several life cycles of being a woman almost simultaneously.

As one mother in her early forties put it, "I feel as if my cycles are being crunched together all at once. Pregnancy, childbirth, and menopause are all happening on each other's heels in my life. I haven't gotten used to the changes in the way my body looks or feels since pregnancy and childbirth, and now I'm facing menopause. These are all such big issues in a woman's life and how she sees herself."

There are no easy answers for this. It is just one more element that has the potential to either enlighten us or wear us down.

ENERGY

Keep this between you and me, but some of us are tired.

Just last week, I led a seminar for a group of eight new moms who ranged in age from their late thirties to late forties. Exhaustion was a hot topic. They were obviously glad to be in a room full of other new mommies who were feeling the same drain on their resources.

Some of the women I've spoken with have hotly denied being any more tired than younger mothers. You know the joke, I'm sure: "Denial is not just a river in Egypt." I see these mothers, even the ones who keep themselves fit as fiddles. A weariness creeps over them. It's not quite physical and it's not quite emotional. It's just a kind of pervasive overall unwillingness to summon up the amount of energy required to get the little bundle of strong-willed needs to change direction. (See chapter 13, "Assuming the Mantle of Parenthood.")

Although all new mommies and daddies feel the effects of disrupted sleep, there is a physical reality connected with each ensuing decade. It is harder to bounce back. It is harder to go days, weeks, and even months with less sleep and rest than your body needs.

Most twenty-year-olds can put in a full day at work, go out at night, carry on, get a couple of hours' sleep, get up, and do it again. And again. Every month or so, they might sleep all weekend, and start back in refreshed. By forty, most people without children physically cannot keep up that kind of schedule, nor do they choose to do so.

Yet that is essentially what it is like having a young child in the house. It is not useful to pretend that we are not faced with a physical challenge. It is more useful to find ways to cope.

POSSIBLE PERK

Here's a tiny morsel of interest for some of us. Statistically, women past the age of forty who have babies unassisted (indicating reproductive cycles on the late end of the scale) are four times more likely than everybody else to live to be a hundred!

I might have another fifty years to go? That's fabulous! That means that at some point I actually might be able to find the time to attack that big closet in the entrance hall. Ba-da-*bump.*

HELPFUL HINTS

Just to reiterate where we are physically: Our reproductive system is beginning to shift. This causes, among other things, a slower metabolism, mood swings, and sleep disruption. Many of us, even though our hormones are shifting, still have enough hormones so that we have

PMS. Because we are aging, we are more susceptible to serious systemic malfunctions. Because our metabolism is slowing, we are more susceptible to excess weight gain. Excess weight gain increases the likelihood of serious systemic malfunctions. We most probably have jobs, we have small children, and whether we have husbands or not, it's clear we might be under some stress. Stress increases the likelihood of serious systemic malfunctions.

So, what's a poor mother to do?

EXERCISE

The most sensible, enlightened, obvious one thing we should do for ourselves with regularity so that we can take care of everybody else is to exercise. This will help keep our bodies young, fit, and trim; will help us sleep; will combat fatigue; and will keep the mood swings of either PMS or menopause—wherever you are in our reproductive drama—in line. It will eliminate, or at least ameliorate, stress. It will keep our weight down or get it off. It will help our cardiovascular systems to stay free and clear and it will boost our immune systems to help fight everything from colds to cancer.

So if we know all this, how come so many of us don't exercise? Time is a big problem. If you work and you want to see your child, going to the gym becomes a logistical nightmare. There aren't enough hours in the day. How can I do my job, run errands, and still see my child?

There are others of us who in fact have built exercise into our lives as a way of maintaining sanity and feeling as if we still "have a life." Some moms I've spoken with are religious about exercise, making sure that on their way to work they go first to the gym, where after exercising they dress and then move on.

I've got some ideas for women in each of these groups to consider, whether you be a gym rat, in a time-management dilemma, or a slugabed.

For Those Who Already Do

If you have already made exercise a regular part of your life, carve your exercise time from your work hours. Rather than going to the gym first thing in the morning (and missing some of the most precious hours you can spend with your child), take an hour out of your work-day. To some that may seem a radical idea. It is a shift in priorities. It implies that you consider time spent with your child and family the first priority, and attending to your own needs your next priority, and that you are willing to keep work, although it is important, in its rightful place in your life. If you have too many things to do during the course of a day and the hour to take care of your body—which is a real need—must be "stolen" from somewhere, steal it from work. The memo that you struggle over for three hours will only be marginally better than the one you dash out in less than an hour. But the regular breakfast time spent with your child, even though some days may feel nightmarish, will be become part of his or her most secure memories from child-hood. You are entitled to an hour every day from every job. Whether we have corporate jobs, or work for ourselves, taking an hour for ourselves during the course of a workday is not only permissible, it's advisable.

For Those Who Need To

For those who have not already made exercise a regular part of your life, here are two thoughts. The first is nearly as radical as what I suggest for gym rats.

There is an enormous adjustment to be made in becoming a mother. For some people, building exercise into their lives is a her-culean task. If you are one of those, although you know you should be exercising—and there isn't anyone who knows anything about health who wouldn't strongly suggest that you exercise—give yourself some temporary slack.

If you are a new mother and the idea of exercising seems com-pletely overwhelming, which it might, take a moment right now and choose a time in your mind when it might not be so overwhelming.

Was your time "When my baby is three months old"? Was it "When my baby is eight months old"? If you chose a time during your child's first year, write it now on your calendar. Make a date with yourself. If you can't imagine being able to exercise ever, I offer you a gift. For your child's first birthday, your gift to yourself, to your child, and to your husband, if you have one, will be that you will start taking care of your body.

Yes, putting off exercising that long flies in the face of enormous amounts of sound research. Yet the stress of overcoming an ingrained habit can be overwhelming to a new mom.

On your child's first birthday, however (or earlier, if the spirit should move you), along with whatever plans you make to celebrate that day, plan to take—listen, this is very simple—a ten-minute walk. Once you start that, you can begin the program listed below. You need to take care of your body so that you can take care of your child.

For Those Who Don't Like to or Can't Find the Time

There are many new programs out now for exercisers who hate to exercise. These same programs are a godsend for people with too many things to do each day, such as the full-time working mom. They address the daunting feeling of simply not being able to find the one to two uninterrupted hours at least three times a week that "serious" exercise entails. The I-hate-to-exercise or I-don't-have-time-to-exercise programs include sensible, bite-size amounts of exercise.

IF YOU WORK OUTSIDE THE HOME AT A DESK JOB

- Walk down the hall to somebody else's office, rather than calling.
- Move your wastepaper basket away from your desk so that you have to get up to throw something out.
- Every time you make a phone call, stand up to dial. If you have to sit down again to take notes, that's fine. If you have a phone-intensive job, where standing up every time you pick up the phone would make you feel like a jumping jack, make up a game. Here are some examples: I will stand up every time I make a call that I know by heart, or that is on speed dial, or that I have to look up the number for. You know your work; just create some game that means you're standing up at least once every fifteen minutes or so.
- Park your car as far as possible from where you need to be, instead of as close as you can get.
- Steal ten minutes here and there during the day to quickly walk around the block, around the halls, or around the parking lot. You can put these breaks to very good use, by the way, because while you walk you can think about things; when you come

back, you may have come up with a better solution to whatever problem you were working on than if you had not taken a break. Thirty minutes of brisk walking divided into ten-minute segments has been proven to have the same beneficial effects as an uninterrupted thirty-minute period.

- Climb the stairs instead of taking the elevator. Begin by walking down one flight for a few days, and getting on the elevator on the floor below yours. Then walk down two. If your building has doors that are locked from the stairwell, take the elevator to the second floor instead of the lobby the first few days, and then add a floor as you're ready to increase.

- Run up and down the stairs in your office building for three minutes every once in a while, every day. Gradually increase this until you can run up and down the stairs for fifteen minutes.

- For regular weight lifters concerned with maintaining or building mass, familiarize yourself with the specifics of the exciting new research that shows that lifting one set, as long as the weights are heavy enough is just as efficacious as lifting three sets.

Once you start making these manageable moves, you may find that your increased energy will inspire you to take on more.

If You're an At-home Mom

Many at-home moms get stuck thinking they can't exercise because they either can't afford a gym or can't find any time during the day. Others think they don't need to exercise because they move enough simply being with a toddler. Both groups are missing out, however, on the beneficial effects, emotional as well as physical, of getting your blood going and of taking a few minutes during the day for you. The easiest, cheapest most readily available form of regular exercise is walking.

- Walk in the morning when your husband is with your child.
- Strap your baby into a Snugli and take a brisk walk.
- For the stroller crowd, take a brisk walk in the park or around the mall, or anywhere without traffic.
- Hook up with other moms with kids in one of the stroller groups forming in major cities. Not only will you get support to help you exercise, but you may make new friends.

- Obtain a tape made by these groups, called "Strollercize," if a group has not yet formed where you are.
- Form your own group of stroller-walking moms.
- If you're an at-home mom who has a sitter and belongs to a gym, choose an optimal time to work out.
- Go after your child has spent the cozy, homey, wake-up-start-your-day breakfast time with Mommy.
- Use your sitter's valuable services for taking your child to the park, for example, while you go to the gym so that you haven't had to forfeit some of the more tender moments of life with a young child in order to maintain your own health.

DIET

The less processed food we eat, the more energy we have and the healthier we can be.

Just as a simple matter of trying to compensate for a mildly diminishing amount of energy as we age, you would do your entire family a service if your eating habits improved. Include in your diet lots of fresh fruits and vegetables, whole grains in place of refined, a modest amount of protein, and some good fat, like olive oil, and consume as little junk food, processed sugar, caffeine, and alcohol as possible.

REFRESH YOURSELF EMOTIONALLY

Lorna, the forty-two-year-old single mother of a four-year-old, expresses what so many of us feel. "You live through days you can't believe you lived through because they're so hard. But they're better than the easiest day you ever had without your child.

"Sometimes, I don't know if I can get up in the morning. Sometimes I have so much to do I don't even know if I can get to bed! But then I think of all those Saturday mornings in your pajamas. You stay home and watch old movies. Would I trade any of that for the worst moment with her? Never!"

For all women with young children, there is a drain on us in some ways. We are meeting the needs of another living being who is appropriately needy. And while hopefully all of us share Lorna's feeling that no matter how exhausted we are, we wouldn't trade one moment, it is useful to find some way to give yourself a small inner cuddle that is just for you.

If possible, try to find time during the day when you do something not work- or child-related, such as reading a novel or a magazine or talking to a friend about things other than child raising and work. Both meditating and journal writing are also very useful tools for regrouping.

Finding the time for these simple acts is often hard.

The Early-Morning Option

Many women, whether they work inside or outside the home, have found that a way to refresh themselves both physically and emotionally is to get up an hour before everyone else. Although this sounds contradictory, it gives them some time to themselves to read the paper, stare out the window, pet the cat, quietly hum, or do whatever before everybody else's needs come crashing in. This will only be a useful idea if your child is not a really early riser. Some babies are up for the day at six, which makes early rising not a viable plan. But as they mature, it becomes more likely that you can find some time for yourself before the rest of the household is up. Usually by the time a child is three, his or her sleeping patterns have become manageable.

For Those Who Work Outside the Home

Women who work outside the home have more options for finding these precious few minutes to regroup.

If you commute, read a novel on the train or listen to a recorded novel while you drive. You might use your reverse commute to write in a journal or use a voice-activated tape recorder. If you have the kind of job where you can close the door and turn over the phones to an assistant or to voice mail, take fifteen minutes a day for yourself. This will give you some time to be off duty from being a mom and a worker. Try to find a time during the day when you are not planning work or home events, but are taking a break.

For Those Who Work in the Home

If you are an at-home mom with hired help, you can usually find a short period of time to slip off and read non-mom material, meditate, write in a journal, or in some way regroup.

At-home moms without help are those who are at the highest risk for never getting a break. There is never any guarantee that the moment you choose to refresh yourself will not be the very moment when your child awakes unexpectedly.

Although you may feel overwhelmed when your children are babies, here is a hint. When your baby naps, give yourself that time. That does not mean clean the house, do the laundry, make all the calls you're supposed to, get on the Internet and find the information you wanted, pay bills, do your exercises, scrub the diaper pail, make a grocery list, and on into domestic infinity. It means when your baby naps, lie down on the couch, put up your feet, and read. Or call a friend, write in your journal, meditate, or sleep! All the domestic chores will be there when your baby wakes up. If you do them during this nap, they will be there again tomorrow. But you will be yet a bit more tired and stretched thin.

Here's a small caveat. Part of what we need to refresh ourselves from, and part of the difficulty of having a young child in the house, is that we cannot really ever plan anything at a specific time. Things change. Children wake up. Children get sick. There is someone in the house whose needs may take precedence over ours.

That's the catch-22. Meeting the needs of someone else means that you need to meet your own from time to time. But it's the time-to-time part that gets hard.

The less desperate and rigid you are about meeting your own needs, the more likely that you will be able to meet them.

Can I be your sort of radical-sounding cheerleader? Let it slide, let it slide, waaaay back! If your hour to exercise or your specified time to meditate get horned in on today, you may have to do either one at a slightly different time, or in a slightly different way. If you are too rigid, you will snap.

During the first few years of your child's life, your time is not really your own. You need to be available as much as you can to your little one. But it is very short period of time. Within a few years, your child will be old enough to go to school, leaving you much more time to take care of yourself.

I'm not suggesting that you cancel your gym membership, abandon your walk, or throw your journal onto the top shelf of a closet. I am suggesting that for a few short years, you pencil in the time you plan to do these things. That way, if your child should have a pressing need, you can take care of that without feeling as if you cannot take care of yourself. You can take care of yourself. You just might not be able to take care of yourself exactly when you planned on it.

Once you realize that, you eliminate a major stress that can really get us down. Things *have* changed. It *is* different. We cannot plan exactly the way we could before. The acknowledgment of that change can free us. And once we are free from the frustration of feeling as if we can never take care of ourselves, we begin to find the time and ways to actually do what we need.

I'm going to jump up and take a quick walk. I'll be right back.

That was refreshing. While I was out, I remembered one last thing I meant to tell you.

Don't forget to get your mammogram and Pap smear. Oh, and floss your teeth.

BEYOND TECHNIQUE: FUN—THE ADDED ENERGIZER

Whether we're in tip-top or not-so-tip-top shape, we have one major "vitamin" in large doses that many other people our age don't. Fun.

It is a lot of fun to be with a little kid. Being silly is fun. Laughing is fun. Playing all the little games that we play with our kids is fun.

An older dad in our working parents' after-hours toddler class recently exclaimed, as if he had just discovered a new truth, "I can't believe how young my son makes me feel! I get to play with him all the time!"

The tonic effect of laughter and the delight of spending time with a little child cannot be overestimated. It more than makes up for whatever physical exhaustion you may temporarily feel.

9

Confronting Life's Cycles

All parents have "special issues" that they must address in order to handle them in a way that is in their children's best interests. Being older is just such a "special issue." It can adversely affect your children if you let it adversely affect what goes on between you and them.

THE BROAD STROKES OF THE POSSIBLE EFFECTS OF OUR AGE

Our age can have a negative effect on how our children view us. In addition, our children may have to face certain life-cycle events, such as death, at a younger age than many.

THE DOUBLE GENERATION GAP

Psychologists and sociologists note that teenage children of older parents have historically experienced their parents' age as a wider distance between them than the distance other adolescents feel between themselves and their parents. In the literature, it's termed a "double generation gap."

Children who are teens today sometimes report that they feel their older parents are "different" from their friends' parents. Since many teens live to be like their friends, "different" can be a curse unimaginable.

A current mother of teens who was in her early thirties when she became a mother (as recently as the early 1980s this was considered old) reports that her children "are furious that she's older." She adds that "it wasn't an issue until recently." But now, they feel that because she's "so old" she can't possibly understand them. There is too wide a "generation gap."

WHY THE GAP MAY NOT YAWN SO WIDE

It is a teen's *job* to resent his or her parents. If it's not your "advanced age," then it's something else. Some teenage girls, for example, have to compete on their own psychological turf with young mothers trying to stay young. I am reminded of my own teenage years, when so many of us felt that our parents, most of whom were young, couldn't "relate" to what we thought, felt, or liked.

A real "gap," or emotional distance, doesn't have to do with age, it has to do with temperament. If we as parents when our children are teens do not have the capacity or willingness to pay attention to who they are trying to become, it is possible they will resent us. If we have trouble listening to our toddlers, it is possible that by the time they're teens, they will expect us "not to understand." (Please see chapter 11 for a discussion of the difference between "understanding" and "indulgence.")

It is also possible that by the time our children are teens, the "double generation gap" will have lost some of its appeal as a bone for adolescents to chew on. There are more and more of us. The "stigma" of having older parents may by necessity diminish somewhat, in the same way that biracial marriage, such an explosive issue merely twenty or thirty years ago, is a nonissue today. Or perhaps to stay with the analogy and the truth, it is no longer an explosive issue in society but probably has a few ripples within the immediate families concerned.

Thus, let us look at ways to smooth our "special issue" ripples, rather than create heavier waves.

WAYS TO CLOSE THE GAP

Here are some ways to handle the issue of your "age" with your child that may preclude their feeling "different" and hopefully sidestep the "you're too old to understand" accusation when our children are teens.

Accept Your Age

Be comfortable about your age. The cheap jokes I made in the last chapter aren't so funny in your child's ears. Don't lie about your age.

The lie will ultimately be discovered, making your age seem negative. Don't brag about your age, which again will emphasize it. It just is what it is. If your children ask you how old you are, tell them. If they don't ask, don't offer it. Take your age for granted and don't make it more than it is.

Avoid Using Your Age as a Crutch

It is useful to make it clear that your temperament and tastes are not necessarily linked to your age. How that translates practically is in what you say. Or perhaps what you don't say. "When you get my age, you'll see you won't want to . . ." is not particularly useful to say to your child.

Should you be physically out of shape, for example, chances are that had you been a parent when you were twenty, you might not have enjoyed sports even then. Perhaps you would have been one of the moms content to sit on the sidelines cheering for everybody and making sure the picnic basket held everybody's favorites. On the other hand, perhaps you would've been like one of the younger moms we see who are fabulously in shape, so fabulous that they are more inclined to lie on a chaise at the pool, working on their tans or keeping their hair and skin protected under a big umbrella. They also are not in the water, doing handstands to see whether they can stay under longer than their kids. There is room in this world for many ways of participating in a family outing.

Make sure that you don't use your age to explain your choice of activities. "I'm having fun reading/being the family photographer/rooting for you" (or any other activity that you're comfortable engaging in) is a better reason than your age to explain why you're not next in line waiting to swing the bat at the Fourth of July picnic.

Avoid Making Your Child Your Caregiver

It is also useful not to slip into reversing your roles and having your child feel as if he or she is the caregiver. Most of you are brand-new moms in your thirties and forties, so this idea might seem very remote. Yet ten years will go by in a twinkling. As will the next ten. This and that occurs. Knees sometimes get out of whack. Backs can go in a second. These things happen to younger women as well. But they happen with more frequency with each decade that passes. Try and choose which tasks you assign to your child and which you find a way around. Sometimes I have seen mommies inadvertently turn their eager, lively elementary school children into what amounts to a fetching device. "Can you please bring mommy that?" I know you think, "Oh, I would never," but I have seen it occur in the nicest homes before anyone quite knows that the change is taking place.

Share Your Stories and Your Child's Interests

Share as many stories from your childhood and teen years as you can. This will make you closer with your child now, and will stick in his or her head later when the accusation that "you couldn't possibly understand" is apt to be leveled.

Once your child starts choosing from the outside world, join in. Watch the TV shows your child likes. Listen to the music your child listens to. Read some of the books your child is choosing to read. Every generation has its own tastes that offend the generation—or generations—before. Don't harp on the things you don't like. Find what you do like about what your child likes. Stay connected.

The truth is, however, that no matter how much we actually understand what our children are going through, separation is necessary. We may understand that. We may even remember how that feels. But no parent, whether twenty or fifty when our child is born, can feel exactly what our child feels, no matter how much we'd like to.

Perhaps this is the greatest strength we can bring to them: the knowledge that they are separate from us, and that as much as we can teach them, each person has to go out into the world on her own.

FACING TRANSITIONS: DEATH

It is quite likely that you and your child will lose someone in your immediate family during your child's early school years.

A very important concept is to be extremely judicious in discussing death so that you do not link it to old age. This is true in raising all children but becomes particularly relevant to us. If you can, before you need to deal with the death of a loved one, try to find the lovely children's book called *Lifetimes,* by Bryan Mellonie and Robert Ingpen. It talks about all lives having a beginning, middle, and end and is quite skillful at not linking death to old age.

Be very sure that "Grandpa was old" is not one of the explanations you give. "It was the end of Grandpa's life" or "It was Grandpa's time to die" are much more reassuring ways to explain death to any child, but particularly to one who within a few short years will be aware that you are considered an "older" parent.

If during a family gathering, another person links age and death—as will no doubt occur—don't make a big deal of it, but quietly reinforce that it wasn't Grandpa's age but that it was the end of his life, and that every life has a time when it ends.

I trust that I don't have to advise you to refrain from jokes, or even serious comments, about when you're "gone."

A comforting discussion on an appropriate level for a young child addressing death is useful and called for. Acknowledge that everyone has an end to his or her life, but reassure your child that your life will probably not end soon. In the best of all worlds, this discussion can occur whenever your child brings it up as something he or she is ready to discuss. In the event that it comes up earlier than when your child might bring it up, you would be wise to have thought in advance about ways to handle the issue with a young child. (In the "Recommended Reading" section, you will find additional titles on this topic.)

PROVIDING FOR YOUR CHILD: WILLS AND GUARDIANS

Perhaps the reason so many parents, regardless of age, do not find useful ways to talk to their young children about death is that all of us at some level have trouble absorbing the reality of death. Of death in general, but our own in particular.

A telling statistic is that between 50 percent and 70 percent of all Americans die intestate, which means they die leaving no will.

While death does, and should, seem remote to people in their twenties and even their thirties, with each decade that follows the gap closes between the "what-if" and the "when." I am not trying to be morbid; death is as much a reality of life as birth. But because of its finality, many of us pretend that it doesn't affect us, or that it is not an issue to be dealt with just now.

Here, I would like to share with you an unedited tape of an older mommy in Seattle. A partner in an enterprising business, she is usually sensitive, smart, and wise when discussing her feelings, her daughter, her marriage and her life.

Married to a lawyer, she was forty and her daughter was six months old at the time we spoke. I think she speaks for all of us who have not been able to tackle this difficult part of our lives.

Do you have a will?

"Yes." Pause. "Well, not exactly." Pause. "We . . . well, there . . . we . . . we did have one but . . . it'll be . . . we had talk . . . no. We don't. Actually. We don't."

Do you have designated guardians?

"Mum . . . yum . . . we don't quite know who we . . ." Pause. "Well . . . uh . . . You know, we talk about it, but we, there's just n . . . it's just so har . . . we can't . . . no."

If you do have a will and guardians selected, as all the single mothers I spoke with did, naturally, and as many of the married couples do, you will be rather shocked at the idea of not having taken care of this. The rest of this section won't be useful.

If, however, you are among the significant number of us who have not worked on this important issue, I ask you to read on.

WHY WE HAVE TROUBLE NAMING GUARDIANS

Although we all have a sense of unreality about our own deaths, for those who do not have a will, it is not the death part that we can't deal with. It is the guardian issue that stops us cold.

For younger families, it is certainly a sensible plan to have a will and name guardians. But it is less troublesome to think they have not taken care of this part of managing their families. Younger families have a likely candidate for guardians. Their mothers. What parents in our age group have to say when asked about our arrangements, however, illustrates why, whether we like it or not, we need to face this issue.

"Both of our mothers are too sick."

"Neither of our mothers is still living."

"My mother's healthy, thank Heaven, but she's seventy-two."

Because our own mothers are not good, automatic choices for guardian, it becomes more pressing to choose.

Here is a sampling of the justifications offered. All the others were variations on the same theme.

"My brother in California would be perfect. He's my favorite and he's financially secure. But his wife is a witch. She doesn't share any of my values. We had a big fight."

"My brother-in-law and sister-in-law are the most likely. But I just don't want my child growing up in the kind of world they live in."

"My sister is single."

"My brother is divorced."

"My friends would be perfect, but they already have three kids/ don't have any kids/hinted that they'd already raised their kids and wouldn't want to do it again/are dirt poor/can be flaky."

"My cousin would be a possibility, but he and his wife already have three children and are barely maintaining their sanity."

What we are all saying, in some deep way, is that there is no one, no one, no one on the face of this planet who will raise my child the way I want my child raised. There is no one, no one, no one on the face of this earth who will usher my child into the world in the proper way. There is no one, no one, no one on the face of this earth who is perfect enough to replace me.

Here's the hard part. If you do not have the *perfect* sister and brother-in-law, or the *perfect* best friend, then you must choose who in your opinion is the *next best thing* to perfect. Why?

What would happen if, God forbid, both you and your husband were hit by a car today? I know, I know, I know, it is an unbearable thought. But I am asking you to push yourself to think about the unthinkable.

WHAT HAPPENS IF THE UNTHINKABLE HAPPENS

If you do not choose, should something "happen" to both of you today, you will have died intestate. Your child, of course, will automatically inherit everything you own.

But here's the next part.

If you die without a will, a *court* will determine who will take care of your child. Not only that, but at the same time, the *court* will determine who manages your child's inheritance, if you left anything, and who will supervise the distribution of any property you leave behind.

So this perfect child, this child who is so perfect that there is no one perfect enough in your mind to take over for you should you drop dead, is now essentially a ward of the state.

Let us really project ourselves for a moment into the unthinkable.

We are beyond the shock of a double funeral. We are beyond both families coming together and rising to the occasion—as all families do—laying aside their differences in order to pitch in to arrange for the funeral. Everyone but our immediate families has gone home. The family members sit in a room shaking their heads in disbelief. Not only are you gone, but you have left them to pick up the pieces.

Someone is holding your child.

It is probably not that wife of your brother who's flown in from California. The brother who is solvent, and torn to pieces because of your death. In his deep grief because you were his favorite, he doesn't notice that his wife is holding their own child and fuming in the corner because they have to decide what to do since you couldn't get it together to organize your affairs.

But they are the only ones in your family who are the *likely* candidates. Your brother will stand in court, and take his rightful place as the one who should raise your child. And, because they are an intact family, they will probably be the family that the court determines should take over. Your sister-in-law will probably be the one to take over raising your child.

Your best friend (whose life is more scattered than you'd like but who has a good heart) is shocked, and would have done it, but won't come forward to say anything because if you didn't ask her, you must have had reasons not to. Or perhaps will timidly step forward and say that although she's single, and doesn't have much, she would do it.

At that point your brother-in-law, the somewhat shady businessman your sister married against everybody's better judgment, will jump into the act because the only thing you did manage to do was leave a hefty life insurance policy. He looks good on paper; he'll step forward to supervise your property.

Your sister, who cannot bear the clutter you call home, and especially despises anything manufactured less than six months ago, cannot wait to get her hands on all that old junk, as she calls your prized vintage collections. She steps forward, offering to clear out the house.

Perhaps a roaring fight will break out at that point. The court, in the best interests of the child, will divvy up the duties. The court will indeed assign your child to the care of the woman in California, control of the money to the brother-in-law who can't speak to the brother, and the distribution of property to that neat, clean, sensible-looking woman talking about the Salvation Army pickup days. . . .

And so it goes, on into whatever dramas your own family circumstances would provide.

Someone will be *assigned* by a stranger to hold your child from that day forward.

And the final legacy that you will have left your child is that you were simply unwilling and unable to properly set up a home in advance that, although *imperfect*, would welcome your child into its fold without reservations, recriminations, or bad feelings.

In case you are lucky enough to come from a family, like ours, where the ones you ask respond simply, "Of course, it goes without saying," please let me reiterate. It does *not* go without saying. If you do not say in writing what your better judgment is, you leave it to the court to decide.

In case you are lucky enough to come from a family as dysfunctional as ours, the one you ask, after seriously replying, will laughingly say, "I guess we all have to pick the ones whose insanity is the most compatible with ours."

If you do not have a will and guardians chosen, please take a minute to pick, right now, which of the *imperfect* choices would be the best.

Even if you purposefully put this book down now, march into whatever room your spouse is in and say, "That's it, we have to pick!" and you manage to pick, it is still likely that the two of you will then allow yourselves the luxury of not moving on the whole issue because you can't make an appointment with a lawyer, can't afford it, can't find the time, can't whatever.

How to Make a Legal Will Right Now

It is far better to use a lawyer to draft a will, particularly if you have any assets, or in lieu of that, to use one of the programs now available, some of which you can even download from the Internet. But the fact that you haven't taken these obvious steps means that you have some resistance to the whole thing. Resistance notwithstanding, you can take care of this enormously important issue today.

Here is what you can do right now to make a *legal* will to protect your child. This will take you about one half hour. (After you have done this, I advise taking better steps by seeing a lawyer.)

Elements of a Legal Will

- It must be typed or computer-generated. (Handwritten wills are legal in only twenty-five states and are subject to nit-picking qualifications.) As soon as you've read the "Content" section below, go to your computer, compose one will, copy the whole file, then substitute the other spouse's name. Or you can type two pieces of paper, one for each of you.
- It must be clearly marked WILL.
- It must be dated.
- It must be signed by you. (Don't sign it yet!)
- It must be signed by *three people* who witness you signing the will. (It is two people in some states, but let's not mess up now, okay? So do three.) They must be people who do not inherit anything in the will. (Don't worry about who's going to sign. We'll get to that.)

Content

- Appoint an *executor*. Anyone in your family or a friend is fine. Write a short sentence: "I appoint So-and-so executor of this will." The executor signs papers and carries out any special wishes you include.
- Write a short sentence saying that all your earthly belongings go to your child—or, for example, all of your earthly belongings except your books, which go to your sister. Obviously, you can specify any things that you want, such as your sister gets your

books, and all that stuff. But that is only stuff. Don't get hung up on stuff. It is your child's welfare that is at stake. You can take time after this to really think about who you want to leave some things to.

- Write a short sentence stating, "I name So-and-so *guardian* for my child." Both parents should name the same guardian.
- Make provisions for handling any property you leave. Either name your guardian *trustee* (meaning to take care of the money) or someone else: "I appoint So-and-so guardian of my child and trustee" or "I appoint So-and-so guardian of my child, and I appoint Thus-and-so trustee of my estate." Different states have different ages when a child can take over managing the money (eighteen, twenty-one, or twenty-five, depending on your state). If you don't want to leave it for the state to decide, you can specify that you are leaving your money in trust, for the trustee to handle, until your child becomes whatever age you think is appropriate. Don't get hung up on this point. There are pros and cons to every decision. Just make a decision now and write a short sentence. "I appoint So-and-so trustee of my estate until my child reaches the age of [you choose]."

After You Have Made This Simple Document

- It must be signed by you in front of three people. Don't get hung up on who is going to sign. Drive to the nearest 7-Eleven, Piggly Wiggly, or whatever convenience store is close by and has several employees. Ask the people behind the counter if they will sign that they have seen you sign this piece of paper. Sign in front of them (you can cover the contents with a piece of paper) and have them sign. Ask them to print their names and addresses under their signatures. On the way there, drive carefully, please.
- Call the person you appointed executor and tell him or her that should anything happen to you, you have left your will in a file folder marked WILL in your file cabinet, your safe deposit box, or anywhere that is an easy place for it to be found.

Within one hour of reading this, you can actually take care of one of the most important, often neglected, parental duties that we have.

That covers the legal part. Here is some advice tailored for those of you who are clearly having trouble with this. Once you have drafted this document, call whoever it is you specified as guardian and/or trustee and ask permission.

Of course, the logical thing would be to call them first. But you have been procrastinating about something vitally important to your child's welfare. It is possible that you could put the phone call off indefinitely. Once you actually type a document, I suspect, you will be more inclined to move forward. Furthermore, whoever you *think* would be a *reasonable* choice, will be a good choice.

The sister-in-law in California who is so mean may turn out to be mad at you for your difference in styles. She may surprise you by being flattered. She may also approve of your having made provisions for your child. Although her values may be different from yours, she may suddenly take a new kind of interest in your child. The shady businessman may be so touched by your request that you begin to see why your sister chose him in the first place. The ditzy best friend who lives alone may become your child's best friend throughout the rest of your long, long life. Without getting too starry-eyed, what you will have accomplished by asking is that whichever imperfect person has been chosen by you, your child, should the need arise, will have an expected place to go rather than becoming a football in a family struggle.

If you don't reach them, leave a message telling them you have something important to ask them, and proceed anyway.

If you happen to die before you reach them, you will at least not have died without a will. It is unlikely that you have chosen someone who would refuse.

INSURANCE

If you don't have a will, you just might not have life insurance, for similar reasons.

Although there are financial planners, and ins and outs and variables and exacting fiduciary decisions, and it is indeed such an onerous, hideous process that Woody Allen has found a nice little sideline for himself making fun of insurance salesmen, call the first major company your finger falls on in the phone book, and buy at least a quarter of a million for each of you so that if something "happens" today, your child will not be a financial burden to whoever raises him or her.

After you do that, at your leisure, you can then educate yourself and make an informed insurance choice, if you choose to do so.

We are "allowed" to be as out of touch with an organized life as we wish when it comes to ourselves. When it comes to our children, we owe them more.

Please appoint guardians, make a will, and get insurance. Think of it as taking an umbrella. If you take it, you won't need it.

BEYOND TECHNIQUE: A LETTER

When you have a moment, write a letter to your child to accompany your will. Touch on the things you think are important. Write as if you will not be here tomorrow and this is your last chance to say to your child what really matters to you.

After you have done this, you may find subtle changes in your life. They will be for the good of everybody.

10

One Is Silver and the Other Gold: Friends

Becoming a mother is like moving. You enter a new world where you look for the best bread shop and try to discover who sells the freshest fish, what's the quickest route from work to home, what's the most scenic. And who are the people you like. Whom do you connect with, whom should you avoid? Whom can you learn from, who knows the local dirt, who knows where the bargains are, who knows where you can get something fixed?

Just as when you move, when you become a mother you stay in touch with some friends while others drift out of your life.

While younger new moms lose some friends, keep some friends, and make some friends, a major difference for us is that the friends we have, and sometimes lose, have often been our friends for a long, long time.

LOSING FRIENDS

Barb is thirty-nine, her daughter about to turn three. A lawyer in Portland, her voice is rather slow and breathy over the phone, with a slight sibilance.

When I ask her if she lost any good friends when she became a mother, there is a really big sigh.

"Well, yeah, I did. I lost my best friend."

I ask her to tell me a little about it.

You can almost hear her shrug before she settles in.

"We'd been friends since college and we went to law school together. Our careers were parallel. We both got ahead at the same pace. We were never competitive. It was great. We were very supportive about work.

"We both got into therapy around the same time and she was the only person I talked to about family things besides my therapist. That made us even closer.

"Then I got engaged around the same time Karen broke up with the guy she was dating. She had a series of boyfriends—she's really beautiful—but none of them worked out. We used to talk a lot about why she'd always pick these people where things just couldn't go anywhere. She would always say she wanted to get married and have children but then she'd start another dead-end relationship.

"When I got married, it wasn't easy at first. But we talked about it and got past it. When I was pregnant, I was pretty self-absorbed and not too available.

"She came over a day or two after I came home from the hospital. I was telling her about the delivery. I was on the couch and started to nurse. I looked up and . . ." She pauses, then goes on. "Her eyes are really big and blue. And I just caught this expression. It was so sad. Those big eyes. Then she said, 'I can't do this. I'm really sorry, but I just can't.' And she left.

"I called, but she didn't return my calls. The worst part is that I really understand. It's not petty jealousy. For her it's painful. And I know she knows I understand. There's nothing I can really do except hope she finds somebody soon and then maybe we can get back into each other's lives. Because I really miss her."

Not everybody is so forgiving. Of course, the reasons and circumstances around losing a friend affect how we feel about the loss.

Jennifer was best friends with a woman who is the biological mother of three. After a long journey through various treatments, Jennifer was finally confronting her infertility. She was going through a painful period of grief.

"My best friend," she says, "or I guess I have to say the woman who used to be my best friend, said to me, 'When are you going to get over this fertility thing?' It did our friendship in."

Libby, another adoptive mother, is a forty-eight-year-old who lives in Cambridge.

"When you're the single woman, you're always available. But things change a lot when you're no longer available," says Libby, whose voice when talking about her daughter is soft. But it is not soft now. It is tight, and it is clear that she is angry.

"The person who I thought was my best friend, who was going to stick by me through this whole thing, abandoned me! It happened immediately, but it took me a couple of months before I could admit to myself that she really abandoned us. When you first come back with your baby you have a million people around you. She just wasn't there.

"When we talked, she said she got 'busy.' She has a child in high school and a sixth-grader. She got 'busy.' She said *I* wasn't a good friend because I couldn't understand that. She had no time in her life for me and my child. She got 'busy.'" Libby says the word with layers of contempt, disgust, ridicule, and incredulity.

"I had to grieve for the woman I thought was my best friend for fifteen years.

"She needs to be the center of attention and the special one. She told me she'd be there every step of the way. She's lazy. If she can sit on the phone and talk to you she can help, but if it means getting off her can to come out and give real help . . ." She trails off. "I got close to some other people, but it broke my heart.

"I know who she is now and for fifteen years I didn't. She's just a selfish, narcissistic woman. She has a glowing, radiant affect, but it's only affect, not a reflection of her heart."

There is a silence. But Libby is spunky. "Onward! I talk to other people all the time. So it's onward."

Here is a mom who almost lost a friend. I will let her tell you about it.

"I thought I was the Madonna!" Diana laughs. "I couldn't understand why everybody in the world wasn't dropping everything to come rave about my baby. I was so hurt that my friend and her husband didn't rush right over to see my son. They had theater tickets!" She mimics taking umbrage. "Theater tickets! This is my baby! We talked about it and worked it out. But in the beginning, I really felt miffed that my baby wasn't the center of the universe."

KEEPING FRIENDS

Many of us, like Diana, work out the initial rearrangements as we add a new person to the mix. Like Barb, Jennifer, and Libby, many of us lose a friend who feels irreplaceable.

All of us keep many of our dearest friends, even though we discover that our time is no longer the same.

"If it weren't for e-mail I wouldn't have any of my old friends," says a thirty-six-year-old working mom who can find time to communicate with friends only very early in the morning or very late at night.

"The only old friends I have really been able to keep," says another, "are the ones who don't reproach me if it takes me six months to return their call.

"I used to hang out with my friends all the time. I had my old girl-friends. My husband and I had several couples we used to see all the time. If it happens at all, it happens rarely now. I try to keep up by phone, but even that gets stretched thin these days."

"The one thing that's nice about my old friends," says another, "is that we go back so long. They know me. It's easy. We can pick right up wherever we left off. Those are my real friends, of course."

For the friend we used to talk with on the phone several times a week, for the friend we used to meet regularly for lunch, for the friend we went to the gym with, went to the movies with, got together with our husbands with, for all these friends, if they remain in our lives it is because they understand that we are temporarily not as available as we used to be.

We have a child, and we have entered a new world. The mommy world. It is a world where we make our way, like all new mommies, toward finding our own little niche.

MAKING FRIENDS

Ronni is forty-three and her daughter, Fannie, is two. When Fannie was born, Ronni left her position as a senior editor in publishing and is now freelancing so that she can spend more time with her daughter. She has a birdlike beauty. Light, tiny, she darts rather then moves. Her straight bangs cover her eyebrows; the rest of her dark hair is in a tight bun. Her severe simplicity and upswept gold earrings give her a very sophisticated, citified look. She appears rather cold. But the minute she speaks—in a surprisingly big voice for such a little woman, and with lots of animation and emphasis on her words, laced frequently with loud long laughs—her warmth and enormous spirit come through.

As she talks, she touches on experiences that so many older moms share.

"I have no mommy friends. I don't know if it's because of who I am, what my career circumstances are, or because of my age. But I don't feel a part of the mainstream. My experience is isolating.

"It's been a real loss for me. There are so many times I've wished to be in a community with women who were in the same stage of life as me and with whom I could share all of the 'girlfriend' stuff. But it's been exceedingly difficult to connect with other mothers.

"I went to a Gymboree class. I didn't take Fannie only for her bene-fit. I thought, 'Well! This is a built-in, great opportunity for me!' But besides baby-sitters, there were only two other mothers. They were substantially younger than me and they knew each other. It's not as if they were exactly pretentious." She rolls her eyes and laughs at the understatement. "But they weren't my cup of tea. Besides, they had no interest in connecting with me! It was hard.

"I've met other mothers with their children playing in the sandbox. It's what I call my new kind of pickup. I pick up mothers!" She laughs. "What's been interesting is that I meet a mother, take her name and number, and inevitably never call! I met one mother who lives on our block. She was definitely younger than me, but she seemed like a nice person who was at home with her baby. I took her name and number. It'll be a miracle if I call her!

"In the winter, I took Fannie to one of those indoor play spaces. It was only us and another mother there with her baby. We exchanged numbers. But nothing ever came of it. Why? Because with all these women, we don't have a *thing* in common except that they have a baby Fannie's age!

"Another thing that makes connecting difficult is that we don't spend time with our children in the same way. I think every experi-ence for me is magnified. Because I waited that much longer, it has that much more meaning. I don't take a second of life with her for granted. Everything is incredible.

"I don't like being a passive observer with my kid. But I notice a lot of the mothers seem to say, 'We're at the playground. You go play. I'm just going to sit on the bench and have my latte.'" I wish you could hear how funny it is when she exaggerates "LAH-tay."

"A lot of people let their children do things that are not okay with me. I look for ways to help children learn good manners and the ability to interact. I find I'm always saying to other kids, 'We don't throw sand.' There are kids who are rambunctious. I look out for what potential damage these kids can do to Fannie. I'm protective, not cloyingly so, but I think some of the younger mothers don't help their children negotiate interacting with others.

"I also find myself in the situation of play leader. I'm there in the sandbox playing with Fannie and other kids'll come over. I'm like camp mom. Which is actually a lot of fun for me. I've seen fathers do that, but not a lot of other mothers, particularly the younger ones. I like playing with my kid.

"But it would be nice to have another adult besides my husband to do kid things with. I would *love* to make friends with other mothers. But the fact of the matter is my close friends are still the same people they always were. My wider network of chums has significantly diminished since I got married and had a family. I dropped off their radar screens. It's been a transition that's been very hard.

"I used to see friends a lot. I never go out with friends anymore. Never! Actually, that's something that Jeffrey felt very left out of. It's more of a husband issue than a kid issue. When I would want to go off with friends, he felt very abandoned. So I deferred in some ways to him. But it's still a need.

"Now I take snippets of time if I want to go grab a cup of coffee with a friend, but I don't do that a lot. I talk on the phone to my friends periodically after Fannie's asleep. If I've had Jeffrey time.

"It's one of the things I'd like to adjust in my life as time goes on. If I still have any friends left!" She gives a big laugh.

She has hit it all for so many of us. The desire for friends. Not feeling as if we have much in common with a lot of the women we meet. Missing our own friends. Hoping they'll wait for us.

Interestingly, she mentions what we're about to explore in the next chapter. She feels that she plays with her child in a way that is slightly different from younger mothers.

She has touched on the way that we are different from younger moms. We are at a different stage in our lives.

What Are We Looking For?

What the older mom means by wanting to "meet people" is that she would like to hook up with other adults to share the *parenting* part of her life in the same way she might look for a gym partner, a dieting partner, or a partner for any other specialized area of her life that would be nicer with the support of a kindred spirit engaged in the same activity. She already has her own set of friends, some of whom she's been close with since her twenties, some even longer.

But the younger mother has a different perspective. Making life-long friends is an important stage of development for people in their twenties and early thirties. Although she definitely views the playground, Gymboree, or any other child-centered activity and place as something fun for her child to do, whether she is able to articulate it or not, she sees these activities primarily as a *social experience for herself.* That is why when the children are in the sandbox, so many younger mommies are drinking their lattes. They are making friends, and connecting with other women the same way we did when we were their age. Just as we made our friends starting in college and then going on into work, they started in college and are now mommies.

The mommy world is their primary world.

But what's hard for us, though not insurmountable, is that we already have a "world," but now here we are, just like everybody else in the new world. We have moved.

"I just haven't found my soul mates in motherhood," says another older mother. "I feel kind of lonely in the playground."

Not all the older mommies I spoke with felt this so keenly. Some lucked out and fell in with a group that felt comfortable. Others figured out a way to make do.

"I don't have time for my friends now," says Barb. "My social life right now is really about my daughter. My best friends are parents of children that she plays with and that's great. I see my other friends, but it's not like it was before. Except for my oldest, best friends, my friends now are those who are parenting now."

Should you be feeling somewhat isolated, here are two ideas to help you out.

It Gets Better Past Nursery School

The early years are somewhat hit or miss in terms of who you meet through going to the playground, or classes, or any other child-centered place. In nursery school, we tend to hang out with the families of the children our children like. But by elementary school, where the pool of people tends to widen, you may find that it becomes easier to get to know women you would be friends with even if you didn't have children. Your children aren't so dependent on you, requiring you to actually be with them during a play date, making more or less comfortable small talk with their grown-up.

By elementary school, there are school functions and events that we start participating in where we can meet other people whom we simply like.

CREATING YOUR OWN SUPPORT GROUP

There is an element in the vast landscape of American motherhood that has changed radically since our own childhoods. People used to live near their families. They relied on their sisters, cousins, and aunts, as well as their mothers, for practical help and shared experiences to make raising children easier. But most American mothers no longer have such a built-in support system.

In many ways, friends, neighbors, and other new parents have taken the place of our extended familes. This accounts in large part for the proliferation of "new mommy" and toddler classes, which provide places for new mothers to meet others. While there are many organized activities, such as the groups we offer at the Y, which I strongly recommend as very fun times for your child, frequently the adults are women who, although lovely, are, as Ronni put it, people with whom you have nothing in common except the age of your children. In order to create a bond that feels truly supportive, we need peers.

Nationally, there aren't that many organized groups of older mothers yet. We have started seminars at the 92nd Street Y in New York during the last several years. I've heard of play groups here and there around the country. But if I were a new mom again, like I was ten years ago, I would try and organize a group of woman closer to my age for social companionship and to exchange ideas about parenthood. Particularly if you work part-time, or are an at-home mommy, and do not have as much adult company as a full-time working mother, your life and the life of your child will be richer if you make it a priority to schedule some time in the company of like-minded others. It is a lot more fun in the playground, at the zoo, and even going out for lunch when you have more in common with the other mothers than simply searching for the best brand of diapers.

Just be advised that as with every other group, if your only thing in common is age—whether your child's age or your own—you may not automatically feel connected. I have seen groups where some of the women feel the other women are "a little sad-sacky," as one put it. I've seen others where mothers didn't fit in because their financial situations were considerably different—to the point where one, who was struggling economically, confided, "I wish I had *their* problems." Basing a group solely on age is no guarantee of instant intimacy. It does, however, give you half a shot!

Likely sources for finding peers would be through fertility doctors, pediatricians' offices, or an announcement in your local parenting paper. You can also approach your local community center to see if they would offer you a room and notice in their bulletin.

Sometimes women within their own fields organize play groups. I know of an older mommy lawyer group and a "Hollywood Mammas" group, organized by people whose faces are well known but would like to maintain the privacy of their motherhoods.

I know from offering our seminar that if you don't specify an age, but simply say "Older Moms," you will find women who identify with you and feel a need to find friends who are closer to them in interests.

I highly recommend that you find peers. Just as all kids go through the same developmental stages, so do all adults. You might find your parenting experience just that much richer when you can share what you and your child are experiencing with people who understand your concerns, your fears, your jokes—and above all your exquisite joy in having started your family later in life.

RAISING OUR CHILDREN: TAILOR-MADE PARENTING TIPS

Rather than focus on the child, on which there is a vast body of knowledge at your disposal, this section will focus on you. On external conditions of your lifestyle and internal conditions of your mind, how these interplay, interlock, and influence how you interact with your child.

Because you are rewarded every day of your life with all the large and small moments with your child that tell you all you need to know about how well things are going in general, here we will concentrate only on the ways that things can possibly go awry.

11

Overindulgence: Our "Special Hazard"

According to Burton White, in *The New First Three Years of Life,* we have a "special hazard." As a group, we have "a tendency to overindulge."

Overindulgence was a theme consistently touched upon by the physicians, educators, psychologists, nurses, baby-sitters, and even hairdressers and retailers whom I consulted while researching this book.

They all said more or less what he said. There is "absolutely nothing worrisome . . . about [older parents'] capacity to do the job."

So if it's so unworrisome, why even mention it?

White hastens to point out that our maturity is "almost always an obvious advantage." They all toss in that "almost," to cover their behinds for delivering the zinger. Not only do we overindulge, but we are "in conflict concerning discipline."

Although it kills me to agree, I have to admit that he has hit the nail on the head. White is the only one I've ever found who mentions *in print* our coyly named "special hazard." And no one ever talks about what we might do about it.

Therefore, from me to you comes tailor-made parenting advice.

THE "BURDEN" OF OUR LOVE

As you read the next few chapters, it may feel as if I'm judging, and even scolding. That is not my goal. What I *am* trying to do is exhort you to be the best parent you can possibly be. While the next three chapters are devoted to all the ways that we might slip up, when all is said and done, in the context of what goes on all over the world, our parenting dilemmas are basically fine-tuning.

Our problem—if we do have a defining weakness as a group—has at its most fundamental bedrock deep, abiding love.

We do not abuse, beat, starve, or torture our children. We do not plop them in a playpen, park them in front of the tube, and ignore them all day or leave them at home while we go out.

Our worst fault is that we kill 'em with kindness. We tend to err in the direction of too much. Too much attention, too much latitude, and frequently too much stuff.

"Too much" is a problem that 99 percent of the children who have ever crawled the face of the earth would joyfully exchange for their own lot in life.

One mother in her early forties put it beautifully. "In our house, we call it 'the burden of our love.' Matthew can't blink without both of us noticing. Even though we're conscious of it, it can get out of hand."

That we love our children does not mean that other families and other groups do not love theirs. That we have a tendency to over-indulge certainly does not mean that we are the only parents who are capable of overindulging our children. Furthermore, no older parent does all of the things that I am about to describe.

With that said, let us look at some of the external factors that might contribute to a tendency to overindulge.

HOW DOCTORS "DIAGNOSE" US

Pediatricians and obstetricians alike said they welcomed how well-informed we are as patients, and how we help create collaborative relationships in place of the doctor-as-God stereotype. They all gingerly tossed in little asides. "Noticeably in love," said one. "A bit hesitant in ways," hinted another. This is code, in case you missed it, for a tendency to be overindulgent and conflicted about discipline.

Their nurses and receptionists were more forthcoming. According to them—confidentially, mind you—we call in a lot more than other families. Not just moms. Dads. The dads were the ones that really surprised the receptionists. We are more noticeable, more "demanding."

One nurse, as if my notebook and questions freed her from all her professional nice-nice, tucked in, in a hearty British manner, leaning forward to make her point. She simply wanted to say to us, "It's just feeding! Babies have been feeding for thousands of years! What's all the fuss?"

I'll tell you what all the fuss is.

We spent years and obscene amounts of money, we withstood untold physical and psychological wear and tear. Many of us not only ran the fertility-mill gauntlet but ultimately discovered that our best path to parenthood was adoption. We laid out another king's ransom and had our gizzards ripped out waiting through various false alarms, dead deals, and trips to the ends of the earth, or at least out of our own neighborhoods, before we were able to actually hold the angel that the universe in its mysterious way had earmarked for our homes and hearts. About a third of us endured all of this without the support of a partner! And even for those of us who didn't have to become mothers through trial by ordeal, judging from what our sisters went through, if you'll pardon the pun, all of our eggs are in this one basket! And you want to know what all the fuss is?!

To put it in the dry lingo of one psychologist, our children are "highly valued." For him this left-handed compliment served to identify predictable problems.

LIFESTYLE FACTORS THAT CAN LEAD TOWARD OVERINDULGENCE

As a group, we say yes frequently in response to our children's requests for material objects as well as to more ephemeral demands on our time and attention. Saying no for the sake of saying no is not a morally superior parenting stance, of course. In all of parenting, balance is what we are striving for.

But there are external conditions that we share as a group that have a tendency to tip the scales toward overindulgence.

Depending on your individual temperament, financial situation, and decade of life, some of the following specifics will strike closer to home than others. None of us has all the factors that we're going to look at here. But enough of us have enough of these factors to create a pattern.

How many of the following characteristics describe you and your family?

Parenthood Was Our Choice

As we already noted, our children are not unwelcome mistakes. We are not unwed teens whose lives will be derailed by motherhood. We are not younger, married women building careers and conflicted about whether this is the right time to start a family. Although there are later-in-life "surprises," they account for a mere fraction of first-time babies. Our children are ours by choice.

Parenthood Was Often Hard to Come By

Not only do we want them, but almost two-thirds of us went through a lot and waited a long time to get them.

When I asked how first-time motherhood was going for a woman in Chicago, she answered, "Are you kidding? We tried for seventeen years to have this child! I love every minute of it!"

Is it any wonder that these children are precious to us?

Of course *all* parents who are happy about being parents, regardless of their age, find their babies to be precious. Biologists and evolutionists theorize that the young of mammals are genetically programmed to be appealing so that they will survive during their long, dependent babyhoods. Thus the big eyes, fuzzy-wuzzy hair, and cute antics.

But where we older parents leave younger parents in the dust in the "precious" department is that we tend to find *every* facial expression, belch, and lisping syllable our children bestow upon us to be brilliant. For a lot longer.

We Have Tasted Life

The tendency to view everything about our children as precious prevails as much for those who conceived with no difficulty as for those who struggled toward parenthood.

An Oscar winner who I know you adore turned down an offer to spend several months on yet another (yawn) star-studded set leading to yet another instance of worldwide acclaim and the attendant fanfare and fabulous parties. All of that paled in contrast to the pure joy of sitting in the sunshine on the floor playing with her daughter. Try to explain that shift in priorities to a struggling actress of twenty or even thirty who would probably sell her own mother—and daughter—for a crack at a leading role in a Hollywood blockbuster.

Similar experiences are reported by many, including a journalist at the top of her field ("Bylines on the front page? Been there, done that"), a producer of a major network news show ("There's no news; it's just the same story, over and over"), and other women who are equally as successful in their fields if less visible publicly.

Our perspective has changed about "what life is all about." For those of us who have spent time in the fast lane, parties, prestige, and "the brass ring" begin to lose their luster in comparison with participating in a miracle and in the love, joys, frustrations, and challenges of being part of a child's life.

But also for those of us in the middle lane, or even the slow lane, a shift in what we perceive as the meaning of life takes place as we mature. What is valuable changes. "Getting there" loses some of its imperative. "Being there" with those we love becomes much more treasured.

The light, delight, and potential in our child's eye when reaching out toward a bubble that we have blown is now more thrilling than the potential inherent in the flashing light of our answering machine.

We are inclined, when our toddler says "more," to give more.

MANY OF US ARE SOLVENT

Many of us, simply by virtue of having one, two, or even three decades of work under our belts, have some discretionary income. Saying no because we can't afford something occurs less frequently in our homes than in many other homes with young children, where the parents are certainly no more enlightened than we, but are simply constrained by their finances.

MANY OF US WORK

After a long day of work-related stress, the last thing in the world anybody feels like doing is coming home to butt heads in power struggles.

"I don't want to fight with them because I only have a couple of hours in the morning and in the evening," says the mother of two in a small town in Washington. During the luxurious, uninterrupted weekends, once again, we don't want to waste our time fighting.

WE WANT OUR KIDS TO HAVE IT ALL

Perhaps due to our age, we often seem to function with a subterranean urgency. We want our children to have it all. Furthermore, we want to *see* them having it all. Right now!

Thus, not only are we less inclined to deny our children's requests, but we also tend to expose them to more than many younger parents have the means or desire to offer.

HOW EDUCATORS MAY SEE US

The director of a nursery school in Boston describes what she regards as typical among the children of older families in her school. It should be noted that the families she deals with are quite affluent.

Here is what she has to say: "Children of older parents are often exposed to culture, such as museums and concerts, at a very young age. The downside, of course, is that the child must fit into an adult-oriented world. They go to the ballet, but not to the park. Sometimes they aren't exposed to kid stuff at all.

"We had a newly-turned-three-year-old who was just starting school. We noticed that the child seemed overwhelmed. When I talked to the mother, I learned that in addition to having just begun school, the child had four after-school activities: Italian, ballet, drawing, and music lessons. The family was very achievement-oriented and the mother couldn't wait to give everything to the child that life has to offer.

"To the mother's credit," the director added, "she heard the feedback and pulled her child out of all the activities—except Italian, which she laughingly confided she just couldn't give up."

HAVE YOU EVER BEEN HERE? IN A STORE

Okay. So we made a conscious decision to become parents and went through hell and high water to get there. We are somewhat world-weary and we're delighted by the freshest experience we've had in a decade. A lot of us have very comfy amounts of discretionary funds available, we want our kids to have it all, and a lot of us work.

These conditions, even if we don't work and don't have that much extra money, have a cumulative effect. Here's a typical example.

In a store, when our child asks for some mere bagatelle, and money is no object, and the exquisite delight on our child's face is so marvelous, and the pure joy and the warm moment and the lack of conflict and the entire delicious gestalt are so perfect, there's no earthly reason to refuse!

Of course, intellectually, you know as well as I that there are many compelling reasons to refuse some requests. We'll get to that.

But if you'll bear with me I'd like to continue digging deeper to see why we might have a tendency to overindulge our children not only with material objects but more critically by honoring every preference they expressed.

MANY OF US HAVE ONLY CHILDREN

The only child is an entire subset of parenting that has spawned its own world of literature and ideas. To distill the theory to its essence, having only one child in a family often gives rise to overindulgence simply because there is no built-in waiting or sharing, nor is there any buffer between parents and child.

MANY OF OUR KIDS CAN TALK RINGS AROUND US

Most only children have highly developed verbal skills as a result of speaking mainly with adults.

In most older families, the adults are more often verbal than not. So even in families with more than one child, our children are very adept with words quite young. As a result, by preschool many of our kids can talk rings around anybody, including their parents.

MANY OF US ARE SELF-CONFIDENT

Another factor that seems to heighten our tendency to overindulge is that we are often self-assured out in the world. We are not embarrassed by our children being children. In fact, we delight in their very "child behavior." Therefore we tend to be less likely than younger parents to rope our children in in public.

HAVE YOU EVER BEEN HERE? IN A RESTAURANT

Here's a scenario, exaggerated to make a point and to have fun, that combines many of the elements we've introduced so far.

A restaurant. A mother and father in their late thirties, a toddler in his late twos. The parents are crowded on one side of the booth, having responded with delight to their child's eloquent request that Mommy and Daddy sit together.

A grilled cheese sandwich is held high over the table while the waitress waits for a place to be cleared among the books, crayons, toy trucks, Magic Markers, and toy phone that rings exactly like a real one. Often. To the vast amusement of nearby diners.

The grilled cheese is whisked away because it is too dark. A glass of milk arrives. It spills. A second glass is requested. The child experiments with placing paper sugar packets in milk. The experiment continues until all the sugar packets at the table are soaked.

A second, more lightly grilled cheese, appears. A bite is taken. The waitress is summoned. A tuna sandwich is ordered with the assurance that the family will gladly pay for all of the sandwiches.

The toddler wriggles down from the booth and starts running. The mother bobs and weaves her head, unable to see her offspring from the inside corner of the booth. The father calls the child's name. The hostess intercepts the toddler and brings him back, smiling politely, but not warmly.

The child wriggles across the father to the mother. Both parents smile even though knees dig into their crotches.

The child gives the mother a huge hug and kiss. She returns it, with an expression of pure love filled with wonderment that such a hug and kiss could be hers. The father leans in, tousles the child's hair, and kisses his wife.

The mother picks up the toddler's sandwich and offers it to him. The child pushes her hand away. The mother says in a chirpy voice, "I see you're finished with lunch."

The father swoops the child up in his arms and the child shrieks with delight as his father swings him up on to his shoulders. They parade through the restaurant toward the exit.

The mother bolts the last few bites of her lunch, and her child's, and catches up to them, lugging a large bag.

They have left their table in shambles. Scattered in the clutter are several toys and a generous tip.

WHAT CAN WE MAKE OF THIS MEAL?

Perhaps three sandwiches, as in our example, is excessive. But I've seen families politely order a second dish when the first one wasn't accepted. I've certainly seen families at home bring out a second dinner if the first is not accepted.

Where the trouble in that kind of accommodation to a child's whims occurs is that while you may be trying to please the child by making sure he has food he likes, he is not talking about food! He is finding out what his boundaries are. So in a funny way, you're having a conversation in two different languages.

He says, I don't want the grilled cheese. You say, Okay, it's only a couple of bucks, what the heck, I never liked it when they burned my grilled cheese either, hang on, buddy, I'll get you a different one. But what he really meant was, Please teach me. Am I supposed to eat this? Can I always do anything I want? Do you have any tricks to show me so that if the grilled cheese is too dark, I can learn how to deal with it?

The alternatives you have at your disposal are, first, to agree that it's darker than you usually make it at home. But then, for example, you can show him how to scrape off the dark part! I'm not suggesting a deprivation-based, make-do kind of arrangement, or a stern you-eat-this-or-starve approach.

I'm suggesting that you teach him how to use his imagination and resources to get what he wants or needs, or to learn how to deal with what is. Not just to use his will or his buying power. Because the more you teach him now how to be creative and elastic about accommodating to minor inconveniences, the better prepared he is for life. If his only options to change things, or to meet his own needs, are to either carry on (which is emotional blackmail) or to pay for something, he's going to be out of luck in any situations where he is poor in the currency of the realm, meaning wherever somebody else has a bigger will or more money. Even more significantly, he will have been given no resources to cope with any situation, whether minor or major, where there simply is no option for change.

Take something like "You two sit together." I've seen more than one family with the grown-ups crowded together on one side of the booth. It probably starts out because they're so delighted that their child has the verbal ability to come up with a plan. But that kind of arrangement, where the child basically determines who sits where, has a flaw. It means the child is in control. The parents, in deference to the child's idea, will sacrifice their own comfort and even good sense. The child is being overindulged.

I'm sure that as you read the lunch scene you saw all that. You realized that too many toys at the table mean that nobody even knows what's there. That a ringing phone in a public place is uncivilized. You realized that it's rude to soak all the sugar packets; that it doesn't encourage his curiosity but teaches a child the bad lesson that he's allowed to destroy other people's property. That when a child pushes a mommy's hand away, he needs to be firmly told that that's unacceptable behavior, and that we leave a restaurant when the adults are ready, not when the child has made it impossible to be there.

The problem is not in interpreting behavior when we read it. The problem is trying in the moment with our child not to let his cuteness interfere with our guidance.

From a child's point of view, there is another side to overindulgence that we might want to think about. If we parents are so loath to disagree with him, might he not be fairly scared when we actually do disagree? So that if we go through our day yessing him to death, when we do say no, he'll probably scream his head off. He'll think some-thing's wrong.

Let's see what other interesting events are taking place in our homes that might contribute to our having a tendency to over-indulge.

THE "SECOND FAMILY"

Where there is a wife in her late thirties to early fifties who is becom-ing a mother for the first time, there is often a husband who has already raised a "first" family. Obviously, this scenario gives rise to tons of fascinating interactions among all the family members. (See the "Recommended Reading" section for sources you might find help-ful.) In terms of parenting this small child, however, the family struc-ture has a specific configuration.

Here are two representatives who fit this paternal profile, both seen here attending a toddler group.

Although I imagine the first was good-looking when he was younger, now in his sixties he's drop-dead handsome. A lot of white hair. A craggy face. One of those good-bone bodies that clothes drape well on. Unlike some of the younger dads who show up for class in full business regalia, he wears wide-wale corduroys and a beautiful sweater. His quiet good taste screams money. He's thoroughly at ease with himself and his place in the world. From the sidelines, he watches his son and wife benignly. He does not interact so much as preside.

When asked the difference between being a father now and the first time around, he smiles. "The first time around, all I did was earn money. This time, whatever the two of them want . . ." He gestures toward the world, his for the buying—and giving.

The other type approaches this second round of fatherhood differ-ently, even though he seconds the opinion that everything is different now because of money.

With his first family, like the other second-family dad, he was a shadowy figure who came home at the end of a long day, often after the kids were asleep. On the weekends, he couldn't be disturbed. Daddy was exhausted. This time around, financially secure and in a position to take time off when he chooses, he is free to play. And play he does. Down on the floor. The toddler smacks his head? So what! The kid knocks his glasses clear across the room? Big deal. He's raising a little tiger, one he can tackle and roll around with. C'mere, you little squirt. This is a very happy father indeed, and he has absolutely no intention of being the distant, cold disciplinarian who never had the time to share so many warm moments with his first kids.

Neither of these fathers is likely to be very big in the "no" department.

OVERINDULGENCE IS NOT RESERVED FOR THE RICH

Lest you think that "overindulgence" is a cryptogram for how the middle- or upper-middle-class older parents spoil their children, I'd like to show you a little scene I witnessed recently.

Amsterdam Avenue, New York City. A mostly Spanish, rather poor neighborhood. A rattletrap truck pulls up to the curb. A tired-looking, middle-aged couple climb out. They wear nondescript, predominantly navy blue clothes. Everything about them has the faded, dusty look of worn-down poverty. Both are short; the man is wiry, the woman stout. Her frizzy gray hair is pulled back in a ponytail. She is missing some side teeth.

I can see she is missing teeth because she is smiling, even though the toddler she holds in her arms is flailing and smacking her in the head.

Never do I assume a gray-haired lady is a young child's grandmother. I know too much! The worst that happens is you flatter somebody by calling a grandma Mom.

"Don't hit your mommy," I joke. (Once a teacher, always a teacher.) The child stops, turning toward the high-pitched voice that all kids and dogs recognize is meant for them. We smile at each other. He is fabulously adorable, with dark dancing eyes and dimples.

The woman laughs, hugs him, and shrugs. In broken English she says, "Is okay. We waited sooooo long for him. Whatever he do is okay."

See what I mean?

I see another mother in a mall in New Jersey. From her hair, her skin, her general appearance, I can tell she's the right age for this book. She is carrying a boy who looks to be solidly in his twos. She puts him down, puts her hands on the small of her back, and leans backward, grimacing. "Brian, you'll have to get back in your stroller. Mommy's back is breaking."

Brian holds up his arms and wails, "Mommy! Carry me!"

She sighs, rubs the small of her back, grunts as she picks him up, and as his heavy body settles, limbs wrapped around her, she staggers off, pushing the empty stroller.

SINGLE MOM/ADOPTED CHILD

Parenting is real life, not a textbook. Although we'd like to divide ideas neatly into sections, it doesn't always work that way.

Here is a sensitive mom who touches on many themes at once. I am including her here, not because I am accusing her of overindulgence, but because she has expressed so beautifully the impulses so many of us share, and she manages to capture the flavor of many of our decisions.

Rebecca is a single mom with an adopted daughter—two elements of the "highly valued child" classification. Her child is now almost five.

In response to my asking if she thought her age itself had affected any of her parenting decisions, this is what she said:

"From the time my child was two and a half, she cried to take violin lessons daily. When she was three, I looked into Suzuki. They made it very clear how much commitment it is for the parents. It is staggering. And I thought, 'I am a single mother. There is no way I can do this.' Had I been younger, I probably would've held to that. But then I thought, 'How can I *not*?' So my business will suffer. I'll be more in debt. I'll have to work harder after she goes down at night. So what?' I don't think at twenty or thirty I would have made that decision.

"Now she's a Suzuki girl. It's very structured and disciplined. Of course, I want to nourish the free spirit in her, so there's an abundance of that in our time at home when she plays with her 'babies' and does art projects."

Here is a mom who reflects what so many of us feel. "I'll have to work a little harder. . . . So what?" As long as the child has what she wants, including being a "free spirit."

Again, let me make it clear. I am not suggesting that Rebecca is overindulging by meeting her child's heartfelt desire. I am instead suggesting that this may be one in a series of many situations where a mom thinks "How can I *not?*" Encouraging a free spirit can get tricky, as we'll examine in the next chapter.

PHILOSOPHICAL FACTORS THAT CAN LEAD TOWARD OVERINDULGENCE

If you are still in your thirties, or early forties, the evanescence of life may be nothing more than an intellectual concept. For most people, however, with each passing birthday, the kaleidoscope of life shifts slightly, altering what seems important to us.

WE ARE AWARE THAT LIFE IS SHORT

As one mother in her mid-forties said with a laugh, "Your defenses sag with your skin." Although many of us don't yet have sagging skin, she was referring to the fact that we feel less invested in holding on to positions. We aren't as desperate about many things. We "mellow with age." Unless you're by nature a fighter, the more experience you acquire, the less inclined you are to "sweat the small stuff." You may, like Rebecca, want to foster the free spirit of your child.

Although not sweating the small stuff is no doubt a sign of growth, it can lead toward overindulgence. If your child wants to wear rain boots on a sunny day, that is hardly an issue important enough to risk causing a meltdown. "Of course, go ahead, wear boots" to many of us is a no-brainer.

But where the "brainer" part comes in is knowing where to draw the line, which we will discuss in the following example in the kitchen.

WE ARE AWARE THAT LIFE IS FINITE

There's a major issue that younger parents simply aren't concerned with. Particularly for those in our late forties and up, we are confronting, if not yet quite coming to terms with, our own mortality.

As the fifty-year-old mother of a toddler said, "When you're older I think you understand the cycles of life more. You understand how precious life is. Maybe you've lost your own parents. And you understand that you're going to have to say good-bye to your children, too, in a way that when you're twenty and thirty is so remote."

How does this understanding affect our moment-to-moment responses to our children? It has a way of making you want every moment to be remembered with a glow. On a deep level, you're aware of how memories are being made. You don't want the memories to be tainted with too much negativity. You want everything to be "nice." This desire often predisposes us to avoid conflict.

One older mother acknowledges that this awareness affects our relationships with our own aging parents as well as with our children. She says, "We see ourselves at some point in the future with our now-adult children taking care of *us*."

HAVE YOU EVER BEEN HERE? IN THE KITCHEN

Your child wants the blue cup instead of the red one.

It's likely that to you the color of a cup is so insignificant in the grand scheme of things as to not warrant a flicker of indecision. You smile, whisk the red cup off the table, and replace it with the blue one.

But where we sometimes hit a snag is that once our toddler, who has a very different emotional agenda from ours, has the coveted blue cup, then which chair she sits in becomes crucial. And once the favored chair has been chosen, then the cow fork rather than the stars-and-hearts fork becomes an issue of passionate preference. Before we know it we're engaged in a series of interactions that are the complete opposite from what we'd imagined. They are not glowing, they are not lovely, they are not nice. They are exasperating and quite possibly enraging. And it's not even 7:30 A.M. No wonder so many working women are not kidding when they say they're more exhausted feeding their toddlers breakfast than running a planning session for a million-dollar ad campaign.

THE DIFFERENCE BETWEEN "UNDERSTANDING" AND "INDULGENT"

An "understanding" mom doesn't insist that her child keep the red cup. She understands that life is short and a cup is not worth fighting over. Her child has made a simple request that's easily met.

But the mom who then goes to the next step—the chair, or the fork, or whatever it is that is not moving us toward breakfast—has stopped being understanding and is close to being indulgent. "The chair you're in is fine" is a reasonable response. "Here's your cereal" is a logical step guiding your child forward into breakfast.

If you watch a child play, it might give you a reference point for helping you decide what your child is really asking for. A toddler will pick up a toy, play with it, and then, suddenly, the object loses its allure. The toddler will sometimes throw it down, or drop it behind him without so much as a how-do-you-do. The toddler has moved on. And so it is with things like cups and forks and spoons. If we will allow it, the toddler will move on.

We have to try and "understand" the subtext in these events. The child's subtext is something like this: Can I get mommy to listen to anything I say? That fork looks interesting. Look at that chair! I like those stars. Look at mommy's face!

Your toddler really truly isn't emotionally invested in the fork with the cows on it. Or at least not permanently invested in holding that fork. Your toddler needs *you* to help him move on.

Let's say that the worst-case scenario occurs. You try to move your child on and rather than being happily distracted, your child pitches a fit. Now it's even harder. I mean, after all, what are we doing here? It's only a fork. Who knew he wanted the fork so much?

Hello. He doesn't want the fork. He is so beyond the fork it's not funny. He's pitching a fit because you said he couldn't have it. And that's the thing that's eating your heart up. Why, you might be thinking, couldn't you just simply have said okay and then none of this would've happened?

This is the hard part. It's okay for him to be pitching a fit. Fits happen. What's not okay is for you either to try to avoid the fit by "indulging" any request he has or to try and stop the fit by backtracking and giving him the fork. In fact, the really understanding mom understands that her child needs to learn how to pitch a fit at home, with you, where he's safe, and discover that at the end of the fit, not one thing has changed except that his nose feels sniffly.

What we have just described is a scene that many of us go through. Some of us handle it with more aplomb than others. But most of us prefer to avoid big fits.

WHY WE AVOID BIG FITS

We don't like them. They are unsavory. They are uncivilized. They are loud. And truth be told, many of us find them frightening.

We feel ill-equipped to know what to do and sometimes we're even afraid of our children. Afraid we'll displease them. Afraid they won't love us. Afraid, way down deep, that we won't know how to climb back from a fury that shocks us with its force.

Afraid that the little glittering smile that we love so well will never again be ours. If we can just keep that smile, with the fork, or the spoon, or by saying okay, then everything will stay nice.

But as we know, it won't be nice. It will probably, unless we do something different, get worse.

Which leads us, of course, to the twin sister of overindulgence. Our conflict about discipline. Or why it's hard to say no.

12

Discipline: Why It's Hard to Say No

In addition to the external factors described in the previous chapter, there are internal factors that we share as a group that contribute not only to our being overindulgent, but on a deeper level to our being conflicted about discipline.

I want to present a major ingredient that I believe causes many of us to tippy-toe around or even flatly refuse to use the N-word.

PSYCHOLOGY IS OUR *LINGUA FRANCA*

A familiarity with psychology flavors much of parenting today. Many people have attended Smokenders, Weight Watchers, or similar kinds of self-help groups. It is no longer considered cutting-edge for a business to incorporate conflict resolution and other forms of discussion into normal working hours. Furthermore, unlike younger parents who have not had as much time to hit snags in life, many of us, for one reason or another, have availed ourselves of individual or group therapy. During the time when we were trying to start our families, for example, many of us made use of the valuable help of counselors to safely make our way through the field of emotional land mines presented by infertility and adoption.

Through this experience, we have learned to make positive use of value-free discussion as a method to explore our feelings, become aware of what we do, and thereby hopefully improve our lives. We have also gained a helpful working knowledge of our child's developmental stages as well as a handle on our own foibles.

But enough of the positive! It's always so much more fascinating to analyze the negative, don't you agree?! So let's jump right on the downside.

THE ANALYTIC "WHY?"—AND WHY IT'S NO GOOD FOR PARENTS

In couples therapy, "Why do you think you forgot to mail the letter?" is a terrific, nonjudgmental way to begin exploring the dynamics in your home. It's a starting point to talk about how it makes you feel when your husband intentionally acts like a stupid, inept, compulsively idiotic bumbling blockhead who thwarts you at each and every turn. Wait a minute! That's not how judgment-free discussion goes, is it?

All silliness aside, asking another adult *why* he or she did something is a civilized method of opening a dialogue that, if it works, will lead to genuine communication.

But this kind of useful discussion with an adult is death in a conversation with a child! Asking *why* your son heaved his dump truck at the cat for the fifth time this morning is inappropriate. *Why* did he do it? Because he's two years old and still relatively feral! The last thing in the world he needs is to have his parents ask him *why* he heaved a truck. What he needs is to have his mommy and daddy tell him, point blank, that he *can't* do it.

Asking *why* your eight-year-old didn't give you the message that Grandma called is inappropriate. She's eight. She's learning. That's *why*. "You know the rule. If you answer the phone, give people their messages. If you can't remember, don't answer the phone" is a useful instruction to a child. If she forgets again, she loses the privilege of being able to answer the phone.

But we are often loath to make judgments, for fear of being critical.

Here is Elaine, the mother of a four-year-old, talking about her parenting style as opposed to her own mother's: "I don't want to be such a critical mother. My mother felt that to love is to criticize. I've tried very hard not to do that. I've tried very hard to meet my son's needs rather than mine and to let him be freer than I was. I grew up in a very controlling, authoritarian home. My view of parenting is that you teach them manners and stay out of their way. That's what I try to do."

She expresses what many of us feel. Yet it is often that very kind of judgment—"You can't," "You may not," "You are no longer allowed to"—that our children need most from us. Many of us confuse criticism, which we may very well have been the recipients of, with guidance, which is direction delivered with love.

"You Must Be Feeling Angry"

There is another therapeutically inspired activity we encounter in parenting literature that older parents seem more inclined than younger ones to incorporate. We frequently try to teach our children how to put their feelings into words. Certainly clear communication is a gift. But sometimes we arm our children with sophisticated methods that obscure real communication.

"You must be feeling angry," for example, is a fairly common response to a heaved truck. There are two problems with this approach.

First of all, you don't know what your child is feeling or thinking. For all you know, he's a budding rocket scientist who's observing an aerodynamic phenomenon as the truck hurtles through space. By suggesting a particular feeling, you may be doing the exact opposite from what you are attempting to do. You may be taking your child farther away from identifying his own feelings by supplying inaccurate names based on educated guesses. Even more damaging, you may be projecting your own emotion. *You* may be feeling angry that your child heaved a truck. But your child is not necessarily angry. There are as many feelings he may be having as there are children. Impish, fiery, testy, curious, thwarted, and peeved are some of the possibilities. But you do not know.

More important, by attaching a "feeling" word to an action, and focusing on expressing that feeling verbally, you are tacitly condoning whatever the behavior is. The *conversation* about what happened becomes the significant event, not the event itself.

Rather than mucking around in adult "feelings," and conversation, you would serve your child best by remembering that you are the parent, not a friend, guidance counselor, or disinterested observer. You have expectations of behavior that your child needs to learn he can rely on. If you provide clear-cut parameters of acceptable behavior when your child is young, you will have established a secure framework within which your child can function as he matures.

What all this translates into in parent/kid talk is: "No throwing trucks!" or "No more answering the phone!"

A GROUP DISCUSSION GIVES US PLENTY TO DISCUSS

Often we overanalyze what's going on in our homes, thereby denying all of us ways to make things feel comfortable.

Just last night, I was lucky enough to be given the opportunity to address a group of parents, which is always a wonderful experience.

During the question-and-answer period, a couple who appeared to be in their mid to late thirties expressed a concern that their three-and-a-half-year-old girl seemed to be mean. The example they cited was that earlier that evening she had left her father's side while he was reading to her and joined Mommy, who was reading to the younger brother. Another mom, who was pushing forty, raised her hand immediately and suggested that perhaps the child was angry about something and that that was why she was being mean.

The example raises many fascinating questions. Why is the family using the word "mean"? Has the child actually been "mean" to her friends, or to her brother? Are the parents using a benign example to open up the conversation? Does the child never want to be with her father? Is the father at work for such long hours that when he comes home he's perceived as the interloper? Does the mother work long hours? Whether it fits with what we think should or should not be, the reality is that many kids want to cuddle up in Mommy's lap, get their batteries charged, and then go to Daddy. Is Mommy quite simply a better reader? Does the little girl want to make sure her little brother isn't displacing her in a territorial coup involving Mommy? Were this couple sitting in a therapist's office, where cigars are rarely cigars and discovering how people think is part of the goal, the very way they posed the question might have led to any number of productive avenues of discussion.

But here in the land of "practical parenting," you wonder why the family members were separated in the first place. Most likely, the family split up, one kid in each parent's lap, to offer "bonding" and "quality time" for each parent with each child.

The Myth of Bonding

"Bonding" is a dental term. Family members don't "bond" like two pieces of plastic stuck together with Krazy Glue. Family members love each other. Sometimes they fall head-over-heels in love instantly. Sometimes their love grows slowly. Some members of families feel closer to some members than they feel to others. Sometimes a preference for spending time with one rather than another is pronounced. Sometimes, suddenly, the preference shifts. But we cannot, or perhaps should not, try to "create situations to foster bonding." We are a family. We live together, hang out together, have fun spending time together, and sometimes don't have fun spending time together.

The Myth of Quality Time

There is no such thing as "quality time." *All* time that you spend with your kid is quality time. You cannot manufacture quality time. You cannot pencil quality time into your date book. All you can do is spend as much time as you can with your child doing whatever it is we do in life. Children don't have anything but quality time. To a toddler, taking the garbage and throwing it in the recycling bin is hot stuff! To a four-year-old, hitting the remote control for the garage door is right up there with winning the Nobel Peace Prize. To a ten-year-old, setting up a "buddy list" on-line is fab. Showing you, in your on-line ignorance, how to set up your own is heaven. Sitting at the breakfast table looking at a cereal box counts. Screaming at each other and making up counts. If you're with your child and you're doing it, from the child's point of view it *is* quality time.

Solutions Are Allowed to Be Superficial

Let's go back to our two families during Q&A. They do what the best among us do. They care deeply. They try their very hardest to do what's best for their children. The parents were worried that their older child felt displaced by the second and the second never got any time alone with Mommy, and Daddy got shunted off somewhere in no-man's-land, and they were worried that everybody didn't love everybody perfectly. So they came up with a plan: "You take her, I'll take him, we'll all feel close and cozy." But the strategy created separation among the family members rather than encouraging everybody to feel closer.

One practical solution, of course, is simply to plan in advance that everybody sits together while either Mommy or Daddy reads a story. But if they planned a separation, and are now faced with their child being "mean" by not wanting to sit with Daddy, a practical response might be to help the child understand that if Sam wants some special time with Mommy, Brittany can have a turn tomorrow, rather than allowing Brittany's carrying on to succeed in getting everybody to change positions.

What was the most interesting part to me in our discussion, however, was that both the family asking the question and the other mom bypassed the superficial and went drilling immediately for something "deep."

In an effort to analyze, they missed planning a wonderful chance to cuddle up together as a whole family. Barring that, they missed a wonderful opportunity to allow their older child to learn to live with things when they don't go exactly as she wants them to. Either of these options is, in my opinion, more valuable for their whole family than trying to analyze whether "anger" was at the root of the child's perceived "meanness."

"ISSUES" WITH OUR OWN FAMILIES

It would take a scientifically controlled study to validate the theory I'm about to propose. But I would like to run an idea by you and see what you think.

The very fact that we are older when we start our families is a predictor that we will be more separate emotionally from our parents than younger first-time parents. I have met many younger moms who describe their mothers as their best friends, who seek out their mothers' opinions and listen to their advice. This is not the common experience among the older moms with whom I've been in contact.

Furthermore, although maturation certainly plays a part in emotional separation, I don't think that this phenomenon is simply a function of age. I know many women in their forties, fifties, and up who speak with their mothers on the phone frequently, if not daily, go shopping together, and share relationships that are similar to those of many younger women.

I am proposing that, in addition to the desire and time necessary to build our careers, those of us who start our families later for the most part had some pressing "issues" to work out about our formative families, that working out these issues was an underlying reason why we have started our families later, and that it wasn't until we got a fairly good handle on our own histories that we were able to go forward to start a new family of our own.

BEING DIFFERENT FROM OUR MOTHERS DOESN'T MEAN BEING OPPOSITE

As we've noted, our analytic frame of reference, if not used properly, can lead us toward inappropriate dialogue with our children. It can also cause us to miss easy solutions in the search for underlying reasons.

There are two other significant areas where our parenting can be adversely affected by an analytic approach. We can sometimes use inappropriate tones of voice and we can respond in a superficially positive way.

Elaine, whom I mentioned when talking about our unwillingness to be critical, touched on a very important topic. She did not want to be critical, *the way her own mother was.*

I think she has hit a nerve. Most of us, like Elaine, are quite clear about what we know we're *not* going to do. We're *not* going to be like our mothers.

Personally, I happen to like your mother very much. But as we're all aware, knowing someone socially or working with her is a very different hill of beans from being her daughter. So if you say you don't want to be like your mother, even though I also happen to like you a lot (so she couldn't have been all that bad), I will accept at face value that you have your reasons.

But this desire to do things differently—which, let me reiterate, I am not suggesting is necessarily a bad idea—can lead us toward questionable responses.

UNSUITABLE TONE OF VOICE

Go back to our two-year-old who has just heaved a truck at the cat. You hear the enraged voice, the whining voice, the reproachful voice, or whatever button-pushing voice your mother used. That is the voice—with all of its reverberations—that springs to your lips. Obviously that is not a voice that you want to come out of your mouth.

But because we are being so careful not to replicate a tone of voice, and by inference quite a bit more, that we experienced in our own childhoods as damaging, what happens to many of us is that the voice that does come out sounds forced, or even inappropriately pleasant.

We sometimes even add polite address: "Please, don't throw the truck, Brandon." Sometimes we even go so far as to ameliorate the dreaded negativity with an added "darling," or "sweetie."

"Darling, please don't throw the truck," said in a loving way, would appear intellectually to be a sensible way to interact with those we love.

But unfortunately it's not. Brandon has not had the benefit of hearing in your tone of voice that he has done something of which you disapprove. Because you do not want to replicate an unpleasant experience from your own childhood, you might be conflicted about discipline. But by being unwilling to come down with authority, you are denying Brandon the opportunity to understand that he has done something unacceptable. He has been denied the right to learn boundaries at home.

While you have spent a good deal of your life trying to step out of the controlling bounds that were placed on you, you run the risk of not setting up enough boundaries for your own child. In other words, you are overcompensating. But while you and I are talking about boundaries and overcompensation, your two-year-old still hasn't been properly taught by appropriate tones and words that WE DON'T THROW TRUCKS!!!

"Darling, remember to use gentle hands when you turn the page." "Please don't put the cat's tail in your mouth." These are all the kinds of small corrections we need to offer our toddlers constantly that warrant a more pleasant tone than we may have heard as children. As our children mature, "Dearest, don't forget to hang up your coat,"

"Honey, please remember to put your lunch box in the kitchen," and an infinity of reminders that help to civilize our children are far from life-threatening and deserve parental guidance free from psychologically damaging, serious undertones. We need to distinguish among the kinds of corrections we make, based on the "seriousness" of where our child has gone astray in order to help our child discriminate between real right and wrong.

If you find that when you correct your child your tone and words do not signal that the child has done something unacceptable, worry less about using an unpleasant tone from your own childhood and concentrate more on making it clear to your child that he has done something bad.

INAPPROPRIATE "POSITIVE" RESPONSES

Unlike parents who are closely connected philosophically with their own mothers, we are obliged to reinvent the parenting wheel. Our role models tend to be our friends, whatever experts we read or meet, and for some of us even our therapists.

A common, and laudable, parenting revision from our own histories is that we try to respond more positively than we felt our own parents did. But sometimes, in our attempt to do things differently, we get stuck in the amber of our own thought processes. In an effort not to repeat our own upbringing, we sometimes ignore our own visceral responses and even our common sense.

HAVE YOU EVER BEEN HERE? INSIDE YOUR OWN HEAD

Take Andrea, the forty-year-old mother of a four-year-old girl. She describes what so many of us go through on a regular basis. Her child wanted to pick out her mommy's outfit. The mother shrugged when telling the story, as if to say, "Why not?"

First her daughter chose a vest. The Mommy explained that she had to wear more than a vest because otherwise her bra and panties would show.

The child chose a dress. Andrea is laughing as she tells the story, but when it was happening she was quite serious.

"I didn't really want to wear the dress. If I wore the dress, it meant I either had to wear stockings, which I didn't want to wear, or go with my legs bare, and the dress is kind of short, and I didn't really want to. What I really wanted to wear were pants. But if I said I didn't want to wear the dress, what would it do to my daughter? I want to encourage her to be free with offering her opinions. I *certainly* don't want to discourage her thinking for herself. Most important, I *never* want her think that I don't approve of the decisions she makes. Finally, I just put on the dress." She looked down at the offending dress, mildly bemused.

If you have never had an internal monologue resembling that one you are not like any of the other mothers I know. It is such a familiar seesaw of variables. If I do this . . . but on the other hand, what about that? And on and on.

Because of her psychological orientation, implicit in her "analysis" in the moment, at the root of most of the reinvention and correction of old patterns is an emphasis on building self-esteem.

SELF-ESTEEM, BOUNDARY ISSUES, AND OVERINDULGENCE

When her child expressed a desire to pick out Mommy's clothes, Andrea had a momentary fleeting thought. Her instinctive, first response was that she didn't really want her daughter to. She had to weigh the request, as evidenced by her shrug as she tells the story, as if to say, "Why not? Big deal."

Someone with less experience and introspection, even this same woman ten years earlier, might have reflexively said "No." Someone less conscious of the effects on someone else, at the point where a four-year-old chose a vest, might have laughed at the absurdity or gotten annoyed at the impracticality. Someone less concerned with the child's feelings might have said something demeaning, or summarily taken the choice from the child. All these kinds of responses can easily occur in homes where the mother hasn't spent a good deal of time thinking about the ramifications of small moments between mothers and children. These are, in fact, the kinds of erosive responses that we try to avoid.

Of course, there are many options besides squelching the child. She could have offered to let her daughter choose between two outfits that the mother wanted to wear. She could have said she wasn't in the mood to wear a dress, and asked her daughter to pick out something else. When you're sitting in the ease and comfort of a chair, *thinking,* ideas come flowing forth. Standing in your bedroom in your under-wear trying to get out the door and spend time pleasantly with your daughter before you leave, however, is a horse of another color.

An effort to bolster self-esteem is the driving force behind many decisions we make. When our children express a desire, whether for a blue cup, a turtleneck shirt, a particular song to be played while driving in the car, or to choose our clothes, we tend to honor their request, associating positive responses with building self-esteem.

We sometimes overidentify with our children emotionally. Perhaps because we have spent so many years analyzing our own childhoods, we operate from the child's point of view. We remember vividly what it felt like to be denied a choice, and we rush to make sure our own child has a different experience.

We do not allow ourselves the option of thinking, "I don't want a four-year-old picking out my clothes," which is what is about to hap-pen. Instead we think, "What a marvelous opportunity to encourage my child to express herself."

IF I HAVE ANY REGRET . . .

What's fascinating in my interviews with people whose children are entering their preteens is that, time and again, the one regret these parents have all expressed is that they wished they had set more limits in many areas from early on.

Listen to Julie, the fifty-three-year-old mother of a twelve-year-old. She is now eight years down the road from Andrea's experience of wearing a dress all day long that she didn't want to be wearing because she wanted to let her daughter express herself.

"I gave her a lot of freedom to express aggression, which I have mixed feelings about having done now. She's extremely well behaved and good in school. It doesn't go out into the world. But I'm the focus of a lot of it.

"It's beginning to bother me more now that she's older. She's become someone I've got to contend with. For example, she goes into my closet and takes my clothes. . . . She shouldn't do that without asking. And so we fight about clothes! This is my closet! But I haven't always asserted those kinds of boundaries because I've taken so much pleasure in watching her try on my clothes, and play with this, and play with that. I've had so much interest in her head and what's in her mind.

"I gave her too much freedom, and too much say, and too much right to speak her mind. It took me a long time to figure out that I didn't want to hear everything on her mind. That there are things that hurt me, and I have a right to say that."

In addition to our propensity to want to bolster our children's self-esteem, sometimes at the cost of our own, and perhaps ultimately of theirs, we have another leitmotif, or maybe heavy motif. Paranoia. Perhaps not as universal as the inclination to build self-esteem is among us, it is certainly around enough to warrant taking a look at.

KEEPING PARANOIA AT BAY

One forty-three-year-old laughingly addressed a nervousness that many of us echo. "I feel like I've got Velcro attached here." She holds her forearm up to her forehead in a vaudevillian rendition of worry. She can't shake the horrible image of her daughter standing alone in a cemetery when she's only twenty, no sibs, no parents, an only-child orphan.

Here's another, who is fifty-two and the mother of a preschooler. "I have the most morbid inner life in the world. I didn't always. I always used to live in the moment. I just wanted to have fun and fight the good fight. Now all I can do is think about my funeral, or my son's funeral. I know intellectually that this is my fear of being separated from him, but I struggle with it almost every day. Do others worry like this?"

"I worry about earthquakes, fires, that something will happen to her and I'll be powerless to help," says a forty-six-year-old mother of a kindergartner.

"I worry all the time. Do you think that's normal?" asks a mother from southern New Jersey. It's normal for every parent to worry.

Some people are more inclined to worry than others. But proportionately, we older parents worry more than younger parents.

"By the time you hit your fifties," adds the mother who is worried about funerals, "you know that bad things can happen in life, so maybe it's made me a bit more cautious."

A mother in her late forties changed her daughter's nursery school when the school's renovation included what she felt was an unsafe method of stripping paint. She was concerned about lead. Another mother reports that when major construction was begun on a building in which her child's nursery school was located, out of some hundred families, twenty decided the risk wasn't worth it and transferred their children to different schools. Most of these families were older.

Within the group of us who tend toward seeing disaster as a real possibility, there may be two things going on at once. On the one hand, there is simply our age. As noted earlier, by the middle of your life, you know you are not immortal. Furthermore, you know that "bad" things can happen because, if they haven't happened to you, they have happened to someone close to you. It is no longer paranoia, worry, or fear; it is probability.

There is another factor, however, that may come into play. For some of us, the last few decades have been spent working on real paranoia, not simply the humorous bandying of the word. We were working on not being timid, on not being fearful. There were many emotions that we needed to bring under control. Sometimes, with the advent of motherhood, which naturally inspires protectiveness toward our young, the worries that we have struggled successfully to contain now well up again, with our child as the new focus of the worry.

As a group, we display a much keener sense of the potential for disaster, or at least for something going wrong.

PROTECTION OR OVERPROTECTION?

Perhaps the difference between paranoia and prudence, from a parenting point of view, is how your mood and behavior affect your child. Often, in small, everyday moments, we can determine whether we are being prudent or overly cautious. In my observation, we sometimes continue to exercise precautions that our children have outgrown. Typical examples include early food restrictions, such as dairy products, strawberries, tomatoes, and other potentially allergy-inducing foods that we wisely withhold from babies. By toddlerhood, some of us are still exercising these precautions needlessly. Removing crib bumpers, moving our children into beds, allowing our children to play out of our sight at home and to walk ahead of us on the sidewalk or in a mall without holding hands are other characteristic places where we tend to continue imposing restraints that are no longer age appropriate. If you notice that other mothers have abandoned a particular precaution, consider that it might be time for you, too, to let it go.

If you find that you are frequently cautioning your child at play to be careful, consider seeing what happens if he actually falls. Falling, crying, and skinning knees are parts of childhood. In fact, your child needs to learn how to fall without becoming unnecessarily afraid. By allowing your own anxiety to course through your veins and spring to your lips when he takes a tumble in the playground, you may inadvertently be creating anxiety in him. I am not suggesting, by the way, that you become cavalier about falls and safety issues, but rather that you try and keep your underlying apprehensions from flavoring your child's reality.

Baby-proofing our homes is another area where we sometimes can become a bit *gung-ho*. A tongue-in-cheek thought that might help is this: Anything that will teach your child to exercise restraint is a useful lesson; anything that will kill your child is not. With that kind of benchmark in mind, attaching a heavy, freestanding bookcase to the wall is a smart piece of baby-proofing, because if it topples over when pulled on, a serious, if not fatal, accident will occur. Installing baby-proof latches on every door, drawer, refrigerator, oven, and toilet in the house, however, is not a sensible gesture. In the first place, it makes your home uncomfortable to live in for the adults. Furthermore, it denies your child the right to learn simple safety lessons. For example, he can't learn that if he puts his fingers in a drawer or door and closes it, he will get hurt. He is not warned away from the oven. Thus, when he's out in the unsafe world, where doors are much heavier and potentially much more dangerous, and where ovens are to be avoided, he is the proverbial babe in the woods! By overly baby-proofing your home, and therefore never having to teach your child not to go near dangerous things, you have given your child a false sense of security. You have given him no experience within the save confines of home to learn proper respect for things that can hurt.

GUIDANCE OR CONTROL?

Sometimes our worry can manifest in a tendency to be quite controlling about what is around our child. "What are the ingredients in these crackers?" asks a mother in one of our classes. "Is this paint nontoxic?"

While it would be remiss to even imply that someone who had a healthy dose of skepticism about the safety of what we eat and drink was overprotective rather than prudent, we do sometimes see a controlling atmosphere brought into play. In our effort to promote our child's self-esteem and to keep things feeling good, we may want to control the world around our child or expect that rules be broken for him or her.

I have seen in our classes, for example, a tendency to allow a child to continue eating a snack even though everyone else is cleaning up. Or perhaps the desire to allow a child to continue working on an art project even though the rest of the group is moving on. We may be inclined to request special treatment for our child because we are focused on making sure his self-esteem and intellectual development will blossom unfettered. Or we may not yet have learned the skills to help our child end one activity and go on to the next, and so we would rather try and bend the rules around him rather than face his wrath.

By the time our children are in elementary school, we sometimes have trouble having a clear take on how they are out in the world. Sometimes when confronted with feedback from school, we will take a stance that there's nothing wrong with Jordan, it's the school that's not doing it the way he likes it.

Ultimately, of course, this does our child a disservice. We would help him more by helping him learn how to move within the rhythms of a benign group rather than by encouraging him not to learn how to function smoothly in the world.

PROVIDING THE RIGHT KIND OF RESPECT

I mind very much when people don't respect children. Those, for example, who need to "show a kid who's boss" always strike me as oppressive, rather stupid noncoms who lord it over the privates the minute they get a chance.

But there is a way of behaving toward a child that is respectful which may be gotten to more easily by starting off with what it is not.

Treating a child like an adult is not treating a child with respect. Treating a child as an equal is not treating a child with respect. Treating a child as your peer is not treating your child with respect. A child has the right to be treated as someone who is learning. That relationship, seen in adults as mentoring, assumes that the adult knows more than the child. It is not a peer relationship, but rather a hierarchical one. The parent is above the child in knowledge, experience, and decision-making rights and obligations.

Your child needs to learn from you. Your child needs you to show him the ropes, to teach right from wrong, to tell him what he can and cannot do in the world in order to live a productive, emotionally secure life.

If you act toward your child as if you are peers, he has no safety net. Because he *knows* he doesn't know anything in the world. If you are treating him as if he knows as much as you, then who is in charge?

"PERFECT PARENTS" ARE NOT PERFECT

We have just spent a fair amount of time looking at all the things that can get in our way. That makes it hard for us to say no to our child and that make us wary of the world around our child. After all that, which as I said in the beginning was really fine-tuning in terms of parenting, I'd like to step back a bit in order to regain our balance before we head into the next, practical chapter.

Although most parents who attend parenting groups and lectures, or who read parenting books, such as you and I, are inclined to want to be "perfect," older parents seem to go at perfection with more brio. As a group, we seem to attack parenting as if it's something we can conquer. Something we can get an A in. Something that is task oriented.

But parenting is not a job, goal, or finite interaction. It can only be based on pure love for another person—regardless of what that person is like—in order for it to be fulfilling for both the parent and child. If you approach parenthood as a milestone of your own accomplishments, you are probably headed for a very rocky road. Parenting is rather formless and unpredictable. It is a dynamic, fluid series of interactions between two people, as well as among however many people make up your immediate family. It is a rich—and very demanding—relationship.

As in all relationships, there can be no perfection. There are times when things go well between us, times when our hearts fill with the pure joy of being in each other's presence. There are times when our hearts feel as if they're filled with broken glass, ice shards, barbed wire. There are times when we are together and not feeling much of anything one way or the other, times when we are barely aware that the other is there, times when we are preoccupied by something else and the other's presence is a minor—or major—irritation, times when we wish we were anywhere but where we are and times when we wouldn't trade where we are for all the riches, fame, and robust good health—or toys, ice cream, and water parks—that exist in all the world.

If your goal is to be a "perfect parent," the first step is to realize that there is no perfection in parenting. Whatever goes on between you and your child that's *essentially* more positive and productive than it is negative and disruptive is as close to perfection as can be. All relationships, including that of parent and child, are unpredictable, growing, developing, dynamic, and individual.

Let us take a lesson from the master ceramicists of Japan. In any piece of pottery they make, they intentionally include a small flaw. This is to remind them that they are human.

So it is with being a parent. The flawed, uneven moments with our children, as important as the sublime, combine to create a perfect imperfection that is a happy family life.

13

Assuming the Mantle of Parenthood

Overindulgence is actually deprivation. While we may feel that we're "giving our children everything," we are withholding fundamental knowledge and skills they need to live a satisfying life.

From a strictly material point of view, we refuse our children the right to treasure objects as well as achievement. By indulging *whims* as if they were *wishes,* we deny our children the pleasure of "wanting." The child who doesn't "want for" anything, doesn't want anything. Not wanting anything can diminish or even rob them of the drive that makes life interesting, as well as fulfilling. We build in a premature jadedness. If you have every piece of primary-colored plastic on the face of the earth, none of them matters very much. If you've got a lap-top in your room when you're ten, what do you have to look forward to in college? If a tutor can be hired to get you through a test, why bother to study on your own? What events, objects, and rewards mark your personal achievement, maturity, and increasing stature in the world?

Emotionally, the price our children may ultimately pay is even higher. We set up false expectations. "You can have anything you want" just is not so. Not in the real world. Not in preschool or elementary school, and certainly not later in life. We deny our children the ability to delay gratification by waiting, striving, and finally achieving a reward.

By not disciplining our children, we skew the relationship between parent and child and take the easy way out in the moment, thereby creating harder times to come.

We don't help our children develop the skills necessary to roll with the punches when they don't get what they want, or to figure out how to get what they want when it's not easy, or to deal with disappointment, being thwarted, or any other of the very real vicissitudes of life. In some instances we create rather tyrannical behavior that sets our children up for lonely personal lives.

Perhaps most significantly, and trenchantly, we deny our children the right to look up to us as firm, consistently fair arbiters of acceptable behavior and boundaries. The parent/child relationship is not a peer relationship. If the child is the one who sets the pace and the agenda of every interaction, we have tipped the balance, putting our children in the awkward, strained, ultimately tragic position of looking down on us.

OUR THREE STICKY WICKETS

There are three major areas that are especially tricky for many older parents. We often rush prematurely to soothe, thereby depriving our children of the chance to learn how to deal with frustration. We confuse liberty with license, allowing boundaries to slip and slide, which ultimately confuses our children. We fail to establish simple routines, thereby turning even the most mundane event into a potential power struggle.

RUSHING TO SOOTHE

Many of us have a tendency to want our child to be "happy" all the time. This desire sometimes causes us to rush in to make things "right." Although we make haste in many situations, crying provides us with a ready-made litmus test of whether we have a tendency to rush rather than to wait.

Infants Should Not Be Allowed to Cry

Any baby under the age of six months needs to be tended to if he or she is showing *any* sign of distress. Telling a parent to let a baby of that age cry, whether to "learn" how to sleep, to avoid the dread "spoiling," or to establish the proper "hierarchy" in the home, is mean-spirited, if not downright sadistic. An infant is not malevolent and has no mechanism for communication other than crying. Hormonally, genetically, and on a cellular level any emotionally secure, decent human being who hears an infant cry will move to find out why, and fix it, unless the adult is ignoring his or her own internal impulses and following misguided advice.

Very young babies (other than those who are colicky) who are in physical contact with their parents rarely cry. Thus a Snugli, for example, is a much better choice than a stroller when you are walking. During these early months, the more in contact with your body your baby is, the less time you will have to spend agonizing over whether to respond to the baby's crying and your own answering heart, or ignore them.

The Cries of Older Babies Are Different

Sometimes, however, we have trouble altering our behavior to match our child's emotional growth. Although our child is developing more sophisticated skills of communication, we may continue to respond to an infant's needs, rather than to those of a maturing baby.

A child over the age of six months or so who is not allowed the privilege of crying *sometimes* for *a short period of time* without having an adult rush in to ameliorate whatever is going on is being denied certain basic human rights. The right to learn how to deal with frustration. The right to learn how to make yourself feel better ("self-soothe" is the clinical term). The right to acknowledge that sometimes things are not perfect and that we do not die in the face of imperfection.

By always moving quickly to alleviate any uneasiness our older child might be feeling, we may inadvertently do two things that are not beneficial. We may deny our child the chance to build up the ability to withstand discomfort and frustration. Furthermore, we may create more anxiety on the part of our child: If minor things are not "right," I must be threatened. Otherwise, why would Mommy or Daddy come running so fast? We have then perhaps built a cycle of distress: If I'm feeling out of sorts, and Mommy and Daddy come rushing, then they must think that out-of-sorts is really bad. So the next time, not only do I feel out of sorts, but I feel upset about feeling out of sorts. And on and on until the child is experiencing intense discomfort rather than mild discomfort.

Raising a child is composed of a multitude of small and large moments, interactions, and events that shape an entire life. There is never one moment that we can pinpoint as being The Moment that characterizes the flavor of the relationship between parent and child.

Yet there is a moment for all of us when our defenses are down that offers us an opportunity to peer into the heart of our interactions. Rather than begin with all the little easy moments with our child, I want to jump right into one of the hardest times, to help us get some clarity on the direction in which we might find our ships listing.

Crying from the Crib: Babies

Sleep is a loaded issue (please see "Recommended Reading" for some book suggestions). It engenders what amount to religious battles over the "best" way to handle what is simply a process. Learning to sleep, like speech acquisition, requires *emotional and intellectual maturation, time, and guidance* for proficiency leading to mastery. It is not a one-time event. Nevertheless, "experts" propose cookie-cutter solutions for "how to handle sleep," some advising us to let babies cry, others advising never to let them cry, as if it were not an individually paced learning process. Although here is not the place to look at the whole subject of sleep, what this complicated process in our child's development offers us is an interesting way to think about *our own response* to our child's cries.

Crying babies need, and deserve, a response from their parents. *How* we respond, however, bears discussion.

If your eight-month-old, for example, wakes up, you do not need to honor the rush of adrenaline you feel, nor the contraction of your muscles that makes your feet hit the ground running as you dash into his or her room.

If you move in to calm the child *prematurely,* the child begins to depend on the parent to always *make things right immediately*. But you can't live up to this false expectation. You can't always make things right. By always trying to make sure your child is happy, you potentially set him up to be miserable.

What should you do? You can actually *listen for a moment.*

I promise, if you allow yourself you can hear the differences in the kinds of cries. You can then respond to the individual communication that your child is making. Here are some probable communications.

Terror or Pain

Terror or pain requires a parent's presence immediately. A young child who's terrified, or hurts, deserves to be picked up and soothed as fast as you can get there. When the child is calm, he or she should be settled back down.

But your child doesn't need *you* also to be terrified; your child doesn't need you to meet the intensity of his or her mood. Your child needs you to be calm and reassuring. Your child needs *you* to know, deep inside, that he or she will not die from feeling afraid. Because here, in the middle of the night, when we hear our child cry, our emotions well up. My child! My child! I have to protect my child! I have to swoop my child into my encompassing arms, and hug him and protect him and let him know that he is safe because Mommy's here!

It is right here, in the middle of the night, that Mommy has to stand straight and tall, knowing that her child's very life is *not* being threatened and that what he needs from her is the real comfort and security of a calm, unfrightened adult. The mommy has to know that the child's terror is smaller than the mommy.

On the other hand, some of us deep in the middle of the night feel something else. Some of us feel rage. It wells up and spills out. I cannot bear being awakened another time tonight. I simply cannot stand this feeling. If I ignore that crying, maybe it will go away. Oh, it hasn't gone away. It has only gotten worse. There's no avoiding it. I have to go. Come. Hush, quiet. Hush. Just like the mommy whose terror matches her child's, the mommy in a rage gives the child's emotions a larger-than-life importance. The child's crying will not kill the mommy. The child's neediness will not kill the mommy. It will not destroy you if your sleep is disrupted. It will only make you tired.

It is right here, in the middle of the night, that Mommy has to stand straight and tall, knowing that *her* very life is not being threatened and that what her child needs from her is the real comfort and security of a calm, unfrightened adult. The mommy has to know that the child's terror is smaller than her adult self.

Dismay

Crying from dismay should be given a few minutes without a parent racing in desperately trying to make everything perfect. Hopefully the dismay will go away and the crying will cease. This means your child has *successfully figured out* that feeling out of sorts is not so threatening and can be ignored. If this has occurred, everybody has turned a corner. If the dismay turns into terror, though, your child needs you. (By the way, there are many practical difficulties, such as losing a pacifier, that can easily be fixed. Here we are exploring the adult's possible feelings, which have a great bearing on how the adult responds. You will find help with practicalities in the "Suggested Reading" section.)

Anger

A child crying from anger should *never* get an immediate warm, cuddly response. If ignored, sometimes it will stop. Hurrah! Your child has successfully dealt with being alone. But let's say you hear outraged crying.

Calmly, slowly, and if possible without a pounding heart, go to the child's room. If you can keep in your head the idea that your child is not dying, you will both be better off. The angry screamer doesn't need to be smiled at, doesn't need to see soft looks of concern. The child needs to see a calm face telling her to lie back down and go to sleep. She can use a rub on the back or any other soothing physical contact that does not include a big, warm hug.

But, you may be thinking, Whenever I hear my child crying, I feel horrible. I feel as if I have to race there, to protect her, to hold her, to make everything perfect.

That's a very understandable feeling. I am not by any stretch of the imagination suggesting that you let your child cry all day and all night. This is not a license to let her cry. I am suggesting that you give her a *moment,* from time to time, to see if she can figure out how to stop her own crying. The reason for this is that if you are the only one who can soothe her, if she never learns how to do it on her own, a time will come when you are not there, and then your child will truly be bereft. You will have given her no way to cope with distress.

I am also trying to give you some perspective based on the knowledge that a cry communicates more than one thing and that learning to respond more to your child's communication than to your own pounding heart will ultimately help your child.

Should you find, as many new parents do, that your response to your child's crying feels very distressing to you, consider getting some help. While all new parents face major readjustments, as we said before, we who are older are not used to feeling incompetent. Sometimes the pressure of a new child's intense needs coupled with our discomfort at being incompetent combines to truly overwhelm us. You would do yourself and your child a world of good to get a handle on those emotions in a neutral setting rather than try to deal with them in the middle of the night.

For those feeling minor, manageable distress, here's a technique that might help.

Technique: Mommy's Mantra

If you are like the mom we just described who is stressed or annoyed by your child's crying, this technique might not be so useful for you. But if you are a mother who rushes in to soothe, here is a technique you might try.

While your baby is not crying, think about this:

If my baby cries, he or she will not die. If my baby cries, he or she will not die. And again, all together. *If my baby cries, he or she will not die.* Very good.

Let's go to the next one while you're in the rhythm.

If my baby cries, I will not die. If my baby cries, I will not die. One more time. *If my baby cries, I will not die.*

Now let's try a really hard one.

If my baby cries, I am not a bad parent. Go on. You can say it! *If my baby cries, I am not a bad parent.* Excellent. One more time. *If my baby cries, I am not a bad parent.*

While you're on a roll, let's go for the gold.

If my toddler cries, he or she will not die. If my toddler cries, I am not a bad parent.

When Crying Is Not an Emergency

It's possible that the next time you hear your child cry, whether in the middle of the night or when you have left the room momentarily to answer the phone and have left him sitting in a safe place, or when your child is hungry and you are preparing his food—or any of the other tiny moments in life that are not perfect, but are not life-threatening—and it is not a cry of pain, you will be able to withstand the overwhelming feeling to *rush* to "make nice." When this happens, if your child learns that if he cries for a minute or two without having someone come desperately rushing toward him that he won't die, and that if he doesn't feel "happy" it's not the end of the world. You have given him an enormously valuable gift. The gift to be able to tolerate real life.

ALLOW YOUR TODDLER THE CHANCE TO BE FRUSTRATED

As a group, we tend to be excellent teachers. When our children play, we often challenge and encourage with questions and instructions. "What color is this?" "What shape is this?" "Show me the blue one, show me the rectangle." Our children, as a group, tend to learn these kinds of things quite young.

Perhaps less productively, some of us become so keen to teach that we can become involved in dictating the "right" way to do things. "Hold the glue stick like this." "Put the sticker there." I have noticed that as a group we show an inability to simply "sit" with a child and allow the child to lead the way. It's rather an ironic twist, since we allow them to "lead the way" in so many other areas of life.

With that in mind, let's try a fun game. "What Would You Instinctively Do?"

Your fifteen-month-old is sitting at a little table playing with a table toy. A piece drops. *What would you instinctively do?*

Choice 1. Pick up the piece and hand it to her.
Choice 2. Do nothing.

If you chose immediately picking up the piece and handing it to her, I ask you to reconsider. Although kind, polite, and totally loving, *it doesn't give her what she needs.* From her viewpoint, she is playing and something happens to change that. She has a problem to solve.

If you do nothing, you get to see what she'll do next, thereby learning something about her. More important, *she'll* get to see what she does next, learning many different things at once.

Here are some predictable responses.

She might pick up the piece. She might push away from the table and move on. In either of these cases, the problem has been solved for both of you.

Or she might peer over her shoulder and look at the piece, thinking. She might—dare I say it?—cry.

Quick. *What would you instinctively do?*

Choice 1. Do nothing.

Choice 2. Pick up the piece and hand it to her.

Choice 3. Point and say, "You can pick it up."

"Do nothing," is a possible response if your child is looking at the piece and thinking.

But if you suppose that "Do nothing" is the best response to crying, you don't have your thinking cap on. You're answering by rote. Who ever said parenting is easy? And why do all those people who have those big jobs like air controller, for example, think they're making more complicated judgment calls than what any mommy or sitter does all day long when she's home with a toddler?

The reason doing nothing is now not a useful response is that your child actually doesn't know what to do. On the other hand, if you hand the piece to your child, you have just taught her that Mommy will make everything better.

If you point to the piece and tell your child that she can pick it up, you have given your child a skill that she can internalize that she wasn't yet able to figure out for herself.

So basically, the idea is this: Let the child see whether she can solve the problem herself. If she can't, point out or show what she can do, but don't do it for her. Even if she cries! Particularly if she cries.

Once again. *If my child cries, she won't die. If my child cries, I won't die. If my child cries, I'm not a bad parent.*

Common Small Moments of Frustration

Here are some questions to ask yourself about whether you move in perhaps a bit too quickly to guarantee immediate "happiness" in your young child's life.

When your thirteen-month-old steady walker is learning how to climb the stairs on a toddler sliding board, do you always hold his hand? Immediately grab his tush if he stumbles? Or perhaps point to where he can hold on to help himself climb up.

When your fifteen-month-old is reaching for a crayon that is slightly out of reach, do you immediately get it for her?

If your eighteen-month-old stumbles, do you reflexively reach out to prevent a fall? If he falls, do you rush to pick him up or encourage him to get up?

When your two-year-old is trying to attach two pieces of giant LEGO, do you reach in to snap them in place?

When it's mealtime, if the food is too hot, do you put some crackers on the high chair tray while it cools down?

If your three-year-old has just had a toy taken from her in the playground, do you watch to see what she'll do, or do you move in to instruct the other child to give it back?

There are as many examples of choices we can make as there are moments in the day with a child. These are just a random few to inspire you to think about whether you allow your child a moment or two to see what will happen, to fail, to fall, or to succeed without your immediate intervention.

CONFUSING LIBERTY AND LICENSE

When writing about parenting for a general audience, authors like to point out that personal preferences regarding such benign topics as a choice between two foods or a choice of clothing are useful areas in which to allow a child to flex some independence muscles.

We older parents, however, don't seem to have trouble allowing our children freedom in those areas. We may be much less uptight if our child is wearing an outlandish outfit, for example. We are more likely to need a reminder of the places where it's inappropriate for a child to choose. As we discussed, we are inclined to foster self-esteem.

I don't mean to suggest that that is not a good thing. Sometimes, however, in our desire to foster self-esteem, we go overboard. We lose perspective on what is the child's province and what is the adult's.

Perhaps this will serve as an overview: The adult is in charge of where we go; when we go; how we get there; all elements of safety, hygiene, health; and all routine events. In other words, the adult runs the house and is in charge of scheduling. The child is then free to make a multitude of personal choices within those parameters, as long as the choice does not interfere with any of the above.

That is all, in some ways, a simple exercise in management and assigning of duties. Where it becomes somewhat difficult is that the child developmentally needs to test limits. Therefore, it is important to keep in mind that you are trying to guide the ship forward even though one of your passengers is throwing pebbles into the engine, shooting arrows at the backup sails, and threatening to jump overboard.

DRAWING A LINE IN THE SAND

Setting limits is essentially the skill of drawing a line in the sand over which your child may not tread. The most important idea to hold on to in setting and holding limits is this: *In any given power struggle, if you, the parent, don't win, you all lose.* Here are some typical scenes where the child is likely to want to test by asking, "Where exactly did you say that line was?"

Diapers: Thirteen-Month-Old

Diapers are often a favorite place for kids to test. I have seen—or excuse me for being blunt here, but I have smelled—four-year-olds who are still not only wearing diapers but carrying on about changing them. Such a four-year-old is in a pickle and in my opinion has been let down by his parents.

Here's how to prevent this from happening to your child. If diaper changing isn't an issue for your child, substitute some point of dispute in your own home.

If your thirteen-month-old does not want his or her diaper changed . . . tough noogies. You're the grown-up. You know that excrement can harm your child's skin. Change your child's diaper. There are tricks of the trade.

- Propping your child's head up alleviates the extreme displeasure some children feel being flat on their backs (not unlike a woman's feeling at the gynecologist's—and even they caught on and put little terry-cloth things over the cold metal of the stirrups!).
- Offering your child something to play with as a distraction sometimes helps.
- For a very active child who detests having his or her diaper changed, changing it while the child stands sometimes is a sensible measure.

But even if the tricks of the trade don't work, the bottom line is that *the diaper has to be changed.*

Changing a diaper is a matter of hygiene and health. It is also a *routine event.* It is, therefore, by definition, not something for which a parent should even consider an alternative. It is not a matter of self-esteem. It is not a matter that it is useful for the child to feel is under his or her jurisdiction. Even though many children will want to test this boundary.

If it becomes necessary (and admittedly this is not pleasant in the least), you can physically hold a small child down in order to change a diaper. If you hold your child down with anger in your body, you have gone into an undesirable zone verging on abuse. But if you hold your child down not with fury but with firmness, you have been the grown-up taking charge, which is your job. If you do not change the diaper because your child doesn't want you to, and because you don't have the fortitude, you have abrogated your duties as a parent.

Note: If you honor the clever bargaining ploy often offered by a verbal child, "Change di-di later!" you have made a deal with the Devil. There are no good "deals" ever to be made about taking care of the necessities of life. If you don't change the diaper right now, when you, the grown-up, know that it needs to be changed, and when you said it was time to change it, there is no earthly reason to suspect that ten minutes later you won't be having exactly the same unpleasant interaction you're having now. Postponing unpleasantness doesn't make it go away. It makes it worse.

Remember while you're changing a diaper on a child who doesn't want his or her diaper changed, *crying does not kill a kid.* Don't hesitate. Don't vacillate, waiver, consider. *There is nothing to consider!* Poop is not a good thing to keep around. Change the diaper.

Depending on how quickly your child learns and on how much temperamentally your child is invested in testing boundaries, if you are consistent and firm, there will come a time when changing the diaper is no longer a problem. If you allow your child to have his diaper changed only when he is ready, you will find your days are a series of struggles.

This particular kind of approach is useful for any routine necessity of life.

Car Seats and Strollers: Two-Year-Old

If your two-year-old doesn't want to get in the car seat . . . tough noogies. It's time to go. Does a piercing scream accompanied by an arched back require you to push your child down and strap him in? It does. As appalling and uncivilized as that may seem. Again, *how* you push him down matters. If you push with firmness, you are holding up your end of the relationship. If you push with fury you are a bully. If you do not push, allowing your child to stall getting into the car, you are a pushover, and you have left your poor child out in the cold with no coping skills for dealing with events that are not exactly the way he or she wants.

If you manage early on to establish *within yourself* the fortitude to do what needs to get done, for your child's sake as well as for your own, interactions will be smoother with your child, who will in turn feel better.

Strapping a Child into a Stroller: Different Versions

Because I think it's illuminating and instructive, I'd like to share with you a phenomenon that I have witnessed often over the last decade.

At the end of any typical toddler class, after so much stimulation, no matter how much fun they had, many children melt down. It is a common sight to see at least one if not more moms and baby-sitters strapping screaming kids into strollers. What is always fascinating to me is how different groups have relatively predictable styles of accomplishing this somewhat unpleasant, yet routine, procedure.

With varying degrees of tenderness or a strictly businesslike approach, most baby-sitters, in short order, get the crying child strapped in and calmed with a pacifier or a bottle.

Most younger mothers exiting a class will get their crying child into the stroller, even if it means taking a few quick steps to grab the running child, strap him in, hand him his teddy, a book, or a bottle, soothe him with a physical caress, all the while talking and laughing over her child's head with the mother next to her who is busily getting her own child settled at the same time.

Most older moms make eye contact and talk to their child. "I know you don't want to get in, but you have to" is a typical older-mom observation as she physically gets her unwilling child into the stroller. She will then hand her child whatever toy, book, blanket, or talisman will comfort, amuse, or distract the child.

A number of older moms, and an occasional younger mom, are extremely uncomfortable when dealing with a child's unwillingness to do something. It takes them several fairly painful attempts before they summon up the courage, or physical strength, to manage to get the child into the stroller. When they finally do get the child in, they often kneel down in front of the stroller, looking very concerned and trying through conversation and touch to get the child to stop writhing. Their attempts to soothe in this way not only fail, but in fact tend to worsen the crying.

In extreme cases, more older moms than younger ones cannot get the child in at all. They will spend as long as a half hour vainly following their child back and forth, trying to coax the child into the stroller, before the child becomes bored with the activity, at which time they are able to move on.

Among the various responses, intuitively and stylistically, I personally "approve" the most of the mother who acknowledges her child's displeasure but doesn't let it interfere with what needs to be done. It is in that one small moment of empathetic understanding that the "maturity of the older mother," as so many professionals pointed out, enriches the child's life vastly.

The approaches of the sitter and of the socializing younger mom are certainly respectable, although they're not quite as "connected" as I personally found pleasurable with my own child.

But the two tentative responses warrant change. With varying degrees of intensity, these moms are allowing a simple, normal, mundane event, such as getting into a stroller, to become more than it is. They are allowing the child to create and win a power struggle. They are forgetting that from the adult's point of view, getting into a stroller should not be a power struggle; it is merely getting into a stroller. They are allowing the child's emotional response and developmental stage to dictate the tenor of the interaction. They are allowing the child too much license, and they are allowing their own fear of unpleasantness to exacerbate an unpleasant situation.

Unless they take serious steps toward readjusting the balance, whether through reading a book like this, or by seeking more immediate help from outside, they are looking down a long road full of potholes, flash floods, and broken bridges.

Bath Time: Four-Year-Old

Testing boundaries, of course, is the prime pleasure of any self-respecting kid. Even if you do know how to get your two-year-old into a stroller without enacting a scene worthy of Dostoevsky, there will still be plenty of times, throughout all of childhood, for your heir apparent to test your mettle and see whether you can stand firm, hands on hips, making it clear that here lies the line in the sand.

If you are the mother of an older child, you may find that many routine events of the day are fraught with disagreeableness.

Here's how it may play out. You tell your four-year-old it's bath time. Your four-year-old gives you a look, as if to say, "Oh, yeah. Right. Bath time," and goes back to Ninja cartoons.

There are tricks of the trade.

- Run the water. When it's ready, turn off the TV, announce that the bath is ready, and walk toward the bathroom. This will be a stunner, if your family is used to long, drawn-out dramas around the simplest events.

- If the typical deal starts, "One more cartoon, five more minutes," don't answer. There's nothing to discuss.
- Wait in the bathroom.
- When the child appears, which may not be instant but *will* occur, remember that specific requests are easier to follow than general ones. If you hold out your hand and pleasantly say, "Shirt please," you are more likely to get a positive response than if you simply say, "Get undressed."
- Some fun-inspiring comment—"Okay, let's see what fun things are in the tub"—and off you go.

A quiet, low-key mention later, such as how nice tonight's bath was, is useful. It acknowledges that something went smoothly. By not lavishing praise, you acknowledge that taking a bath is an expected, routine event.

Hard part. Bottom line. If you didn't have success right away, it's still bath time.

It is not sensible to suggest that you physically put a four-year-old in the tub. The truth is, by that age, they are big enough for that kind of wrestling match to end in real disaster. But if you have gone on for four years struggling over many mundane events, it is possible that your child will not eagerly get in the tub.

If you have to, stand in front of the bathroom door. Try and stay as unemotional as possible. Simply point out to your child that it is bath time and that you'll both stay here till he takes a bath.

No long speeches about how hard this is. This isn't that hard! This is taking a bath when the grown-up tells you to! Millions of children all over the world can accomplish this simple task!

Once your child realizes that you are in control of yourself emotionally, that you are not angry but determined, and that you truly have no intention of leaving the bathroom until he takes a bath, he will get in and he will feel relieved. Even if he is screaming his head off as he gets in. The next night, he may scream again. But there will come a night when you say "Bath time" and he gets ready for a bath without a fuss.

Technique: "Phobia" Control

Think about how behavioral therapy helps phobics. Essentially, for a person with a phobia, the brain is hardwired to have a fear response, which occurs subconsciously. For example, a person afraid of elevators will have a terrified response that may arise seemingly out of nowhere, but in fact arises from some earlier experience. The best practical approach behaviorists have found so far is to ride with the person in the elevator. The therapist, by his or her presence, helps ride out the waves of terror until eventually the person can go it alone.

If you have an older child who's basically been conditioned to expect to be "happy" all the time, which translates to getting his own way, you can think of yourself as the therapist who will ride the elevator with the terrified, screaming phobic.

I am not implying, by the way, that your child is a screaming phobic. Nor am I implying that you are your child's therapist. I am trying to give you some imagery to hold on to in your mind that may make a difficult task easier.

Your child has been conditioned not to take a bath, to fight taking a bath, and to be afraid of the consequences of doing things in any other way.

Now you both need to break those bad habits.

WHO'S REALLY IN POWER?

We throw a word around a lot when talking about a way we'd like our children to feel. The word is "empowerment." I've begun to not like the word. Not because I don't think our children should be empowered, but because I think they are too empowered.

Our children are overempowered, and we are underempowered.

Here's empowerment: When *you* say it's bath time, it's bath time.

If your child screams and hollers, begs, pleads, wheedles, or deals, hang tough.

There is no reason on the face of God's green earth why the child's desire to take a bath five minutes later is more salient than your desire to be done with the bath routine so that you can get on with the evening!

The fact that you, the parent, deem bath time to be seven o'clock, for *your convenience,* is reasonable. The fact that your child's bedtime is in the early evening is reasonable.

If you want bath time to be at three in the afternoon and your child to go to bed at four-thirty because you're busy, that is off-the-wall. It denies the child a life. All of us recognize that. Why, then, do we have so much trouble recognizing the other, equally distorted schedule of allowing bath and bedtime to drag on? Of having the children awake basically until the parents are so exhausted that everybody ends up with the same evening schedule? Just as children should be allowed children time, parents should be allowed parent time.

Should you find that your entire time with your child is a series of power struggles, choose one mundane, routine task, such as the bath, and master it completely. Then choose another, until your day is back where it ought to be. Your child will only be happier.

REAL-LIVE MOTHERS WITH REAL-LIFE DILEMMAS

I'd like to introduce you to two mothers whose outward styles are very different yet who have similar issues in their homes. One has a two-year-old, the other a five-year-old.

A TWO-YEAR-OLD WHO WANTS TO BE HELD

A sensitive, caring, smart thirty-nine-year-old whose daughter is two, Lori reports that both her husband and her baby-sitter say she holds her child too much. With lots of curly blond hair, she is casually chic in a short white top and tight jeans. She has an angel's smile when she talks about her daughter. "How can I hold her too much?" she asks. To me, that is a completely understandable question. How could you possibly hold that delicious creature too much?

More talk reveals that her sitter feels that the mommy messes up the sitter's routines. This is probably true. Sitters have a job to do. Mommies have a lifelong relationship with their offspring. The mommy and child have much more invested in the emotional relationship they share. This major investment frequently—as it must—gets them into roiled waters that the sitter and the child won't find themselves in if everything is as it should be.

The father feels that the child wants to be with the mommy more than she wants to be with him. This, too, is understandable, even though we may not like it. Many babies want their mommies above all else.

So then we get to "holding."

"Sometimes around the house, if my sitter or my husband is home, she just says, 'Mommy, pick me up.' And she screams if I don't."

Before we say anything else, does that ring bells for you? Does your child just want to be held? Does your child, out on the street, cry and beg to be picked up, the way Lori's does? Do you, as this lovely mommy does, have all the marginal thoughts so many of us share running through your head? "My child is making a scene. These people must think I'm abusing her. If I pick her up, she'll stop screaming." And so we pick her up.

At home, when the mommy and daddy are trying to get ready for work, for example, the child wants her mommy to pick her up.

What would you do?

If you are like so many of us, caring, tender, and in love with our children, you would probably pick her up. After all, what a simple request it is. How easily met. Why shouldn't we take a few minutes to pick our child up?

Perhaps in fact it's not such a simple request. Perhaps, rather than being a request for a hug, for affection and closeness, which it may in part be, instead it is an attempt to get mommy to do what baby wants.

Doing what baby *wants,* however, is not always the same as doing what baby *needs.* And therein lies the problem.

Baby, unless she's just fallen down and hurt herself, for example, doesn't necessarily *need* a hug. What she probably needs is to learn that at this moment, mommy is doing something else. Mommy is getting dressed. Mommy can hold her in five minutes, but not now. Daddy can hold her if she wants a hug. Vanessa can hold her, or take her out to play. But Mommy can't hold her now.

Lori must grapple with learning to recognize that what her daughter really needs right now is to learn how to live with a manageable amount of distress at not getting her own way. Furthermore, Lori must take into account her *own* needs, which we frequently make second fiddle during these small, tender moments in our home. On a practical level, she needs to get dressed. What is more important, the mommy needs to know that they both won't die if the mommy doesn't hold the child right at this moment. The mommy needs to allow herself to separate a bit emotionally, to not feel as if their connection will weaken if it is not heart responding to heart like fireflies in the dusk. The mommy needs to allow *herself* to not need to hug the child, so that she can allow her child to experience not getting what she has asked for but does not need—and live.

It is in this tender area of the heart that so many of us lose ourselves and perhaps lose our way toward aiding our child's growth.

The mommy must emotionally integrate that *not liking something* is *not life-threatening.*

Even if her child cries. Especially if her child cries. Her child needs to learn to live with a frustration that mommy can assuage in the moment, by holding her. That momentary placation will lead toward more difficulty later.

From a family point of view, if the mommy and the daddy were to regard the "pivotal hug" as something that they need to figure out a solution to together, they would do themselves a world of good. But this couple, like so many couples, sometimes point fingers at each other. The dad "accuses" the mom of holding the child too much. The mom feels guilty. They are a new family working their way toward adjustment; as new parents, they are working their way toward meeting their child's needs at the same time as their own.

It is good to note that, at least outside the home, Lori did finally put her child down. After carrying her through the streets for several blocks, when they got to their block, she said, "Now you can walk." Although her daughter did not *like* it, she did it.

Within every interaction there is ebb and flow as we learn how to assume the mantle of parenthood.

A FIVE-YEAR-OLD'S MORNING

Here is another woman. If you were lucky enough to meet Jeannie and talk to her the way I have been, you would know how smart, kind, and sensitive she is. Stylistically, she doesn't share Lori's casualness, but leans more toward linen shirts and skirts. Yet Jeannie's family, too, is confronting domestic moments that are not exactly the even-flowing moments of our dreams. Like Lori, Jeannie's heart overflows with love for her daughter.

Jeannie's child is now five. Their family spent the morning in what has become a daily horror. The child won't brush her teeth. The child won't put on her clothes. "She won't wear her seat belt," Jeannie ticks off on her fingers. "She won't wear sun block, she won't do her homework, she won't go to bed. She is not respectful in the least," says this woman who has such beautifully effortless, charming manners that in her presence you feel totally soothed.

"This morning, she threw a tantrum. 'I want Daddy! I don't want Mommy!' She was kicking her feet!" Jeannie says, in consternation and annoyance. "I don't know how we got here. I don't know how to get out."

Picture Jeannie's family that morning: a tall man in his shirtsleeves and trousers, a tall woman wearing her underclothes, makeup, and robe, standing looking down at a small child lying in the middle of their bedroom floor kicking her feet. As all parents who have found themselves in that situation will tell you, it's a lot easier to get there than it is to get out.

So for those of you with two-year-olds, you can learn from Jeannie's situation. If your child is the same age as Jeannie's or older, I imagine that your child, like hers, "holds it together in school," as she described, "but loses it at home." You may remember Julie, whose twelve-year-old also does well in school and verges on disaster at home.

That our children do well in school is to our credit. We value learning. We tend to equip them with sharp minds and wide vocabularies. There are many things we do that are undoubtedly good for our children.

But sometimes, confronted by the treasure of our heart lying in the middle of the floor kicking her feet, we feel blue.

Take heart, ye who have let the reins get a little looser than you meant to and now see the horse stampeding toward a stone wall. You can grab the reins, it's not too late; but it requires jumping on the horse, and possibly using the stirrups and the bit to skillfully guide the gallop over the wall—not into it. Since you haven't been riding lately, you may take a couple of bruises yourself along the way.

A FAMILY IN CRISIS—STEPS THEY CAN TAKE

There are some practical steps that Jeannie and her husband can take with their daughter—some tricks of the trade.

- Both parents talk together without the child, to agree that the mornings are abysmal, and plan a strategy. (I'll present some specifics for this family soon.)
- Hold a family meeting when you are not in screaming mode.

Do this together so that the child has the comfort of knowing that both parents are in agreement and working in concert. In Lori's family, in Jeannie's family, in my family, and, if you are a two-parent family, also in yours, children are very adept at playing Mommy off Daddy. We saw the two-year-old not wanting Daddy growing into the five-year-old who only wants Daddy. But none of this is really about wanting Mommy or Daddy. This is about control. We have seen that in two actual families, talking about exactly the same morning routine, the child requesting one parent instead of the one who's available. Our first family is quite new; the other is already fairly entrenched in their troubles.

For either family, it is important that the child knows that the grown-ups are in agreement. During your family meeting, the following are the kinds of ideas to present.

- Explain that the mornings have become very unpleasant.
- Present a new way of making us all feel better.
- Notice that we are not pointing a finger at the child and saying "You are impossible." We are, in fact, stating the truth. Mornings such as these *are* unpleasant.
- Spell out the new rules.

You can make up any rules that suit your home, but here are some ideas.

- Jeannie's little girl carries on about who wakes her. If Mommy wakes her, she wants Daddy, and vice versa. Therefore an alarm clock, rather than a parent waking the child, will signal the beginning of the morning.
- This particular child carries on, changing her clothes over and over. Therefore, the child can pick out her clothes the night before. That is what she will wear. Explain that if she's not dressed, you're all going to leave the house at the right time, so she'd probably rather go to school in her clothes than in her pj's. Because she is such a big girl now, she will be in charge of making sure that she is dressed (at five she can easily do this). This will circumvent all the screaming about not wanting to get dressed. When a certain number appears on the digital clock, she should be dressed. Introduce what a fun game it could be to see if she can be dressed before the clock gets to the number.
- Some families make charts that the child either checks or puts stars on. "When you get your shirt on, check it off on the chart."
- While the child gets dressed, so does everybody else. Mommy and Daddy won't stay in her room while she gets dressed (this cuts down on all the screaming they have in her room about dressing).
- We come down to breakfast when the digital clock says a certain time.

TV IN THE MORNING: A NARCOTIC, NOT A WAKER-UPPER

In this particular family, they had also gotten into the habit of having their daughter watch TV every morning. It began when she was a toddler and it seemed easier to have her watch a video than to entertain her while both parents were trying to get dressed and before the sitter came.

Now that she is five, the TV, like everything else they are describing, has become a major power issue. One more show, one more tape, one more half hour and on and on into negotiation swamp. Also, she gets into that zombie state known so well to parents, so that when you finally do break through, she's screaming. This family could make another radical change, which, if you are a newer family, you might consider instituting now, rather than having to change later.

No TV in the morning. Instead, they put on music. That way everybody sings and dances as they get ready for their day.

The challenge for Jeannie and her husband will now be to model a new kind of behavior. To go about their business happily getting dressed, humming to the music, and not angry with other family members.

As each of these new events is completed successfully, which they will be in the beginning because of the novelty, make sure you acknowledge your child's success in a low-key way. "That was better," as all sit down to breakfast. You don't need to "praise" how splendidly the morning went. In fact, the morning is simply going the way it should go. It is not necessarily exemplary. It is merely free from disagreement.

The specifics will vary but the emotional underpinnings need to be the same.

What it requires is that the parents find a way to *shift the mood* by rearranging the habits everyone has grown used to. Thus, alarm clock instead of Mommy waking the child. Music instead of TV. It requires that the parents withdraw from the fight to allow everyone the space to back off and regroup.

RELEASE THE TENSION AND BREAK THE CYCLE

Although I've made some specific suggestions about how Jeannie's family can change their morning, the specifics are less important than your attitude. If you find that you have an older child and that things have gotten way out of line, I don't want to insult you by oversimplifying this, but I have some suggestions. Think of this as a puzzle. Think of it as a tricky situation that requires finesse. If one approach doesn't work, perhaps another will. If the alarm clock doesn't take away the screaming fit engendered by waking the child, perhaps music being turned on in the child's room first thing in the morning will. If the child is always tired in the morning, an earlier bedtime is in order. But again, it's not the specifics so much as your mood.

Sometimes, we feel downhearted and discouraged. Or we feel furious. But while our feelings are human and understandable, they don't get us where we want to be. What we need is to withdraw a bit emotionally, to try to be a bit more dispassionate. If you skipped the part about a baby crying in the crib, go back and glance at it. Take a look at the idea that your child needs to know that you are calm and secure, and you need to know that your child's mood is not bigger than you are.

If we tackle one event, such as the morning, and manage to shift the mood and break some bad habits, we can then tackle the next small moment. It is not too late at all to set limits and stick to them in your home.

Once any given habitual interaction, such as the morning routine, has been changed, you can tackle the next small segment of life. For example, dinner.

Change may be slow, but it will occur.

ESTABLISHING A ROUTINE

What we have seen in Jeannie's home is a routine of sorts. They have established, in fact, a very solid routine. They argue every inch of the way. They are not alone in this kind of morning. Mornings for most families are hectic and bordering on the nightmarish. Part of the reason is that we all have too much to do and not enough time to do it in.

But part of it also is that we didn't start young enough with our children building the kind of habits that would make all of our lives a bit easier. Just remember that it's never too late to change your routine as long as you do it one step at a time.

A CHILD'S "DIFFICULTY MAKING TRANSITIONS" IS REALLY AN ADULT'S DIFFICULTY SETTING LIMITS

A lot of parents I've spoken with mention that their children have "trouble making transitions." Trouble making transitions translates into everyday behavior like so: Whenever you need to do something else, particularly something *you* want or need to do, your child freaks. Although Jeannie's five-year-old now has such established habits of confrontation that she is somewhat beyond merely having trouble making transitions, when she was younger, that is what we might have called it.

In my experience, however, there aren't nearly as many children who temperamentally have trouble making transitions as there are children who have not been *taught* how to make them.

There are two areas where transitions can become an issue: if a child doesn't know what to expect and if a child is very engaged in an activity.

Teaching a child what to expect is a major way to prevent the pickle that Jeannie's family finds themselves in. She can teach her child new habits, for sure, with persistence, love, and patience, but it will be harder than it would have been if she'd done it when her daughter was younger.

How Does Routine Work in a Group?

We can gain some insight into what happens when a child doesn't know what to expect by first looking at a toddler class. Once we see how the process works in a group setting, we can apply it to home. I will describe ours, which will be similiar to those near you.

During the first meeting, for children who have never been in any kind of organized group activity, transitions are often difficult. The children who respond readily to all the "clean-up" songs familiar in so many programs know what's coming next. The first-timer, however, is often horrified. There is a general bustle that comes over the room as the toys start to disappear. The individual toddler may or may not know what to make of the bustle. However, there's a moment when his or her grown-up tries to indicate that it's time to put the toys away. The child doesn't know what that means. Sometimes the grown-up takes whatever toy is in his or her hand. Most children begin to scream, some cry, some, more in keeping with their temperaments, withdraw to observe. But none of them seem to respond nonchalantly to the fact that all the toys are disappearing. They don't know that *after* we clean up we have a snack. All they know is that they were doing something fun and someone moved to stop them.

Usually during the first class, there is shrieking for every transition, from clean-up to snack, from snack to art, from art to bubbles, from bubbles to circle time. Oh, the carrying on that is possible from a first-timer! By the fourth class, or sometimes sooner, there is no more screaming. The children, *as young as nine months old* (who only have to make a transition from toys to bubbles), know what to expect. They know the routine and find comfort in knowing it. Furthermore, they feel quite competent in knowing what's going on. They have gained comfort and mastery from something as simple as knowing that bubbles follow art.

How can this be used productively in your home? Your child will have many fewer so-called problems around transitions, which ultimately translates as tantrums, when he knows what to expect. In the home this means establishing a ROUTINE.

DOES THIS DESCRIBE YOUR HOME?

Many parents tell me that they have such hectic weeks that on the weekends they really like to lighten up. They eat when everybody's hungry; bedtime is at the end of the day, whenever that is; bath happens when it happens; and breakfast might be brunch.

Rigidity should be reserved for fascists and corpses. But. And this is a big but. The child who has no *basic* routine constantly feels like the child on the first day of class—freaking, screaming, and miserable because he has absolutely no idea what's going on or what's coming next. Furthermore, if you child has a baby-sitter who maintains a somewhat steady rhythm to the day, the child is very confused and upset without it.

Reader, I love you dearly. But I have to tell you, when you brag about the fact that you're raising your child to be able to accept whatever goes on in life, that you and your husband are very clear on not wanting to make your home dance around the children, that the child has to fit in with your schedule—which might mean getting up at seven on weekdays and eleven on weekends—that you eat when you're hungry, and that you encourage your child to eat when he or she is hungry—which very well might not only be anytime but also *anyplace*—I want to say, "Get a grip!" You're denying your child the right to know what's going on. By not having a routine, you are keeping your child almost a prisoner in an odd way, never knowing what to expect when, and therefore unable to have real mental freedom because he has to worry too much about the practicalities.

Some families aren't that loose in the way they envision their day, but because they don't stick to their guns on limits, the routine they establish is subject to controversy. For example, if you change diapers in any of the ways we described earlier, other than simply changing the diaper when the diaper needs to be changed, that is the routine your child grows to expect. Mommy says diaper-change time. I carry on. We put off changing diapers. Mommy talks about it some more. I carry on some more. We talk some more. If I really carry on, we put it off until it becomes an entire new event in my mind and we start all over again.

The way this will play out in the everyday mood in your home is that from the moment you awake until the moment you go to sleep, you might very well find yourself having to "deal" with a child who has to be forced, kicking and screaming, to do the most mundane task.

Thus, we have created an unpleasant mood in the home which is a direct 180 degree difference from what we thought we were encouraging.

Furthermore, if Mommy is *real* loose and the sitter is not so loose, and after all Mommy is Mommy, then loose must be the way things should be. So what's the sitter doing?

Then you have a potential situation where your child is carrying on with you because that's the routine you've established, and your child is carrying on with your sitter because she's not doing it like Mommy. Another very unpleasant possibility is that it actually feels better to your child to be with the sitter, because then your child knows what to expect.

MAKE A ROUTINE YOU CAN FOLLOW

Should any of this ring true in your home, you can introduce transitions gradually, which the grown-ups as well as the children will need since you all have developed habits that need some rearranging.

Pick any daily event, it doesn't matter which. Getting up, getting dressed, eating breakfast, any of the mundane repetitive tasks of life. Let's begin with putting on pj's. When it's time to put pj's on, it's time to put pj's on. This is not a battle, it is not an emotional duel, it is a simple, daily task. What will keep it from turning in to a confrontational power struggle is your declining to be part of the fight.

There are tricks of the trade for doing this. You can make it a game. You can say, "I'll race you to your room." You can challenge your child to put on her own pj's. You can count to ten and see if she can get them on before you uncover your eyes. Try anything that you can think of to make it fun to get the pj's on without carrying on. But when you say it's time to put pj's on, it's time.

Once you have conquered pj's, add something else. You will see that if each of these tiny tasks starts to occur with more harmony, you will establish a rhythm in your home that, like having a key in music, will allow the whole band the freedom to improvise on more important parts of life.

Soon, you will be able to move through the routine parts of any day with less and less conflict.

TRANSITION FROM AN ACTIVITY

Besides the daily routines of everyday life, there are the more standard transitions that all children need to learn how to make. Depending on their temperaments, some can shift from activity to activity more easily than others. But parents who have trouble setting limits sometimes have trouble helping their children learn how to make transitions.

It might be useful to put ourselves in the place of a child who is engaged in an activity. If you, the adult, are working hard on a project under deadline, for example, and are completely focused, should the doorbell ring unexpectedly, you will very likely jump with a startled rush of adrenaline. If then told by a giant to save your file immediately, even though you're not quite done, you will probably not be happy with the command. You might even start screaming. That's pretty much the way a young child might experience being interrupted just at the moment when she was about to make the connection that that little squiggly line on the puzzle piece matches the squiggly cutout on the puzzle frame.

Grown-ups, however, have methods to deal with ending one activity to begin another. We glance at the clock on our screen, realize we have only another half hour left, and move to finish the paragraph, leaving ourselves five minutes to make notes about where we want to pick up, another few minutes to save the file onto a disk and to shut down the computer. Of course, this analogy has nothing whatsoever to do with my own process in writing this book. This is all hypothetical, mind you.

At any rate, your toddler doesn't have those skills. Your child of two or three has only the rudiments of a sense of time, and that is part of what makes transitions difficult. Here are some tricks.

- In a gentle voice, tell your child five minutes in advance that she will need to put the puzzle away soon because you're going to go out. A child who is concentrating hard will only half hear you.
- Remind your child two minutes in advance that you will be putting the puzzle away shortly.
- When it's time, allow your child to put the last piece in, or complete whatever small activity she was engaged in. Then say, "It's time to put the puzzle away."

Now here's where we get to the tricky part for parents who are conflicted about discipline. *When it's time to put the puzzle away, PUT IT AWAY.*

If your child has the temperament to then put it away, make sure you acknowledge her: "I love how you put the puzzle away" or "I love how you got ready to go."

But even if your child cries and screams, as unpleasant as it may feel in the moment, it is time to put the puzzle away. If you give in to the screaming and hollering, what you have taught is that when you say something you don't mean it. You have taught that screaming and hollering is the proper response to being told it's time to do something else. What you have guaranteed is a series of power struggles through-out the day every time there is a practical reason to shift gears.

Is this harsh? I don't think so. Snatching the puzzle away unexpect-edly is harsh. Giving a child warning in advance to teach the concept of time and then following through on what you said was going to hap-pen not only isn't harsh. It's kind. You are teaching your child that there are limits.

If your child knows that when you say it's time to put the puzzle away you mean it's time to put the puzzle away, you will have taught your child to respect your words. Once you are straightforward and reliable about meaning what you say, you won't have to face, time and again, relentless fights over what goes on in your home.

STAY CLEAR ON WHAT YOUR CHILD IS REALLY LEARNING

Frequently, going hand in hand with our ways of approaching life, our children tend to be intense. Therefore, when they do a puzzle, *they do a puzzle.* This intensity notwithstanding, or perhaps because of this very intensity, they desperately need us to arm them with the equip-ment to be able to back off and then pick up the threads of what they were doing later.

Often, we hesitate to interrupt something such as finishing a puz-zle, or looking at books, or doing an art project, because we put such a high premium on the learning process. We want to make sure that our child has all the time in the world to develop her mind. And surely puzzles are one of the fundamentals of problem solving, aren't they?

What's interesting here is that in most cases, your child is not nearly as involved in the puzzle in front of her as she is in the puzzle of trying to figure out, when you say it's time to go, does it really mean it's time to go, or will it be time to go in ten minutes, or if she carries on enough, will it not ever be time to go because you'll put off the errand until tomorrow?

By ending the activity when *you* need to end it, you are not damag-ing your child's ability to reason by depriving her of the freedom to follow her thought processes completely until she's done. You are teaching limits. In the long run, that is a more important skill than any intellectual pursuit in the moment.

She can return to the puzzle when she gets home if the need is still as strong. If she does return to the puzzle with the same intensity, then she is indeed following a line of intellectual pursuit, which I, along with you, applaud. If she does not return to the puzzle the moment she is able, you will know that you taught a magnificently important lesson, which is how to make a transition, and that you did not have to teach that lesson at the expense of the one synapse of understanding that would ultimately have been the only thought process necessary to cure cancer and to bring peace on earth.

Although I have used the phrase "put the puzzle away," for the sake of discussion, it is not *putting it away* that is crucial. It is *ending the activity when you, the adult, know that it needs to end*. As children mature, their play becomes more involved. It is useful for them to leave out their trains, LEGOs, or many-piece puzzles so they can return to them and develop their play. But even as they mature, and are deeply engaged in ongoing intellectual pursuits, there are still moments when they need to stop doing what they're doing because the adult knows that it's time to do something else.

No Negotiating

I often hear parents, when confronted with their children's engagement in an activity, waver from their initial plan by giving the child what looks like a way to make a smoother transition. When the child expresses unwillingness to end the activity, which any child in his or her right mind would do, because playing is fun, the parents will offer something like this: "I can see that you're really involved with that puzzle. Why don't you take another minute."

What happened here, unfortunately, is that you have taught the child the art of making a deal.

The next time around, having learned that it's acceptable to be "really into something," he is now inclined to make a deal on his own: "Two more minutes." Thus, by wanting to be accommodating, you have unwittingly armed your child with skills that will lead you down the dark and dusty path toward that clinically recognized state, the Nightmare of Negotiation.

THE FUNDAMENTALS OF SETTING AND HOLDING LIMITS

Whether your child is beginning to crawl, beginning to read, or beginning puberty, there are fundamentals that remain the same. *You* know more because *you* are the adult. Because you know more and are the adult, you know best how to set up the everyday environment, including all routines.

If you hold up your end of the bargain, and maintain a home where what we do is not always under discussion, you will then have freed everyone, the adults and the children, from the potential tyranny of the everyday, therefore freeing everyone to follow their true interests and intellectual pursuits.

If we get to read after lunch, for example, it is only after lunch that we get to read. If our parents allow us to spend our entire afternoon screaming and fighting about not wanting to get into the high chair, and not wanting to change our diaper, and not wanting to get dressed, and so on into an infinity of domestic quarrels, we never have enough time to read! But if we manage to learn how to make our way fairly smoothly through lunch, because all the little possible points of contention are not taken up by the adult, then we have a glorious afternoon stretching ahead of us where the child is free, as he should be, to choose which books we'll read. Not to choose when to read, not to choose for how long we can read, but to choose what we can read, at what pace we can read it, whether to finish this book or drop it and choose another, whether to read this book ten times in a row, or any of the other perfect places for a child to have the right to choose. Within the safe, secure boundaries of routine events that are non-negotiable the child is free to discover the universe.

Without those safe, secure boundaries, the child must spend his day trapped in a cyclical replay of the same interaction.

LESS IS MORE: MATERIAL EXCESS

Our overindulgence, of course, is often manifested by the number of "things" we accumulate for our children. Although somewhat less troubling developmentally than a lack of tolerance for frustration, or an inability to accept limitations, and some rather serious issues are raised (beyond the bad taste implicit in excess purely for the sake of excess).

If a child has too many things, eventually none of those things matter. If a child expects to be "rewarded" simply for drawing breath, he misses out on the opportunity to strive for something, to have the bar raised and to jump even higher, and then to feel the deep satisfaction not only of having jumped higher but of knowing that his parents are applauding him every inch of the way.

In terms of intellectual development, the child who is spoon-fed every thought, instructed in each new moment, and provided with perfect equipment for any given task may not have the opportunity for the freedom of thought that ultimately leads to real creativity and intellectual growth.

The child who is prematurely exposed to events or ideas that he is not intellectually ready to appreciate loses out on the thrill of discovering how marvelous something is when you have yearned to be able to take part in it.

Below is a list of typical overindulgences. If they ring true for your home, you are not alone. In the event that they do feel familiar, you might want to make some adjustments for the emotional welfare of your child.

These adjustments include saying no even when you can afford something, and even when "everyone" else has it and your child is screaming, begging, or pleading that he or she wants it, too. If you are aware that by saying no when it is appropriate you are really giving your child a gift, it becomes easier.

- *Too many toys.* So many that the child doesn't know what's there and plays with less than half.
- *Too many clothes.* The child doesn't wear things more than three or four times.
- *Too many classes.* More than two a week for a toddler. More after-school activities than an elementary school–age kid can master.
- *Too much planned time.* No free time to daydream, space out, hang out, initiate play, or develop a fantasy life.

- *Certain activities introduced too early.* These might include going to the movies the first time, or seeing movies with more mature content than the child is ready for; sleepovers with friends (which I've seen started as young as nursery school); sleep-away camp. "Not now. When you're big enough" is a marvelous response to requests for inappropriate activities. By saying this, you have given the child something to look forward to.

If your child is always the first in his or her circle to do the kinds of things mentioned in the last item, maybe you ought to slow down and follow the pack rather than lead for a while. Why? It's possible you're rushing your child. More important, you may be denying your child the right to long for something, to yearn to get to do something, or to be big enough to be allowed to take part in whatever the activity is.

SECURITY IS NOT A BLANKET THAT WE CAN BUY

Ultimately, it's less important which limits you set and more important that you set them. Your home should not revolve around your child's whims, whether you can afford them, whether it is pleasurable to indulge them in the moment, or whether you prefer to avoid confrontations. Of course, we all know that intellectually. But sometimes in the moment we lose our way.

Our children are blessed. They are adored and doted upon. Every child on the face of the earth deserves what ours have: to be loved from head to toe-sie. And every child, including ours, deserves to learn, in the comfort and security of his own home, that he will get everything he needs, including not always getting what he wants. Every child is entitled to the right to know that when his loving parents say "No," they mean no. No matter what he does.

There is a security built into a family where mutual respect arises from the fulfilled expectation that parents will meet their children's real needs and that children will do what their parents expect.

Epilogue

It is the day before my fifty-second birthday.

This morning in the park, I ran into one of my dog-walking friends. She is a Swiss psychologist who recently turned forty. I mentioned that tomorrow is my birthday.

She asked, "Is it the big one?"

I said I had already passed my "big one."

Trying to find soothing small talk, she murmured, "It's all attitude."

I laughed. "No it's not. At forty it's attitude. By fifty it's mathematics. It's finite."

It is autumn. We were walking along a path that leads by a garden. It is in its October state, much as I am. Everything has long passed being dewy-fresh buds. It has progressed beyond the full, rich, blowzy state of splendid overgrowth. It has begun to get leggy in places, empty in others. The colors are no longer as rich as they were even a few weeks ago. This garden, in its natural course, may make a hauntingly beautiful photo, but it will never be on the cover of a gardening catalog.

She seemed to have a moment's epiphany.

"You mean this is it?" It was a real question, with gut-wrenching understanding.

"This is it," I said quietly.

"My God," she said, her Swiss accent somehow making it a more heartfelt exclamation. "This is all there is?"

I, too, have reached a new level of understanding. "This is *everything*."

"But how can you stand that it's finite?"

"We don't really know if it's finite. We just know that this is finite."

She smiled. "That's true."

"Because this is finite, everything you do should be the best you can. You should try and enjoy."

"You mean don't sweat the small stuff?"

I laughed. "There is no small stuff. The annoying parts of life are meaningless. Ignore them."

Just then we met a dog I'm particularly fond of. An overfed tan-and-white bulldog wearing a lavender scarf jauntily around his neck. "Winston!" He wagged his entire body, sidling around to get his hindquarters scratched.

Like so many moments of life, if you pay attention, it is marvelous.

Was it a gift that this morning I was thinking about mortality?

Another small miracle occurred.

My husband drives my daughter to school every morning. Sometimes I go with them, walk her into the playground, and stand around talking to the other moms. Sometimes I wave them off so I can go about my day.

On the days when I wave good-bye, my daughter and I have a ritual. We blow each other kisses, catch them on our cheeks, and then give each other the sign language signal for "I love you."

There are some mornings so hideous that my daughter swings her ponytail away from me as she buckles herself into her seat belt and won't look at me. There are other mornings when she's so busy discussing with my husband what tape they're going to listen to that it's all a rather perfunctory exercise. She blows a kiss, pretends to catch it, and throws the "I love you" sign over her shoulder without looking backward as the car pulls away.

But today, oh, today. A beautiful crisp fall morning. Sparkling clean air. We had had an easy morning, everyone in a pleasant mood going about our morning rituals, no hysteria, no recriminations, no hissy fits, by my daughter, my husband, or me.

My husband looked so handsome in my eyes, waiting in the driver's seat, his arm resting on the open window, smiling as we came out the front door of our building.

My daughter jumped in the backseat, buckled herself in, and turned to me.

We both blew kisses at the exact same moment.

We both caught the kisses at the exact same moment.

We both gave the "I love you" sign at the exact same moment.

She was delighted, as only a nine-year-old can be by a small, lovely moment of synchronicity. Then she gave me the "thumbs-up" sign. I returned it.

Then she gave the "thumbs-up" sign with one hand and the "I love you" with the other.

I tried to return it and fumbled.

She lowered the window. "That's hard! Try again!"

I did, and managed. "Good," she called in a voice that I realized I must use with her. It was loving, rewarding, encouraging.

I had a powerful moment of realizing that somehow I have given her something that is not all the "bad" we always worry about.

My husband said, "Love you," as he slid the car away from the curb.

And my daughter threw back her head and laughed with rich delight as she held the "thumbs-up" and the "I love you" out the rear window all the way up the street until I could no longer see the car.

Sometimes, you see your family not as they relate to you, but as who they are in the world. She is a truly neat human being.

And it is that, if anything, that I would love to give to you.

A way to realize how marvelous your child is. Independently of you. What a neat human being your child is.

Sometimes, and especially if we're working at a demanding job, we find our position less a gift and more a burden.

We find our child less an interesting human being whom we're privileged to have time to spend with and more an annoying, demanding drain.

We find our husband less a partner and more a bully, a baby, or a little bit of both.

But you cheat yourself dreadfully if you operate from that place more than once in a while.

Because you have entered the realm of motherhood with an extra decade or two under your belt, you have some strengths—and some weaknesses.

If you are truly mature, there will come a moment when you, too, face and address your own mortality.

Hopefully, this will snap you out of your dream state.

Sometimes, for those of us who are older, we have our lives "in order." I put that in quotes because there never really is an "order" in life. No matter how much you may think you're in control, you aren't. No matter how much planning you do, you are not in control of life. You are too far from being in control of your own family, let alone all the outsiders, your neighbors, your bosses, government—even the occasional crackpot who enters your life unexpectedly—to entertain the notion that you are in control.

What you are in control of is how you respond.

Now that you have this child in your life, you have a choice of routes to take.

You can try and slot this child into an already highly organized, orchestrated lifestyle replete with schedules, contingency plans, and legions of support staff to keep in line. In other words, you can pretend that nothing has changed now that you are a parent.

Just be advised, however, that if you take this path, there will inevitably come a moment that you couldn't possibly have planned for.

There will come a moment where your child will have a need—either sickness or something not going smoothly in his or her life—where no amount of support staff will do the trick.

And you will have to choose. Your seemingly well ordered life. Or your child's need. And even more significantly for you, perhaps, your marvelous opportunity to meet your child's need. Your chance to seize life, to really live it, to interact with your child, and ride the waves of his life with him. If you relegate dealing with him—and all his unsavory, disorderly claims on your life—to someone else, you will have lost out. You will have missed the boat. You will have given up your one chance to be a mother.

That is what happens to the woman who believes that deep down inside she may be a mother, but nothing has really changed. And she is going to keep her life on the well-paced, orderly track she set it on some time ago.

There is a different route you can take. You can acknowledge that your life has irrevocably changed. Better? Worse? Who's to say. But the advent of a child in your life has changed you. Permanently and profoundly.

The gift of motherhood is so rich. But sometimes, we experience it rather painfully. We seem to spend so much of our effort trying to avoid or circumvent or navigate around motherhood. How can I arrange my schedule to fit everything in? How can I get my child to stop crying? How can I get this interaction over with smoothly?

You *can't* fit everything in. Once you have a child, you can no longer comfortably continue doing everything that you did before you had a child. Plain and simple.

You have been a child. A teenager. In your twenties, either a college kid or an apprentice to some body of knowledge. During your thirties, you most likely worked on building a career. It is possible that you have made your mark somewhere in the world. You may even be in charge of many, many people.

You have been a daughter. A friend. Perhaps a sibling, niece, cousin, granddaughter. I hope for your sake that you have had the opportunity at least once in your life of being a grand, passionate lover. I also hope for your sake that you have had the opportunity of living on your own somewhere during these years, not as a member of any family, whether by blood, marriage, or arrangement. You may have been a spouse more than once by this time. You may still be one.

Notwithstanding all these things, *you have never been a mother*.

Allow yourself the luxury of really experiencing this relationship and role.

Spend as much time as possible with your child. Do as many mundane, run-of-the-mill, ho-hum household chores with your child as you can. Bathe, feed, dress your child. Play with your child. Walk down the street with your child—even when it takes you fifty-seven excruciating moments to get ten yards down the block.

Hold your child when she is ill.

Clean up poop, pee, and puke.

Sit on a little chair that you are sure you will need a helicopter to drag you up out of when you are ready to stand, and watch as your child uses the wrong end of the paintbrush!

Read *Goodnight Moon* until you want to scream.

Lie down on the couch with your child and watch *The Wizard of Oz* because the witch is scary. Even when you have so many things to do around the house and for work that you think you're going to bust a gusset. Allow your blood pressure to go down, down, down so you can smell the top of that little head, and feel those little shoulders pressing into your ribs, and hold your child, because your child needs you to hold her because the witch is scary, and because you need to hold your child—for you—because the witch is scary.

Jung once said that the only mistake parents can make is not to have lives of their own. That is still so very true. Yet were he writing now, he might have noted that there are two mistakes we can make. Not having a life of our own. And not having a life with our child.

I wish you and your family all the health and happiness in the world.

May you know when to give, and when to give by refusing, when to stay close and when to let go. May you have the grace to acknowledge what's working and the common sense to change what's gone wrong. May your maturity make you keenly aware of the instant that is childhood—and life itself—so you can treasure them as the precious gifts that they are.

May you use your head to chart your course through parenthood; may your heart always be your ballast. May your knowledge be the stars that guide you, your experience the lighthouse that keeps your family safe from rocky shoals. May your wisdom be the buoy that carries you lightly over places that would've snagged you years ago, and may the love for your child be your port in every storm.

May you hold your dearest darling's essence close to your heart so that whatever you do, you do with love.

REFERENCES

These works, among others, were useful in preparing this book.

Belsky, Jay, and John Kelly. *The Transition to Parenthood*. New York: Delacorte Press, 1994.

Borges, Gretchen. "Women Who Wait: The Phenomenon of the Middle-Aged Mother." Unpublished article, 1994.

Carter, Betty, and Monica McGoldrick, eds. *The Changing Family Life Cycle: A Framework for Family Therapy*. 2nd edition. Needham Heights, Massachusetts: Allyn & Bacon, 1989.

Creasy, R. K., and R. Resnik. *Maternal Fetal Medicine*. 3rd edition. Philadelphia, Pennsylvania: W. B. Saunders, subs. of Harcourt, Brace, 1994.

Cunningham, F. Gary. "Childbearing Among Older Women—The Message Is Cautiously Optimistic," *New England Journal of Medicine* (1995) 333:1002.

Cunningham, F. Gary, et al. *Williams Obstetrics*. 20th edition. East Norwalk, Connecticut: Appleton & Lange, 1997.

Ladies' Home Journal, September, 1998.

National Vital Statistics Reports, U.S. Department of Health and Human Services, National Center for Health Statistics, vol. 47, no. 18, April 1999.

Newsweek. Special Edition, "Health for Life." Spring/Summer 1999.

Statistical Abstract of the United States, 1996.

The following experts from various fields were kind enough to answer many questions:

Susan Bayer, M.S., Codirector, Communication Network, coauthor, *The Caregiver's Manual*

Trudi Berkowitz, Ph.D., Mount Sinai School of Medicine. Advanced-maternal-age mothers, follow-up study of 1,400

Ellen Birnbaum, Assistant Director, Nursery School, 92nd Street Y

Melinda Blau, author, *Families Apart*

Gretchen Borges, M.S.W., C.S.W., Assistant Director, Center for the Study of Social Work Practice, Columbia University

Ellen Bravo, Executive Director, National Association of Working Women

Leslie Davenport, C.S.W.

Catherine D. DeAngelis, M.D., Vice Dean for Academic Affairs and Faculty Professor of Pediatrics, Johns Hopkins University

Ronny Diamond, M.S.W., Director, Post-adoption Services, Spence-Chapin, Faculty, Ackerman Institute for the Family

Margorie Engel, President, Stepfamily Association of America

Susan Etes, Head of Lower School, Allen-Stevenson School, New York City

Madeline Fisher, C.S.W.

Steven Friedfeld, C.S.W.

Ruth Jones, R.N.

Betsy Schur Levy, Ph.D.

Ellen Lukens, Assistant Professor, School of Social Work, Columbia University

Pam Madsen, Executive Director, American Infertility Association

Ramon Murphy, M.D., Associate Clinical Professor of Pediatrics, Mount Sinai School of Medicine

Tanmoy Mukherjee, M.D., Assistant Professor of Obstetrics, Gynecology, and Reproductive Science, Mount Sinai School of Medicine

Rebecca F. Nachamie, M.D., Clinical Associate Professor of Obstetrics, Gynecology, and Reproductive Science, Mount Sinai School of Medicine

Laura Popper, M.D., Assistant Clinical Professor of Pediatrics, Mount Sinai School of Medicine

Richard L. Saphir, M.D., Clinical Professor of Pediatrics, Mount Sinai School of Medicine

Gary Schlesinger, Ph.D., clinical psychologist

Nancy Shulman, Director, Nursery School, 92nd Street Y

Ilene Stargot, National Director, National Infertility Network Exchange (NINE)

Nancy Wahlin, Coordinator, Korean Program, Spence-Chapin

Susan Wartman, C.S.W.

Patti Wollman, Director of Early Childhood, JCC, of the Upper West Side, New York City

Janice G. Yamins, Ph.D., clinical psychologist

RECOMMENDED READING

Chapter 3. TRANSFORMING FROM A COUPLE INTO A FAMILY

Why Parents Disagree & What You Can Do about It, by Ron Taffel (New York: Avon, 1994). A down-to-earth, practical book. Offers many useful solutions and, more important, gives you a jumping-off point for thinking how you might do something differently in your family.

STEPFAMILIES

Yours, Mine, and Ours, by Anne C. Bernstein (New York: Norton, 1990).

How to Be Smart Parents: Now That Your Kids Are Adults, by Sylvia Auerback (San Diego, California: Silvercat Publications, 1995).

These two books have sections about handling an "older" first family and the addition of a new baby into a stepfamily.

Chapter 4. THE ONE-ADULT FAMILY

Although you probably know these two classics, *Single Mothers by Choice,* by Jane Mattes (New York: Times Books, 1994), and *Single Parents by Choice,* by Naomi Miller (New York: Plenum, 1992), the following, written by single mothers, cover a wide variety of issues.

The Complete Single Mother: Reassuring Answers to Your Most Challenging Concerns, by Andrea Engber and Leah Klungness (Holbrook, Massachusetts: Adams Media Corporation, 1995). Addresses your specific issues more fully than I could here.

Two of Us Make a World: The Single Mother's Guide to Pregnancy, Childbirth, and the First Year, by Sherill Tippins and Prudence Tippins (New York: Holt, 1996). Although limited to pre-baby and first year, and including divorce, custody, etc., offers very sound advice about practical matters such as money and support systems.

And Baby Makes 2: Produced and directed by Judy Katz and Oren Rudavsky, 1999. A documentary film that chronicles the lives of three women who chose to be single mothers. Available through www.IMDB.com.

Chapter 6. KIDS, CAREER, AND COMPROMISE

FULL-TIME WORK

The Working Parents Handbook, by June Solnit Sale and Kit Kollenberg, with Ellen Milinkoff (New York: Fireside/Simon & Schuster, 1996). Full of practical tips from women who have obviously juggled responsibilities successfully.

When Mothers Work: Loving Our Children without Sacrificing Our Selves, by Joan K. Peters (Reading, Massachusetts: Addison-Wesley, 1997). A very intelligent discussion of the advantages of working to all family members, including the child.

The Job/Family Challenge: A 9 to 5 Guide, by Ellen Bravo (New York: Wiley, 1995). Many practical tips from the executive director of the National Association of Working Women.

PART-TIME WORK

The Part-Time Solution, by Charlene Canape (New York: HarperCollins, 1990). Out of print, but many copies are still easily available. The best around for practical and tactical advice.

Turn Your Talents into Profits, by Darcie Sanders and Martha M. Bullen (New York: Pocket Books, 1998). If you want to stay home, and your profession doesn't lend itself easily to part-time work, here's a good practical help to get you rolling on earning a living outside of the corporate workforce.

MOTHERS AT HOME

Staying Home: from Full-Time Professional to Full-Time Parent, by Darcie Sanders and Martha M. Bullen (Wauconda, Illinois: Spencer & Waters, 1999). Addresses some of the problems you'll come up against and gives you thoughtful solutions.

Chapter 7. HELPING HANDS: CHILD CARE

The Working Parents Handbook and *When Mothers Work* (see above) both have very sound advice about how to choose child care. For additional information see the following.

The Good Nanny Book: How to Find, Hire, and Keep the Perfect Nanny for Your Child, by P. Michele Raffin (New York: Berkeley Books, 1995). Very straightforward on the business arrangement, with very good practical advice for the employer/employee part of having child care in the home.

The Nanny Book: The Smart Parent's Guide to Hiring, Firing, and Every Sticky Situation in Between, by Susan Carlton and Coco Myers (New York: St. Martin's

Press, 1999). More of the same, with a bit more advice about how to handle awkward situations.

Chapter 8. BIFOCALS AND BARNEY: OUR CHANGING BODIES

Obviously, this is a huge topic beyond the scope of this recommended reading list. *Prevention* magazine (Rodale Press) stands out for practical exercise routines and sound information, including both Western scientific data and advice, backed by research on herbal remedies. Includes a section on caring for aging parents.

Chapter 9. CONFRONTING LIFE'S CYCLES

Here are a few books that might help when there is a need. The first three are for adults; the fourth is for children.

How to Survive the Loss of a Parent: A Guide for Adults, by Lois F. Akner (New York: Morrow, 1993).

Mid-Life Orphan, by Jane Brooks (New York: Berkley Books, 1999).

Caring for Yourself While Caring for Your Aging Parents, by Claire Berman (New York: Holt, 1997).

Lifetimes, by Brian Mellonie and Robert Ingpen (New York: Bantam Books, 1983).

Part 3. RAISING OUR CHILDREN: TAILOR-MADE PARENTING TIPS

On our six-week checkup with our daughter, our pediatrician gave us this brilliant advice: "Throw out all the books and enjoy."

Marvelous advice. We ignored it. You will, too.

There are more parenting books available than anyone can read. Here is a list of what I consider ought-tos ("must-have" is stronger than I'm comfortable with).

GENERAL DEVELOPMENTAL BOOKS

All of the following books have useful, perceptive, and often beautiful things to say about children and their development. All the authors might as well be living on another planet when it comes to the actual, day-to-day realities of our lives (many gained their experience in another country or decades before now). While they offer some useful practical advice, their real strength lies in their accurate presentations and important insights into your child's internal workings. Choose one or all, perhaps beginning with a book in the series *Your One-Year-Old, Your Two-Year-Old, Your Three-Year-Old,* and so on, by Louise Bates Ames and various coauthors. These are published by Dell.

Touchpoints, by T. Berry Brazelton, M.D. (Reading, Massachusetts: Addison-Wesley, 1992).

The Magic Years, by Selma H. Fraiberg (New York: Scribner's, 1959, Fireside/Simon & Schuster, 1996).

Your Baby and Child, by Penelope Leach (New York: Knopf, 1997).

The New First Three Years of Life, by Burton L. White (Englewood Cliffs, New Jersey: Prentice-Hall, 1975; New York: Fireside/Simon & Schuster, 20th anniversary edition, 1995).

MEDICAL REFERENCE

Caring for Your Baby and Young Child: Birth to Age Five, by Steven P. Shelow, M.D., et al. (New York: Bantam, 1991). Best all-around practical medical reference, with regard to shots, fevers, etc. Includes some straightforward parenting advice.

FOOD

What to Expect the First Year, by Arlene Eisenberg, Heidi E. Murkoff, and Sandie E. Hathaway (New York: Workman, 1989).

What to Expect in the Toddler Years, by Arlene Eisenberg, Heidi E. Murkoff, and Sandi E. Hathaway (New York: Workman, 1994).

These books, beloved by many for their wealth of material, offer the very best information about food.

SLEEP

The Baby Book: Everything You Need to Know about Your Baby from Birth to Age Two, by William Sears, M.D., and Martha Sears, R.N. (Boston: Little, Brown, 1993). The Searses are advocates of the family bed, which in many cases turns out not to be as blissful as it sounds in theory. They do, however, have the absolute *best ways to get a child to sleep.* Their attachment parenting ideas are marvelous and most of their advice on all issues, not just sleep, will offer you a more pleasant home and a healthier, happier child.

PRACTICAL PARENTING

Although there are many parenting books on the market, I am not objective. In *Big Lessons for Little People: Teaching Our Kids Right from Wrong while Keeping Them Healthy, Safe, and Happy* (New York: Dell, 1997), I tried to cover the practical areas that occur in modern life that were not covered adequately by others. The chapters on learning, the "Gimmies," sleep, sex, death, and TV will probably be very useful to you. One mother said she liked it because it had a lot of "What do you do in a restaurant? What do you do in an airport?"

IMPORTANT THINKERS

When you have the time and inclination to read beyond the initial how-tos of parenting, these books say extremely important things about the world around us with regard to children.

Children First: What Our Society Must Do—and Is Not Doing—for Our Children Today, by Penelope Leach (New York: Knopf, 1994).

It Takes a Village, and Other Lessons Children Teach Us, by Hillary Rodham Clinton (New York: Simon & Schuster, 1996).

MAGAZINES

Parenting, Parents Magazine, Working Mother, and *Child,* to name just a few, have very valuable practical tips. Subscribe to one or two; you'll always find at least one applicable idea for your family in every issue.

Selected Web Sites

Research has just started affirming what anyone with any common sense knows: there is a direct correlation between the amount of time people spend on the Internet and how depressed they are. (Another large amount of research money that could have been put to better use making a clean, nice free space available for people to meet face to face.) Advice: Have a goal for the specific information you want, set an amount of time you will spend, log on, get your info, and get out.

Since the Internet is so new and fluid, this is a very short, probably incomplete, and possible already outdated list.

OUR OWN WEB SITE

www.sogladwewaited.com. I have set up a Web site for us. You can reach me there. Hopefully it will evolve into a place to find other older mothers in your area and provide you with any specialized information you may seek.

ALL-PURPOSE INFO, CHAT ROOMS, ETC.

ivillage.com. Women's network with all kinds of information, including two popular parenting resources:

- Parent soup **(www.parentsoup.com)**. The name says it all; chat groups and message boards.
- Parents Place **(www.parentsplace.com)**. Supportive site; Q&A.

www.oxygen.com. A fun women's network, with a useful Kids and New Baby section, Moms Online, and lots of other interesting, often funny articles by experts and writers in many different fields.

Moms Online **(www.momsonline.com)**. Personal stories from other women, menus, etc. Working and at-home moms.

Main Street Moms **(www.mainstreetmoms.com)**. Two former career women now give you access to advice and shopping from home.

Formerly Employed Mothers at the Leading Edge **(www.female home.org)**. Support for women who changed careers after becoming moms; local chapters (membership fee to receive newsletter and go to meetings).

Mom's Refuge **(www.momsrefuge.com)**. Ways to juggle and ways to pamper yourself.

AT-HOME WORKING MOMS

There are many sites to give you people to connect with, including both parenting and work-from-home ideas.

Home-based Working Moms **(www.hbwm.com)**. Business tips, how to avoid business scams, where to hold meetings outside your home (membership fee to join and advertise on site; not necessary to join in order to use Web site).

Mom's Village **(www.wahm.com)**. Links to other sites of working moms.

Work-at-Home Success **(www.workathomesuccess.com)**. Lists companies that hire at-home workers.

iVillage **(www.ivillage.com/work)**. Business tips.

KID ACTIVITIES

Family Education Network **(www.familyeducation.com)**. School and educational information.

"Go Local!" Click on your state; many schools list activities and calendars.

Family.com **(www.family.com)**. Disney, therefore ads—but good local guide to kids' events.

INDEX

ABOUT THE AUTHOR

Lois Nachamie is the author of *Big Lessons for Little People* and coauthor of the Parents' Choice Award–winning *Entertain Me! Creative Ideas for Fun and Games with Your Baby in the First Year*.

She writes for parenting magazines and newspapers, has appeared on national television and radio, lectures, and runs workshops. A staff member of the Parenting Center of the 92nd Street Y in New York City, she leads many groups, including the popular *For Older Moms* series.

She lives in New York with her husband and her daughter.